HONORING GOD
with Body and Mind

HONORING GOD
with Body and Mind

Sexual Ethics for Christians

Steven D. Hoogerwerf

CASCADE *Books* • Eugene, Oregon

HONORING GOD WITH BODY AND MIND
Sexual Ethics for Christians

Cascade Books
An Imprint of Wipf and Stock Publishers
199 W. 8th Ave., Suite 3
Eugene, OR 97401

www.wipfandstock.com

PAPERBACK ISBN: 978-1-5326-8706-8
HARDCOVER ISBN: 978-1-5326-8707-5
EBOOK ISBN: 978-1-5326-8708-2

Cataloguing-in-Publication data:

Names: Hoogerwerf, Steven D., author.
Title: Honoring God with body and mind : sexual ethics for Christians / Steven D. Hoogerwerf.
Description: Eugene, OR : Cascade Books, 2019 | Includes bibliographical references.
Identifiers: ISBN 978-1-5326-8706-8 (paperback) | ISBN 978-1-5326-8707-5 (hardcover) | ISBN 978-1-5326-8708-2 (ebook)
Subjects: LCSH: Sex—Religious aspects—Christianity. | Sexual ethics.
Classification: BT708 .H66 2019 (paperback) | BT708 .H66 (ebook)

Manufactured in the U.S.A.   11/08/19

To my students, who for many years have challenged me to think and speak more clearly about the sensitive issues of sex and Christian life.

Contents

Preface

WHILE ADDRESSING ISSUES OF sexual ethics in my college courses over the past twenty-five years, I have encountered many students who were uncertain and confused about their own moral commitments regarding sex. This seems largely due to the fact that many of them had found insufficient resources for sorting out the relationship between their Christian faith and their sexual desires and practices. I have heard many sad stories of brokenness and regret, many of which end with the same refrain: "I wish I had an opportunity to think about these things prior to becoming sexually active!" But even stories fraught with less sadness have included a journey of uncertainty or confusion about sex. Listening to these stories and engaging in conversation with countless students through the years, both in and outside the classroom, has helped shape my own reflections about this topic over the years.

I am also a happy participant in a marriage of more than forty years and a father of two married young adults. The opportunity to share life with people who have had to find their own ways through the challenges of adolescence and young adulthood has helped me understand that lived realities in a complex world are not always a full realization of our ideals, thus creating the need for love and grace, always.

I hope that life lessons learned in work and family have helped me become a good listener and a good student who can bring an understanding of Christian moral commitments into conversation with the lived practice of our sexuality so that people who want to practice faith in every dimension of life will find at least a small measure of wisdom here.

1

An Introduction
and an Invitation

ONE SEMESTER A FEW years back, a group of my students who were assigned to lead a discussion about sexual ethics introduced their segment of the class with an old song entitled "Let's Talk about Sex." It was sung by the American hip-hop trio Salt-N-Pepa, and from what I could tell, everyone in the class had heard it—except me. Popular music is one important part of my students' lives that I'm not in close touch with. But the need to talk about sex is one that I *am* in touch with. And the invitation to talk *and to think* about sex is an important part of the invitation I offer at the beginning of this book.

WHY?

Well, for one thing, students are *doing it*—they are sexually active on a variety of levels, often beginning in their early teens. Sometimes that activity takes place in a relationship that seems like one of love, while at other times it takes place in a setting where teens are seeking love—and using sexual activity as an invitation. Sometimes it has taken place in past relationships and is regretted as part of someone's past "brokenness" or as an experience of learning one's lesson the hard way.

And while it doesn't get one very far morally, I have often said, "If you can't talk about it, you shouldn't be doing it!"

I wish I could tell you how many times my students have begun papers explaining their sexual ethic with a sentence that goes something like this:

1

"I've never really thought about this before." I can tell you that it has been frequent enough that I have often thought about having an old-fashioned rubber stamp made so I could emblazon in red ink the phrase "Well then, it's about time!" because these same students usually report being sexually active.

I still find it a bit mysterious that our bodies develop sexually well before the rest of us develop intellectually and emotionally enough to make thoughtful, carefully considered, and well-informed choices about how we will respond to the sexual urges welling up in us. But that's the way it seems to work. As a result, youthful sexual activity often outpaces our ability to do the kind of moral reflection that is required to guide our behavior by our convictions. When it does, people often look back at their experience feeling that they have been taken advantage of, used as someone's sex toy, or have given an important part of themselves when neither they nor their partner could appreciate the meaningfulness of what they were doing.

But if you are reading this book, you are likely past that point. Now you are asking hard questions and seeking resources to help you formulate an honest and effective sexual ethic.

THE AUDIENCE

If my readers are anything like my students, there will be a variety of stories to be told about personal sexual experiences. Some stories might be told as happy ones, even if they include the violation of some traditional sexual norms. Others will include regrets, painful memories, and even serious hurts not yet healed.

Here are some brief stories of real people.[1] They were all in college when I heard their stories and were self-identified Christians. I expect that many readers will find themselves among these stories, though they may need to make a few modifications to create a variation that fits.

1. Anna has dated just a few people through her college years, in hopes of finding someone to eventually marry. She doesn't believe in simply dating for fun anymore but only dates people who she could possibly see herself marrying someday. Even after several months, sexual contact is limited to a kiss, an embrace, or cuddling while watching a movie.

---

1. Though the events are real, the names are fictional; I have changed them to protect the confidentiality of those who shared their stories.

2. Mark was having a very hard time writing a paper about his sexual ethic. He explained that part of the challenge might be due to the fact that he has had sex with more women on his college campus than he can count. These encounters occurred almost exclusively after weekend parties when both he and his partner had been drinking. He wasn't in a relationship with any of them and didn't have contact with them at any other time.

3. Sarah and Michael have been in a relationship for more than two years and expect to get married someday. They both readily admit that they are in love and in a relationship that is "seriously committed." They intentionally moved slowly with the sexual side of their relationship. As Christians, they had been taught that sexual intercourse outside marriage was sinful, but little had been said about any other form of sexual contact. While they didn't think that the silence implied blanket permission, they did gradually progress to more intimate forms of sexual activity, involving nudity and genital stimulation. Even though they find their sexual activity to be a responsible expression of love, they still feel guilty about it.

4. Amy is part of the hookup culture on her college campus. She is dissatisfied with all the casual sexual activity that never leads to any serious relationship that values her as a whole person, but admits to finding some satisfaction in knowing that guys find her attractive. It makes her feel good to be chosen, even though it makes her feel bad to be discarded afterward. But it's a habit she can't seem to break, and it's such a big part of weekend social life among her group of friends that it's hard to see any alternatives. She described her situation as being similar to spousal abuse. She willingly consents to let guys use her sexually by returning to the same situations over and over again, even though she finds herself feeling unfulfilled and abused afterward.

5. Jim is engaged to be married to Grace in a few months after a long-term dating relationship. They've been "doing everything but" sexual intercourse for a long time and recently decided they can't think of any good reasons not to go all the way, now that they are engaged. In reflecting back on that decision, they affirmed their choice to engage in sex and even wondered aloud why people make such a big deal about sex before marriage. They are now married.

6. Angela had sex with her boyfriend a couple of years ago in a moment of passion—even though she would have told you she intended to wait until marriage. Soon afterward, that relationship ended. In her next

friendship, she didn't wait so long to have sex. After all, she reasoned, she had already lost her virginity, so what did it matter? She's now had sex many times in several short-term relationships. She never really decided that this was a good thing to do. It just sort of happened along the way. But she's not really comfortable with it and is still plagued by guilt.

What's the point of telling these stories? While I haven't heard or included every possible story that could be told (for example, I've omitted stories of abuse and date rape, even though, sadly, I hear at least one every year), I want you to know that in the pages that follow, I'm not presuming that every reader comes to this book with the same experience.

Someone recently recounted her experience of being part of an organized discussion about Christian sexual ethics. The presenter assumed that no one had engaged in sex yet and made a case for abstinence before marriage. If you didn't "save yourself" for the person you'd one day marry, you would be "spoiled goods" and would have to settle for whoever would want someone like that. "Well, then, I guess it's too late for *me* to have a Christian sexual ethic!" she thought. Of course it isn't too late—and I can't help wishing the presenter was more sensitive to the variety of stories her listeners could tell. Obviously, we don't all start from the same place when thinking about sexual ethics, and as a result we come to the topic of sexual ethics with a variety of questions and sexual experiences.

FORMULATING MY OWN SEXUAL ETHIC? WHAT DOES *THAT* MEAN?

Deciding what sexual ethic you want to live by is an important task because it helps you become conscious of the kinds of standards, values, and virtues that you want to characterize your sexual life—even if you sometimes fall short of living them out. If we don't know what our sexual ethic is, it's easy to be manipulated by the culture around us, by our peers, or by people who are seeking a sexual encounter. Sometimes people are hesitant to develop a sexual ethic because their behavior doesn't correspond to what they expect their ethic would demand. But a sexual ethic is not simply a description of what you now do; it's a description of what believe you *should* do. In a sense, your sexual ethic describes the ideal that calls you to be the kind of person you want to be.

But describing your sexual ethic can be difficult if you have never even thought about the concept before. There's no need to worry about that yet!

In the pages that follow you will be introduced to several ways of thinking about sexual ethics. These will provide you with resources for articulating your own sexual ethic in ways that reflect your theological perspective and Christian commitments.

One of the easiest ways to begin to understand what it means to engage in the task of ethics is to think about it like this: ethics is the way we explain the connection between *creed* and *deed*. So at its most basic level, in a Christian context, we are articulating a sexual ethic when we explain how the things we believe about God, ourselves, human relationships, and the purpose of sex should shape the way we engage in sexual behaviors.

This means that we have to think very carefully, first of all, about what it is that we actually believe and which of our beliefs can be used to shape our behavior. Then we need to figure out what those beliefs actually imply about the ways we conduct our lives—in this case, our sexual lives. We'll begin to explore this matter of beliefs in more detail in chapter 2. Subsequent chapters illustrate how a variety of models of Christian sexual ethics link Christian convictions with sexual behavior.

We don't always act in ways that reflect our convictions. You already know that. But ethics isn't a description of what we *do*. It's an explanation of why we *should* do certain things and *shouldn't* do others. When people tell me they can't develop a sexual ethic because they don't live and act the way they think they ought to, this implies that they already *have* a sexual ethic, at least at a subconscious level. Some standard is already at work in the background, telling them what they should be doing and providing a means for measuring their actual behavior against it. One of the tasks of ethics is to bring that standard into the open so that it can be stated, evaluated, possibly revised, or consciously adopted.

WHAT COUNTS AS SEX? (OR: WHY I USE A BROADLY INCLUSIVE APPROACH)

"What counts as sex?" might sound like a strange question! Doesn't everyone reading a book about sexual ethics know what sex is? If someone asked you, "Have you ever had sex?" you would probably assume they meant sexual *intercourse*—penile penetration of the vagina. This response could just be a reflection of what the word usually means to most people.

What if you were asked, "Are you sexually active?" Perhaps you would import the same definition and answer the question on that basis. Aside from sexual intercourse there are other forms of sexual activity. Consider this list, developed by my students:

- Gazing into each other's eyes
- Holding hands
- Giving or receiving a back rub
- Hugging (romantically)
- Caressing (non-genital)
- Kissing/making out
- Caressing intimate body parts
- Genital stimulation
- Genital stimulation to orgasm
- Oral genital stimulation
- Sexual intercourse (penetration)

Perhaps now the question about being sexually active gets harder to answer, because you'd have to decide what forms of sexual activity "count" as being sexually active. Someone still might want to reserve the phrase "sexually active" for sexual intercourse, but at that point it becomes clear that we may need another term to cover a wide range of significant sexual behaviors.

That becomes even clearer if in response to the question, "Are you sexually active?" someone who has done almost everything on the list *except* engage in sexual intercourse answers no. While they might still be technically accurate (if we accept that sexually active = sexual intercourse), the negative response seems to convey something less than a truthful response.

When you decide what counts as sex, you need to decide what range of sexual activity to include. I'd recommend a broadly inclusive approach, and here's why:

1. In our actual experience, a wide range of physical expressions of love have a high degree of meaning and significance. To the extent that sex is a language of love, a wide variety of sexual activities express love—not just sexual intercourse. If we include this wide range of actions in what counts as sexual activity, we can include the entire continuum in our sexual ethic. In other words, it enables us to think morally about what it means to kiss or caress a person or to share the intimacy of nakedness. If those are significant and meaningful human activities, then it makes sense to protect and nurture them with a moral framework.

2. Omitting most other forms of sexual activity from "what counts as sex" carries the danger that we will demean them rather than affirm

the richness and depth of their meaning and role in our lives. To say that only intercourse counts as sex may increase the value we place on sexual intercourse, but it threatens to cheapen the value of everything else and to leave us without any way to think morally about a wide range of sexual activity. If "all that other stuff" doesn't really count as sex, another step is to assume that none of it really matters all that much. And sometimes people choose to see actions like intimate caressing as actions that don't really matter and that don't need to be considered from an ethical perspective. Narrowing "what counts" to sexual intercourse can encourage us not to take the rest of our sexual activity seriously enough. Saying that nothing except intercourse "counts" may on the surface be a statement about definitions, but emotionally it may come to mean that the rest of our sexual activity "doesn't count for much."

A well-known public example of this is former President Bill Clinton's response to charges that he had a sexual relationship with a White House intern, Monica Lewinski. One of his famous defenses was "I never had sex with that woman"—technically true, if sex means sexual intercourse, but in light of the admission that eventually told the fuller story, not very truthful. (She had performed oral sex.) I wondered if President Clinton had received the same kind of sex education that many of my students had received— one that only addressed sexual intercourse ("don't have sex before you're married") and left a huge void when it came to everything else.

If only sexual intercourse matters, and if it alone deserves to come under moral scrutiny, then there would be no moral problem with other forms of sexual stimulation, right? But we seem to know intuitively that many forms of sexual activity matter, so we need to think morally about all of them. And if we don't know it intuitively, the approaches to sexual ethics we'll explore in subsequent chapters will provide some engaging moral arguments!

3. Starting out with a holistic sexual ethic that applies to a wide range of sexual behaviors also reduces the likelihood that one will have moral regrets in the future. One of my students, who was taught that only sexual intercourse is wrong (because her church was silent about everything else), put it this way: "The absence of rules and values for all sexual activity preceding 'sin' allowed me to experience these steps rather (too) quickly, leaving sex (sexual intercourse) knocking at my door." A sexual ethic that says little more than "don't have sex" (i.e., intercourse) seems to have the effect of permitting everything else, especially in dating contexts when the excitement of romantic feelings and the natural urges of human biology combine. People experience the common phenomenon of "going too far too

fast." When we think about the moral meaning of *all* of our sexual activity, it gives us the opportunity to make moral choices about our sexual lives.

Having a broadly inclusive sexual ethic is no guarantee that one will never experience regret. Sometimes what we regret is that our actual behavior fails to live up to the standards we set for ourselves. But there is another category of regret that we might avoid. If we know why certain behaviors are wrong and why they ought to be avoided, then we have a greater capacity to make choices that coincide with our commitments.

If our sexual ethic gives clear permission to some kinds of sexual expressions of love, an inclusive sexual ethic can increase the likelihood that we will express ourselves sexually in ways we can affirm rather than regret. A sexual ethic is not necessarily a set of rules that keep us from expressing our love through physical actions, so that we have no experience of sexual activity at all. Let's take kissing as an example. You might be able to avoid regret if your ethic says no to kissing and you are able to abide by it faithfully. But a sexual ethic can also help you avoid regret if it helps you understand what it *means* to kiss someone, in what types of relationships kissing makes moral sense, and what kind of character and intention you and your partner should bring to this form of loving gesture. Then, although you might have kissed several people during the course of your dating life, you could look back on it with a sense that it was appropriate and meaningful because it reflected your moral values in ways you could explain!

A FEW PRESUPPOSITIONS BEHIND THIS APPROACH TO SEXUAL ETHICS

1. Our experience of sexuality as male or female persons and our experience of giving and receiving the pleasure of sexual acts is all part of the wondrous way God created us.

To put it simply, sex was God's idea, and it is one of the blessings of our lives when our sexual practices are guided by moral values that seek God's good intentions for human sexuality.

Almost every contemporary treatment of Christian sexual ethics begins with an affirmation that sex is a good thing. I'm following the crowd here and you might actually wonder why it's even necessary to say this. Isn't this already an obvious fact that doesn't need to be underscored? But there are at least two common reasons it might not be so obvious.

The first is that there is a long tradition in Christianity of seeing sex as something other than good. As a result, there are plenty of Christians alive today who have internalized the tradition of a negative attitude toward sex. I once heard a summary of Christian sexual ethics that seemed to capture what I realized I had been taught, perhaps mostly through subtle messages. It went like this:

> *Sex is dirty.*
> *Save it for someone you love.*

That's obviously a confusing message! But the idea that sex is dirty isn't uncommon. In fact, as William Countryman points out in *Dirt, Greed, and Sex,* there is a long tradition in many cultures of using the idea that things are "dirty" as a means of conditioning people to avoid them. In the sexual arena, Christianity has done the same thing for a long time.

The problem, as implied in my two-line summary of sexual morality, is that teaching people that sex is dirty might help them avoid it when they are supposed to, but it does not serve us well when sex becomes an appropriate way to express and celebrate love and create new life in the context of marriage.

A second reason someone might not find it so obvious that sex is a good thing is that people sometimes experience sex in contexts of human brokenness, where it lacks the goodness I want to affirm. When sex is experienced outside relationships of love—for example, as experimentation, manipulation, selfish pleasure, a way to fill a void in one's life, or as a form of sexual abuse—people might find sex something they need to *recover from.* To say that sex is good in the face of very negative experiences of sex is a reminder that what some of us have experienced is a perversion of a very good thing and is not what God intended.

2. The morality of sex cannot be understood apart from the meaning of sex.

Sex is not only something we do. By claiming that it has meaning I am saying that it is more than simply a series of physical activities that can be explained descriptively. Perhaps it makes sense to think of sex as sacramental—in a lowercase sense. A sacrament means more than the physical action. An uninformed observer of a baptism might say, "Look, they are dunking that person under the water!" or "They're sprinkling water on that baby's head!" And an informed observer might say, "Yes, this is true, but that's not really the point . . . let me tell you what that action really *means.*"

What does sex mean? I'll propose thinking about sex as having multiple meanings, both intrinsically (what did God intend?) and as determined by the intentions of the people involved. Each dimension of this meaningful encounter helps enhance and support the other, so that it's best understood as a whole, even though it also makes sense to talk about each part separately. *Sex is an activity that communicates and symbolizes the bond of two individuals in a communion of committed love and, often, their willingness and desire to share in the creation and nurturing of new life.*

Sexual activity is a form of communication—it's a language of love and a form of human communion. It's a way that we use our bodies to say what we also mean with the words and actions that express our love. Sex and these other forms of communication should all be saying the same thing! This way of thinking about sexual ethics undergirds both a boundary ethic and a relational ethic—models discussed in chapters 3 and 4.

3. Sexual ethics is grounded in the created goodness of sex; whenever we say no, we do so to affirm a God-given gift and to affirm people God loves.

It's hard to imagine a sexual ethic that doesn't say no to some things. There are many ways that individuals and groups have distorted sex, because even good gifts can be used in ways that demean and distort them. But at the heart of every prohibition is an important affirmation, and hopefully the reader will always see that affirmation as the central theme. Sexual ethics is more about what to seek than what to avoid.

Of course, it's possible to focus only on fears and prohibitions. A limerick that summarizes (or perhaps caricatures) a Christian approach to sexual ethics illustrates this:

> There was a young woman named Wilde
> who kept herself quite undefiled,
> by thinking of Jesus,
> infectious diseases,
> and of having an unwanted child.
> [Source unknown]

It's a sexual ethic based on the fear of detection, infection, and conception. But when sex is shrouded in fear—even legitimate fear—it's easy to lose sight of the deeper and more positive affirmations that undergird these fears but also point beyond them. You'll be invited in these pages to consider the positive meaning and purpose of sex as the basis for thinking about how your moral convictions can guide your sexual practices.

4. Sexual ethics may be a resource for moral discernment.

This book is not designed to tell you what to think. It is designed to *invite you to think* and to be a conversation partner with you as you explore how your own beliefs can be used to shape a sexual ethic for your life. That doesn't mean that I express no viewpoints here. There are plenty of those. As in any serious conversation, I hope you will consider them carefully.

But you will not find in these pages a ready-made blueprint for a sexual ethic that you can simply adopt and employ. You'll have to sort things out, engage in some honest self-reflection and moral discernment, and make some choices. Instead of telling you what to think or what to do, this book is an invitation to explore, investigate, and talk about sex. It's meant to be conversational rather than dogmatic. It will offer you a variety of approaches, though unavoidably with a personal slant.

If you are left wondering, "So, now what am I supposed to do?" that's just about where you should be! Then it will be time for you to do the hard work of owning a sexual ethic that will help you implement the kinds of convictions and practice the kind of moral character that is most likely to guide you into a way of living that honors God.

5. Sexual ethics and LGBTQ+ Christians

Readers will be aware of the fact that people identify themselves as part of the LGBTQ+ community, and that this is an inescapable reality in today's culture. Some Christians are affirming and others are not. This is still an unresolved question in many Christian communities, and it often creates discomfort and conflict.

This book does not address the question as to whether or not same-gender romantic relationships are appropriate. That is an important question that many capable authors have dealt with, and a question that deserves its own book. I often recommend William Stacy Johnson's *A Time to Embrace*.

While this book is primarily intended for a heterosexual audience, Christians with a same-gender attraction can also benefit from developing a sexual ethic that is consistent with their Christian faith. Too often gay and lesbian Christians have been driven away from the church and consequently from their faith.

Students in my courses have identified themselves as gay, lesbian, bisexual and queer. I hoped as I wrote this book that the approaches to sexual ethics discussed here could be applied, perhaps with some creative imagination, to their lives as well. Many such students have told me that they found the ideas in earlier drafts to be a helpful way to think about their own sexual ethic.

2

Christianity and Sexual Ethics
Theological Reflections and Orienting Convictions

WHAT MAKES SEXUAL ETHICS *CHRISTIAN* SEXUAL ETHICS?

APPLYING THE LABEL "CHRISTIAN" to any approach to morality should always be done with humility and the willingness to explain oneself. After all, there are many books on "Christian" sexual ethics, and they say many different things, offering a broad spectrum of ideas about sexual morality. So what makes any of them "Christian"? What does it mean to place the word "Christian" in front of "sexual ethics"? What is implied by saying that someone has a Christian sexual ethic? I can't speak for others, but what I can do here is explain what I mean when I say that I intend to do *Christian* sexual ethics.

Calling a sexual ethic *Christian* is a way of distinguishing that there is a particular narrative and tradition that is being drawn on as we think about how to live out our sexual lives. The adjective points to the content of the fundamental convictions that affect what people believe they *ought* to do. In contrast, one could describe a Greco-Roman sexual ethic, a Jewish sexual ethic, or a libertarian sexual ethic. As you will see, I'll argue that there are certain things Christians believe that we'd expect to influence what Christians choose to do. In that sense, Christian sexual ethics could be expected to look different from a sexual ethic informed by a different set of religious or nonreligious beliefs. That's simply a description of how things are: our morality reflects the faith and worldview that has shaped our way of thinking about things.

But it's also the case that not all Christians see things the same way. As a result, there are a variety of ways Christians approach sexual ethics. So there are many approaches to sexual ethics labeled "Christian." Chapter 6 briefly discusses a few of these with a critical bent. But I hope that you will see that discussion as an "in-house" conversation with others who share many—but perhaps not all—of the same theological presuppositions. When I label a sexual ethic "Christian," here's what I have in mind:

Embodying Theological Commitments in Sexual Practice

A Christian sexual ethic *seeks to embody Christian theological commitments in sexual practice*. Serious ethical reflection addresses questions like, How do we channel the natural, sexual urges of our bodies in ways that express and honor God's intentions for sex? It invites one to consider how the things Christians believe shape their sexual practice. In the section that follows, some of these key theological commitments will be described as a set of orienting convictions.

Other approaches to sexual ethics that embody other worldviews and values might include insights that are compatible with a Christian sexual ethic, since some people who don't identify themselves as Christians sometimes still share similar beliefs. For example, people with a wide range of religious affiliations believe in the importance of respecting an individual's right to make choices about their own body without being coerced by others. This belief typically leads to a requirement that all sexual behaviors be the result of a person's freely given consent. Physical force, emotional manipulation and intentionally misleading a partner are ruled out. We shouldn't be surprised, then, if some elements of a Christian sexual ethic overlap with those of other religious or philosophical traditions.

Acknowledging the Authority of God's Will

A Christian sexual ethic acknowledges the *authority of God's revealed will* for human life and well-being, and specifically for sexual wholeness. Just how we gain access to God's revealed will is a complex issue in ethics. Yet, the idea that our moral life is not simply a reflection of our innate desires or what's popular in the culture around us means that Christian sexual ethics involves allowing one's sexual life to be shaped by a narrative outside of ourselves. It means acknowledging that there is an external authority to which our lives are accountable.

You'll notice that the Bible plays a key role in my understanding of what God intends for human sexuality and is a prominent source for the orienting convictions that shape a Christian way of thinking about sex. The Bible says some very clear things about the value of persons, the goodness and role of sex in human life, and also the possibility that this gift of God can be distorted. The cluster of insights, guidelines, and principles don't give us an instruction manual or an answer book. But insofar as they do orient us to a way of thinking about and embodying our sexual practices, it's certainly not the case that we're left to our own imaginations or passions or that it's up to each person to decide for herself. Orienting convictions are grounded in what the Bible does say and they help us fill in the gaps about what it doesn't say. They point us toward more specific ways to live out sexual lives that honor God.

"Who says?" is a common challenge to moral authority. We don't like other people telling us what to do. We prefer to make those decisions for ourselves! We value individual moral autonomy—the freedom and responsibility to make our own moral decisions based on freely chosen values. We even see doing so as a sign of moral maturity. How does that idea fit together with the authority of God's revealed will?

It fits like this: Christians respond to God's call on their lives with heart, soul, and mind. Developing a Christian sexual ethic does not require checking at the door our capacity to think carefully about what God asks of us or our capacity to give heartfelt assent to God's ways. When Jesus said to would-be disciples, "Follow me," he was issuing an *invitation*. But it was not an invitation to do one's own thing. It was an invitation to follow the way of *Jesus* rather than other ways. A Christian sexual ethic is meant to be a compelling way of thinking about sexual life in the context of the Christian faith that invites your own careful thinking and your own heartfelt assent.

A Communally Shared Understanding

A Christian sexual ethic is a *communally shared understanding* that allows those who confess a shared faith to uphold shared moral commitments, to call each other to embrace particular standards of practice, and to embody particular moral virtues. In fact, developing and sustaining a Christian sexual ethic is best thought of as an exercise of communal discernment, rather than an internal and individual process conducted in isolation from others.

But contemporary Christians don't always experience the kind of community that makes this easy. When I regularly ask college students whether they have had opportunities to have open, honest discussions about sex in the context of their church community, only a few say yes. And the whole idea of communal discernment can be scary, because sometimes that gets translated into others being "judgmental" and condemning. Sometimes it feels safer to just make our decisions privately. Still, there's much wisdom to be gained when we avail ourselves of the tradition, understanding, and varied insights of a community of fellow Christians seeking guidance on difficult moral issues. Communal discernment is an ideal to strive for. Sometimes that might mean reading a book like this and talking about it with close friends, family members, or other trusted adults.

An Ongoing Conversation

A Christian sexual ethic is an *ongoing conversation among a diverse body of believers* whose understanding of God might reflect different traditions, education, or experiences but who believe that it is important to seek to honor God in our sexual lives. Proponents of a specific moral stance often make positions sound firm, timeless, and beyond question. It's true that in order to put a moral viewpoint into practice, especially when it demands risk or sacrifice, one needs to have a high degree of certainty that it's right. If you think about your moral heroes, they probably weren't people who approached morality as if what one person believes is as good as what the next person does, or as if no one can ever really be sure about what's the right thing to do. Living out our morality requires that we be reasonably sure about it—and sometimes willing to put our lives on the line for it!

But there's a tension here, too. Sometimes moral traditions change (slavery is an example), and sometimes people change their minds about what's right and wrong (you can probably think of a personal example here). Morality is in flux, and when people engage in ethical reflection about what ways of behaving are implied by their beliefs, that reflection often looks more like an ongoing conversation between people trying their best to figure out how to lead lives that are faithful to God. When people are asking those hard questions and having the conversations that arise out of them, they are doing Christian ethics—and if sexuality is the topic, they are doing Christian sexual ethics.

ORIENTING CONVICTIONS

What are the theological commitments that Christians embody in their sexual practices? That's a complicated question that most of this book will try to help you answer. The source of those convictions is complicated too! They come from the Bible, but not necessarily in a literal way. And they come from the tradition, but the tradition is always in a dynamic process of change and reformation. And these sources of moral authority merge with our reflection and discernment about how our experience of love and sexuality yield helpful wisdom and guidance.

Let's begin by thinking about some general moral principles that I prefer to call "orienting convictions." There are some arenas of the moral life that are lived in ways that are responsive to the Bible but are not directly the result of explicit biblical instructions or examples. Why? Because in some areas of life, the Bible does not offer explicit instructions. Or if it does, there are other cases where our principles of interpretation do not allow a direct application of the literal text to contemporary life. The requirement to marry the childless widow of one's dead brother is an example of this (see Deut 25:5)!

Even when people believe that the Bible offers important and authoritative guidance for living out one's Christianity, it can still be confusing to look to the Bible for specific guidelines for sexual expressions of love in romantic relationships. Consider, for example, that in the moral world of biblical Judaism and of early Christianity, dating isn't part of the picture—but arranged marriages are! The idea that marriage is the choice of each partner and that they prepare for it in the context of a developing relationship of love is a modern alternative. Biblical admonitions are sometimes directed toward people whose lived experience did not quite match our own. This does not mean there are no important biblical resources for sexual ethics, but it does mean we must take care in deciding how texts apply to contemporary life.

These orienting convictions are beliefs Christians hold that prepare and predispose us to see the world in particular ways and that prepare us to act in the world in ways that embody those beliefs. They give us a perspective that in turn shapes the way we see ourselves and the sexual component of our lives. Even more, they point us in a direction, suggesting a connection between believing and doing. The word *orienting* brings a compass to mind. If you want to go in a particular direction, the compass points you there. Taking a compass reading implies more than simple interest in knowing which way is north. It implies that one wants to use the knowledge to head somewhere. It's a purposeful form of knowing. But it's not a GPS map with instructions about the precise route and every turn—although sometimes it probably seems like life would be easier if a GPS guided us step by step to our destination. But even though a compass doesn't do that in this analogy, it does have truth value and, therefore, an important level of authority. It tells us something we need to know, even though we have to figure some things out for ourselves. Which trail to take might be up to you, but north is more than a matter of opinion.

If you want to follow Jesus in the way you live out your sexuality, orienting convictions point in that direction. The specific steps you take or the trail you follow will be a response to those convictions. They enact one's way of acknowledging that the convictions really matter.

Orienting Conviction #1: God created us as sexual beings, and our sexuality is included in God's declaration of the goodness of creation.

Christian sexual ethics begin with an affirmation that comes from the Bible's own book of beginnings:

> So God created humankind in his image,
> in the image of God he created them;
> male and female he created them.
> God blessed them, and God said to them, "Be fruitful, and multiply . . ."
> God saw everything that he had made, and indeed, it was very good.
> (Gen 1:27, 28a, 31a)

The book of Genesis elaborates further in the next chapter:

> Then the LORD God said, "It is not good that the man should be alone; I will make him a helper as his partner" . . . So the LORD God caused a deep sleep to fall upon the man, and he slept; then he took one of his ribs and closed up its place with flesh. And the rib that the LORD God has taken from man he made into a woman and brought her to the man. Then the man said,
>
> > "This at last is bone of my bones
> > and flesh of my flesh;
> > this one shall be called Woman,
> > for out of Man this one was taken."
>
> Therefore a man leaves his father and mother and clings to his wife, and they become one flesh. And the man and his wife were both naked, and were not ashamed. (Gen 2:18, 21–25)

Whatever Christians believe about the *how* of creation, there's general agreement that the initial words in Genesis proclaim that our world exists because God called it into being. We are God's creatures. The world belongs to God because it was divinely created. And because God declared it to be good, there is a God-given goodness in all that God has made.

Why do we begin here, and how does this affirmation help orient us? The creation story is at the heart of a Judeo-Christian way of seeing the world, and our way of seeing things is at the heart of Christian morality. Our ways of seeing are shaped by a complex web of traditions, influences, and experiences—and often without our full awareness. Not all of those formative influences are healthy, nor do they reflect the way the Bible teaches us to see things. One of the tasks of Christian ethics is to remind us of the narratives that are meant to shape our moral vision. The story of creation is one such narrative. In a world full of messages about our bodies, sex, and relationships, the story of creation orients us to think about these within the context of a particular way of seeing.

First, it tells us that *sexuality is something to celebrate,* rather than *something to be ashamed of.* One thing that is very clear from the story of creation is that sex was God's idea. Whether you understand the story literally or as a theological affirmation that God is the source of all things and this world belongs to God, the creation narrative contains powerful images of the human bond between men and women. It is a deep bond grounded partly in our differences and our complementarity—but also in our profound sense of commonality. And virtually inseparable from the description of this unity is the recognition that the social and emotional bond is also expressed in the one-flesh union of sexual intercourse. This story serves as an important reminder that the shame about sex that we might have acquired isn't what God intended.

There is an important moral insight from this text that is meant to shape our vision of ourselves, of each other, and of our urges for sexual union. As many others have said, we live as embodied people because that is how God created us. It's our way of being human in the world, and our holiness is expressed *through* our embodied lives, not in denial of them. Since sexual union was part of God's creation, and declared to be a good part of creation, it is one of the areas of life we are meant to celebrate. And it is an area of life in which we can honor and glorify God as much as any other.

A second important insight we draw from the creation story is that *people (including ourselves) are created in God's image and deserve always to be treated with love and respect—in a way that honors the image of God in all of us.* For a very long time people have tried to figure out what the creation story means when it speaks of humanity being created in the "image of God." Is it our ability to reason? Is it our capacity to create or to engage in self-conscious reflection? Is it all of these? Since the Bible consistently describes God as love (in a whole myriad of ways), one way it makes sense to see God's image reflected in us is to see it in our capacity to love and be loved. We were created as an expression of God's love—and created to love God and each other with our whole being (body, soul, and mind). Our ability to love is at least part of what makes us reflections of our creator, because God is love.

love

When this affirmation shapes our moral vision, it teaches us to see ourselves as creatures of great worth who deserve to be loved and who deserve to be treated with respect because we were created by God to be loved. And it teaches us to see others through the same lens. However else we see each other, everyone is at his or her core a beloved creature of God, created to love and be loved. So we treat others with the respect due to one who is made in God's image.

Seeing people in this way honors the image of God in them, acknowledging it to be the truth in spite of appearances, since God's image isn't always apparent when we encounter people—or when we look in the mirror. This cuts both ways: one who seems ugly in disposition, behavior, or appearance is in fact created in God's image, and therefore a person of great worth. But someone who appears to be little more than a physical body exciting lust can never be reduced merely to external appearance either. What is more real about him is that he is created in God's image; she is a person of great worth to God.

Let's think about how this Christian moral vision might shape our way of looking at sex by considering a modern alternative. You might start by thinking about the way contemporary media or popular culture teaches us to look at physically attractive people: they are alluring bodies, there to satisfy our sexual urges (pornography); they represent a challenge, waiting to be seduced by means of manipulation or intoxicating substances; they are conquests that boost our self-esteem or characters in the stories we tell to enhance our image in the eyes of others. Each of these familiar ways of seeing is a distortion because it is reductionist. Seeing people like *that* isn't seeing people in the way the narrative of creation teaches us to see them. And it's not a distortion because physical attractiveness or sexual desire is involved! It's a distortion because not much more than sex is involved. Somewhere, the whole person has been left behind. What's left out is the kind of seeing that acknowledges the image of God in each one of us. When we see someone through the lens of God's image, we transform both our appreciation of their beauty and our sexual desire.

we should see them for the person, are, not just sexual desire

Orienting Conviction #2: Seek to honor God in all things.

Seek to honor God in all things. It's a simple and straightforward notion on the face of it. It's simple until we notice that we can't actually *do it* unless we have a clear sense of what God is like and, consequently, what kind of life *honors* God. Yet, as an orienting conviction, it reminds us that sexuality is one area of life in which Christians seek to follow Jesus. Honoring God in what we do with our sexual selves reminds us that sex isn't just about our bodies or the deep love we feel for another person. There is also a sense in which it is about God and our relationship to God. To honor God in *all* things is to avoid the temptation to compartmentalize sex.

This is a consistent theme in the Pauline portion of the New Testament, and it is perhaps the heart of Paul's sexual ethic. In his first letter to the Corinthian church, we become aware that there must have been some pretty serious abuses of sexual freedom taking place. In responding to their "sexual immorality" (translating the Greek term *porneia,* which can refer to a range of sexual practices), Paul points to one specific example people must have been talking about: a church member living in an incestuous relationship with his stepmother. He most likely had a cluster of other behaviors in mind as well.

Paul's primary concern in this text is the health of the church body. The Christian community is to live as a sanctified community where God's standards of holiness are embodied. When members of the community flaunt accepted standards, like the long-standing prohibition of incest, their immorality affects the whole body. But in this context Paul also helps us understand something important about the importance of sex. He develops what we might call a "body theology" that helps us understand the significance of honoring God with our bodies.

His starting point is a strong affirmation of our physical bodies, which were created by God and will be redeemed through resurrection. Rather than assuming that bodies don't matter, Paul understands Christian life as embodied life where bodies and what we do with them matter to God. Because our bodies will be raised as Christ's body was raised, we ought to think of our bodies as belonging to Christ.

> Do you not know that your bodies are members of Christ? (1 Cor 6:15)

In fact, they are temples in which God's Spirit dwells:

> Or do you not know that your body is a temple of the Holy Spirit
> . . . and that you are not your own? For you were bought with a
> price; therefore glorify God in your body. (1 Cor 6:19–20)

It is important to notice here that Paul's disapproval of sexual immorality is not based on the fact that there is something dirty or disgusting about sex; rather, it is grounded in the insight that there is something very good about our physical beings! In all that we do, we should treat our bodies with the respect due to God's indwelling Spirit.

One further step helps us understand Paul's views here. It is his understanding of what we might call the mystical, spiritual nature of sexual intercourse. Paul draws on the deeply affirming notion that sexual intercourse is a "one-flesh union" that creates a unique bond between people. It's not just a fleeting act of pleasure.

The combined affirmations of our bodily existence and the deeply meaningful nature of sexual intercourse lead to Paul's conclusion that we honor God with our bodies (1 Cor 6:20b). What we do with our physical, sexual selves matters to God because our bodies matter to God and sex matters to God.

There's a familiar ring to the moral argument in these texts. You can probably recall someone (perhaps a parent) justifying some piece of moral instruction or social norm with a phrase like "We don't do that kind of thing" or "We're not that kind of people!" It might have sounded like a lame reason when you heard it, but the deeper insight here is that *identity* (who we are) is connected to morality (what we do). So a first step in getting our behavior right is remembering who we are.

The same theme is repeated when Paul writes to the church in Ephesus, "But fornication and impurity of any kind, or greed, must not even be mentioned among you, as is proper among saints" (Eph 5:3).

These texts do not tell us exactly what to do or what to avoid, except in general terms. They don't say what counts as "sexual immorality," nor do they tell us what makes a person "impure." The author probably took for granted that people already had existing categories in mind. We'll need to sort out those kinds of details later, when we move from orienting convictions to some specific applications. What these texts *do* say is that the way we use our bodies to express love or to seek pleasure ought to have a clear connection to Christian identity. These texts point toward the development of a sexual ethic that honors God because that's what it means to be people of God.

What Does It Mean to "Honor God"? A Few Additional Reflections

If a Christian sexual ethic is framed as a God-honoring ethic, one of the first things to figure out is what the idea of *honoring* is all about. The word designates a cluster of attitudes that point to a particular way of relating to God. Let me briefly suggest a few overlapping dimensions of what it means to honor God.

Allegiance: Honor implies that we acknowledge our belonging to someone outside of ourselves. The reminder that "your bodies are members of Christ" is an invitation to recognize and give allegiance to Christ and to see what we do with our bodies in a wider context. That's the nature of allegiance. It's a way of seeing ourselves as responsible not just to ourselves but also to someone or something beyond us: a nation, a cause, an organization—or God. To give allegiance doesn't yet tell us what we need to do, but it orients us to the context in which we figure that out.

Imitation: While there is no explicit biblical connection between honoring God and imitating God, the concept of honor includes what Paul says to the Ephesians: "Therefore be imitators of God, as beloved children, and live in love, as Christ loved us and gave himself up for us . . ." (Eph 5:1–2a). The argument goes like this: we know what God is like because we have seen Jesus. He has taught us the way he wants us to live. The fourth chapter of Ephesians includes many reminders of that. Christians are urged to lead a life worthy of their calling, to distinguish themselves from the world around them, and to live the way they have learned from Christ. They are invited to imitate the way they have learned.

Obedience: Doing what God expects of us and acknowledging God's authority over our lives is another dimension of honoring God. When God gave the law to the Israelites, who had just been delivered from slavery in Egypt, God reminded them that their obedience was a way of honoring who God was: the gracious and powerful Lord who had delivered them! When Jesus interprets the law in the collection of sayings we call the Sermon on the Mount, he exhorts his hearers to be obedient to the way of life he describes. Obedience to Jesus honors him as Lord and affirms his authority to define what is good and what is expected from his followers.

Orienting Conviction #3: Sexual activities seek to express love in the context of covenant relationships.

Looking at the Bible from beginning to end, there is no uniform model of marriage. What marriage means takes different forms in different cultural and historical periods, and many of the characteristics of marriage in the Bible are absent from contemporary Western Christian understandings or have undergone significant shifts.

While arranged marriage was once the norm, marriage today is understood as a choice—a profound one, to be sure—of the individuals entering into the covenant. The transaction between the groom and the father of the bride is no longer a financial one, nor always even a real gaining of permission. When it still takes place today (reflecting an old tradition from an era when brides were the ones to be "given"), it is more likely to be a polite expression of respect for the family of the bride who have nurtured and loved her. But in contrast to the cultural context of Scripture, we don't believe that there's a sense of actual ownership connected to the way daughters belong to their fathers. Today, both daughters and sons belong to their families on the basis of things like gratitude and loyalty and bonds of love.

Even though social forms of marriage change through the history covered in the biblical texts, there is a consistent biblical affirmation that sexual union, understood as sexual intercourse, was meant to take place in the context of covenant relationships, and the Christian tradition has maintained the idea that God intended sexual expressions of love to take place within a covenanted love.

A long-standing way of expressing this idea is embodied in the tradition that sex serves two primary purposes, accompanied by corresponding intentions: procreation and unity. As a procreative activity, sexual intercourse brings with it the possibility of new life. The birth and nurturing of children takes place in the covenantal community created by marriage. As a unifying activity, sexual intercourse communicates, celebrates, and nurtures the deep unity that is Christian marriage.

Biblical admonitions about sex, and especially the prohibitions, seek to protect us from the harmful consequences that typically arise from sex in contexts other than those of covenanted love. While there is no certainty that sex will always have harmful consequences outside marriage, nor any guarantee that it will not sometimes introduce conflict or distress even within marriage, there is a long-standing wisdom that sexual intercourse is most likely to be an experience of meaningfulness and joy within a covenantal relationship. This is a good place to remind ourselves that a Christian sexual ethic doesn't simply set out to say no to a good thing or to take all the fun out of life. On the contrary, when sexual expressions of love honor God in the context of covenanted love, we are more likely to thrive as sexual people. Consider some reasons why.

1. Covenantal promises give meaning to sexual expressions of love. When we describe sexual intercourse as the consummation of marriage, for example, what we mean (at least in part) is that there is complete agreement between the unity we proclaim with our words and the unity we enact with our bodies. To the physical pleasure of sexual intercourse we can add the emotional pleasure of knowing we are loved exclusively, unconditionally, and forever (words typically found in a marriage covenant) by the person with whom we share our love.

2. Sex in a setting of covenanted love provides the security of a "no matter what" acceptance. Sex is a mutual expression of the passion we associate with *eros*, but it is also grounded in the security of knowing that our lovers have promised to love us no matter what—the *agape* love the New Testament describes. This kind of covenant-love eliminates performance anxiety, comparisons, and expectations. Instead, it provides the security of incorporating sexuality into the whole journey of learning to love each other more deeply and fully.

3. When sex takes place in a covenant relationship, most of the reasons to feel guilt and fear are removed. Sexual expressions of love, while appropriately private, don't need to be hidden. Sex is permissible and acceptable, removing the fear of detection, acquiring a bad reputation, or disappointing others. Privacy in a covenant relationship is now motivated by mutual respect, not by fear of getting caught.

4. Covenantal relationships actually enhance freedom in many important ways. This is especially true when there is a high level of trust and respect—two key components of a healthy marriage covenant. Partners have the freedom to say yes or no to sex without this needing to "mean anything" about the relationship as a whole. Partners have the freedom to learn, experiment, feel awkward, and even laugh at themselves. This freedom is grounded in a covenant of love that holds them together.

Orienting Conviction #4: Sex is good (a gift of creation), but not *all* sex is good (*porneia*).

Readers familiar with the story of creation know what follows: the story of the temptation of Adam and Eve and their disobedience to God. The story tells us that in a profoundly mysterious way, sin became a part of human existence, serving as a powerful reminder that even when we have every divine gift we need to flourish as God's creatures, we choose to disobey and dishonor God. Some of the sexual distortions that exemplify this are easy to identify: seduction and manipulation that seek to use others only as means to our own pleasure; sexual violence and rape; sexual practices that harm people physically or emotionally, and those that demean the image of God in us.

Does the reality of sin undo the goodness I've previously described? No, but it does introduce a tension into human reality that Christians have tried to explain for a long time. Lewis Smedes put the challenge well when he said, "Keeping the good of creation separate from sin's distortions of creation is no easy job."[1] On the heels of proclaiming that sex is part of the goodness of God's creation, the pervasive reality of our fallenness introduces another reality that is equally true of us: we are all caught up in the sinfulness that is part of our human existence and must constantly be aware that sex is subject to many distortions. It doesn't *always* reflect the goodness God created us to experience. There is brokenness in our sexual practices just as there is brokenness in our economic lives, our political lives, and our social institutions. So we must be constantly vigilant in discerning between the goodness God intends and the ways we violate those intentions.

Talking about sexual sins, distortions, or brokenness implies that there is a standard we can use to measure our sexual practices. In the biblical tradition where sin can be understood as "missing the mark," this measuring can be a way of gauging the distance by which we have missed God's intentions. Figuring out God's intentions for sex is the topic of most of the remaining chapters. At this point it is important to affirm, despite the different viewpoints expressed within the Christian tradition, that sexual ethics is about discerning what is good and, by implication, what isn't. It's about acknowledging a standard by which we intend to measure our sexual lives, and it's about identifying sexual practices we'll seek to avoid.

There are several different ways the Christian tradition has identified sexual sin. If we think about God's intentions in terms of *sexual boundaries* (see chapter 3 on a "boundary ethic") we can understand God's intentions, at least in part, this way: sexual expressions of love fulfill God's purposes when lived out in the context of covenanted relationships of love. From the story of Adam and Eve, through the evolving forms of marriage in ancient Israel, to the New Testament's affirmation of marriage and continuing through the dominant ethic of Western Christendom, marriage has been the appropriate context for sex. When the Bible identifies sexual sin, it almost always has in mind violations that refuse to honor the marriage boundary: adultery,

---

1. Smedes, *Sex for Christians*, 14.

incest, prostitution, or sex with an unmarried person.[2] Exhortations to "avoid sexual immorality" aim to uphold the conviction that God intended sex to be expressed within the boundary of covenanted love.

If we think about God's intentions in the framework of a relational ethic (see chapter 4), God intends sexual expressions of love to serve the ends of human well-being. They express love in ways that nourish romantic relationships. Relational qualities like mutuality, respect for autonomy, honesty, and commitment undergird the kinds of sexual practices that contribute to health and wholeness. In contrast, a relational ethic helps us see that there are many ways in which some sexual practices do the opposite. When sex is combined with coercion, manipulation, or dishonesty, for example, it degrades and demeans people. A relational ethic illustrates how the same sexual actions that God intends for human flourishing can be mis-used for selfish or destructive ends.

How does it help us to orient our thinking about sex by keeping sinfulness in mind? Sometimes the moral life involves steering a middle course between two extremes. You'll know that's not an original claim if you've read Aristotle. Let's think about those extremes as two sets of tensions. If we veer too far to either side we end up not telling the truth about sex, so the goal is to find our way down the middle.

The first set of tensions is between what I'll call, on the one hand, an anti-material form of *dualism* that sees sex only negatively and, on the other hand, an overly optimistic *romanticism* that sees sex uncritically as holding the promise for human fulfillment.

Dualism

There's a long tradition of associating sex and sinfulness. Sometimes this is linked to the idea that original sin is passed on in the act of sex. Some suggest that Augustine's treatment of sex is partly responsible for the way tradition has developed an anti-sexual bias. Augustine taught that after the Fall, sexuality became associated with bestial, passionate, and fleshly sexual desire and could easily take over one's whole being. Sexual passion was associated with lust and viewed as having the potential to turn one away from God. From this dualistic perspective, celibacy is recommended as the best way to avoid lust and the dangers associated with it. Following this reading

---

2. The tradition is not quite as uniform as a generalized summary makes it seem. For example, interpretations of Paul's advice not to marry—generally understood as a reflection of his expectation of Christ's imminent return—and the long tradition that exalts celibacy as a higher calling complicate the story.

of Augustine, he considered sex a lesser good. Its purpose was procreation, not pleasure. It's easy for us to learn to think about sex in this negative way, since remnants of this ascetic tradition have found their way into popular contemporary Christian attitudes toward sex.

An even more subtle form of dualism finds its way into popular consciousness. When we're young, talk about sex is often associated with "dirty" talk and sexual words are typically dirty words. When we grow older, talk about sex is often kept private, which can give us the sense that it's something to be ashamed of. Sometimes that private sex talk is also degrading, as in what we refer to as "locker room talk." And since there is plenty of negative sexual behavior in our culture, it's not surprising that we sometimes associate sex with sin. This way of thinking about sex forgets that it is part of God's creation and was intended to be part of the human flourishing that God desired for us.

Romanticism *overemphasizing*

The other extreme might very well be a reaction to this negativity. But an overly optimistic romanticism is more than simply rehabilitating an appropriate positive regard for God's good gift. It goes far beyond that to glorify sex, even to flaunt it, and to suggest that healthy sexuality must be free from traditional regulations. This way of thinking about sex forgets that human sin touches all of God's gifts.

There is a danger in *over*emphasizing the goodness of our created sexuality, just as there is a danger in denying that goodness by focusing only on the reality of the brokenness sometimes present in sinful sexuality. The goodness of sex doesn't imply an endorsement of unbridled pleasure-seeking, nor does it imply that restrictions are always a symptom of outdated negative views of sex that would have us flee from bodily pleasure and live as disembodied souls. The dual affirmation of created goodness and human sin leaves us always living in the tension between the celebration of sex and its potential abuses.

This first pairing of tensions leads to a second one, which has more to do with how we respond to the first tension. It's about how we engage the world knowing that sex does not belong only to the category of sin but it shouldn't be overly glamorized either.

Christian Discipleship Characterized by a Sense of Sinfulness

Christian life should be lived with an honest awareness of how easily we mess up God's world even when we're not intending to. But we can be overly cautious just as we can be insufficiently cautious. If life is too much about saying no to sin, about resisting evil, about avoiding impurity, it's possible that we will miss the very adventure of Christian discipleship. That includes the adventure of celebrating and expressing love through sexual activity. Knowing what can go wrong and sharpening our skills at discernment helps keep us on a path that leads to health and wholeness. But being afraid to take the next step because it might be the wrong step is paralyzing. Life is about more than simply resisting evil.

Christian Discipleship Characterized by Redemption and Grace

To live with an awareness that our lives are empowered by God's redemptive action allows us to maintain an awareness of the reality of sin (because after all, it is sin that makes redemption necessary) without being paralyzed by it. Our sexual lives, like all of life, can be lived in responsiveness to Jesus' invitation to follow the way of discipleship. God's grace makes us new creatures. A redemptive orientation allows us to live toward a vision of redeemed sexuality even while being honest and vigilant, given our imperfections.

It's helpful to be reminded that our embodied existence is affirmed in Jesus' incarnation and resurrection and also in the role people play as the "people of God." Embodied humans are called to be Jesus' disciples, called out of the world to form communities that are a witness to God's saving grace, and called to live out in earthly life the signs of God's Kingdom. These include some very bodily acts, like feeding the hungry, clothing the naked, and healing the sick. Christians respond to God's call as embodied creatures. God's Spirit inhabits embodied creatures and enlivens us for ministry and mission in God's world.

Christian discipleship is lived in hopeful confidence when the reality of God's transforming grace is the dominating feature of life. This doesn't deny the reality of sin, but affirms the reality of sin and redemption, admitting the brokenness that invariably creeps into our sexual practices, just as it does into all of human life. The goodness of embodied life and of human sexuality is a fragile goodness. It is always vulnerable. But still, Christian life, including our sexual lives, can be lived with the faith that God redeems our brokenness.

Orienting Conviction #5: Christians expect that living in faithfulness to God's intentions for human sexuality will often cause them to look different from the world around them.

The expectation of distinctiveness is not peculiar to the Christian tradition. Since religion is virtually inseparable from one's worldview, and since morality is usually grounded in religion and worldview, it's not surprising to find moral distinctiveness from one religion to another. In the Judeo-Christian tradition, some level of distinctiveness is expected. This is sometimes expressed in terms of "holiness" and a church-world distinction.

> But fornication and impurity of any kind, or greed, must not even be mentioned among you, as is proper among saints. (Eph 5:3)

Paul's exhortation to the church in Ephesus gives us a clear example of expected distinctiveness, including distinctive sexual practices. As soon as we begin to talk about holiness as a characteristic of human identity, there's an implied differentiation going on—between *us* (those who are God's people) and *them* (those who are not.) The distinction is intentional. It's meant to say that people who follow the way of Jesus can be expected to live out sexuality (among other things) in a way that is different from those in the surrounding culture. To use another Pauline image, Christian sexual practices honor God (1 Cor 6:20). Or, to put this in terms of Paul's idea that Christians are God's holy people, holiness means letting Christian morality shape the way Christians live—quite likely in distinction from those who don't share Christian convictions or a way of seeing shaped by such convictions. The conviction that Christians seek to honor God in all things is thus a call *to* something and a call *away from* something.

The image of holiness in Paul's writings doesn't imply perfection, but it does imply an intentional journey toward an ideal. Consider how this is described in another Pauline letter:

> For this is the will of God, your sanctification: that you abstain from fornication; that each one of you know how to control your own body in holiness and honor . . . (1 Thess 4:3–4)

Raymond Collins' study of New Testament sexual ethics reveals a diversity of material that could only be synthesized by undertaking what he calls a "foolhardy endeavor." However, Collins also says there is a dominant motif among all of this diversity:

The dominant motif might well be that the disciple of Jesus is called to live with his or her sexuality in a way that is different from the way that others live with their sexuality . . . Those who have embraced the gospel of Jesus as adults might be able to contrast the way they live out their sexuality as disciples with their own previous sexual behavior. The sexual mores of the Christian are to be different from the rampant pursuit of sexual pleasure that often characterizes those who are not Christian.[3]

What is the point of living a holy or sanctified life? It isn't meant to be a reason for self-congratulation or for looking down on outsiders. Instead, it is meant to be an affirmation of one's identity—as people who know God and seek to honor the God they know. Leading lives that honor God shouldn't result in pointing down at others in an attitude of superiority. Lives of holiness don't point down at others; they point toward God. They are a witness to the kind of healthy wholeness that reflects who God is and what God wants for those God loves.

IN CONCLUSION: MERGING SEXUALITY AND SPIRITUALITY

Our attitudes toward sex and our sexual practices do not need to be tucked away in a hidden corner of our lives, far removed from Christian convictions, spiritual disciplines, or a personal relationship to God. Many of us have been taught to feel that way, having internalized the idea that "sex is dirty." I'm not suggesting hanging a picture of Jesus in the bedroom. But I am suggesting that God smiles on the idea of expressing our love in sexual ways, when those expressions are God-honoring.

Christian spirituality has been described as "the outworking in real life of a person's religious faith—what a person *does* with what they believe . . . It is about the way in which the Christian life is conceived and lived out. It is about the full apprehension of the reality of God."[4] Understood in this way, spirituality is the way Christians practice the presence of God in every area of their lives—including the sexual realm.

An incarnational theology of the body helps us understand why it makes sense for Christians to live out their sexuality in ways that practice or embody the reality and presence of God. God created us as physical, sexual beings and declared this to be good. James Nelson affirms this idea when he writes, "Sexuality is crucial to God's design that creatures not dwell

3. Collins, *Sexual Ethics and the New Testament*, 183.

4. McGrath, *Christian Spirituality*, 2.

in isolation and loneliness but in communion and community."[5] But even more, Jesus took on human flesh, and in flesh embodied godliness. Again, in the words of James Nelson, "The most decisive experience of God is not in doctrine, creed, or ideas, but in the Word made flesh—and in the Word still becoming flesh." One way God's word becomes flesh is in the life, death, and resurrection of Jesus. Another way God's word becomes flesh is in the lives of God's people, we who seek to honor God in every aspect of our bodily lives.

The merging of sexuality and spirituality makes it possible to celebrate our sexual lives as part of life lived in response to God. It makes it possible to let God speak to our sexual lives and for us to answer, not by fleeing from sex but by bringing our sexual practices into harmony with what we believe and profess. Even our sexual expressions of love are a way to honor God.

5. Nelson, "Reuniting Sexuality and Spirituality," 187–90. Nelson has written extensively on the relationship between sexuality and spirituality.

3

Some Ways to Think about Sexual Ethics

Boundary Ethics

BOUNDARIES AND THE RULES that define them are a common part of life. While we sometimes resist them, we also realize that they are often an effective means of keeping us safe. Traffic laws are an example of this kind of boundary. We may wonder, "How fast may I safely drive on this road?" and the speed limit sign offers the answer: 45 mph.

To offer another example, fences keep us at a safe distance from dangerous places, and "Do Not Enter" signs aim to keep us out of such places. The boundaries limit our freedom, but they do so in the name of our safety and well-being. There is also a comfortable simplicity accompanying these kinds of boundaries. We don't need to do a conscious assessment of the risks, because that work has already been done for us. We don't necessarily need to ask for reasons or justifications or calculations; we can simply observe the boundary, trusting the wisdom and authority of whoever established it.

Boundaries also tell us what is right and good in a more explicitly *moral* way. When we are told not to steal, we are told to recognize the boundary between what belongs to us and what does not. The moral rules that begin "Do not . . ." typically draw boundaries: do not kill, lie, or commit adultery. Moral boundaries like these are designed to limit our freedom too, and they do so in the name of providing moral guidance that helps people distinguish right from wrong and that regulates our common life.

WHAT IS A BOUNDARY ETHIC?

The morality of sexual activity is often explained in terms of boundaries, and many of the familiar, traditional approaches to Christian sexual ethics take the form of a boundary ethic. A boundary ethic establishes a line that distinguishes right from wrong and explains why the line exists where it does. This way of framing moral issues is based on the belief that *abiding by God-given boundaries for sexual practice is the way we acknowledge and affirm God's sovereignty over sexuality and the way we experience God's blessing on our sexual lives.* We'll examine some examples of this approach to sexual ethics in this chapter.

Almost all of the Christian college students I've encountered in more than two decades of teaching have learned a boundary ethic from their church or family—if they have learned any kind of sexual ethic at all. Here's part of a student's story that illustrates some key issues we'll address:

> My identity as a Christian was and still is incredibly important to me, therefore I placed great value on following God's commands. My youth leader talked often of God's very strict boundaries for sexual morality: there should be no kissing before marriage, and of course absolutely no sex before marriage. There were no alternatives to this high standard of morality; any physical activity was considered sin. I was an extremely passionate, impulsive, and romantic kid, a lethal trio. Given that my first kiss occurred at the age of thirteen on a youth group mission trip, it is not hard to imagine why the subject was wrought with confusion. The strict boundary ethic my church demanded was violated over and over throughout my teenage years. In my eyes I disappointed God continually. My natural desire for sexual intimacy led to a lasting sense of guilt and shame . . . I felt like an out-of-control, sinful, strangely passionate, awful, immoral girl.

There are several themes in this story that are commonly found when sexual ethics takes the form of a boundary ethic. My student learned that God is the source of behavioral boundaries and that to cross these lines is a violation of God's commands. The boundaries have clear behavioral references—for example, kissing someone or engaging in sexual intercourse. When the actions take place on the wrong side of the line, they are sinful. And in spite of the serious nature of boundary violations, we find ourselves easily tempted to cross the line anyway. When we do, boundary violations result in guilt. But sometimes confusion replaces guilt, because it's not always clear *why* it's wrong to cross a particular line.

While this story contains oft-recurring themes, not every boundary ethic draws lines at the same place. Often the boundary simply says that sexual intercourse belongs only in marriage. People are then left to figure out the other lines (if there are any) for themselves. This generates a commonly heard boundary question: How far is too far? (We'll look at how a boundary-ethics approach could help answer that question later in the chapter.)

Wherever the lines are drawn, and however specific they are, staying within them seems to be a struggle for people with natural sexual urges, especially in the context of romantic relationships. Of course, keeping within other moral boundaries is often difficult too. Guilt and shame are not accidental within the framework of a boundary ethic. They typically serve as reminders that a standard has been violated or that one's moral identity has been compromised and as motivators of a renewed effort toward greater obedience.

Here are some examples of boundaries gleaned from a variety of contemporary books or articles on Christian sexual ethics:[1]

Some boundary examples

- The covenant of marriage is God's intended context for the pursuit of full and joyful sexual and relational intimacy. (Gushee)

- There is no getting around it: biblical teaching places a clear veto on sexual intercourse for single people. (Foster)

- Oral sex is sex and belongs in the intimacy of a marriage, not in the explorations of physical intimacy outside of marriage. (Hollinger)

- A couple who is casually dating ought not to be engaging in activity that is leading them to sexual union. (Grenz)

- A couple should not engage in any sexual acts in private that they would not do in public. (Winner)

- "I am recommending virginity. Virginity for both men and women. If virginity is to be preserved, lines must be drawn. Why put yourself in a situation where the lines become smudged and obscure? Why take the risks? Why accept the pressure of tremendous temptation when you can easily avoid it by refusing to be anywhere where compromise is possible?" (Elliot)

1. Examples come from the following sources: Gushee, "A Sexual Ethic for College Students"; Foster, *Money, Sex, and Power*; Hollinger, *The Meaning of Sex*; Grenz, *Sexual Ethics*; Winner, *Real Sex*; Elliot, *Passion and Purity*; Ludy and Ludy, *When God Writes Your Love Story*.

- Save yourself completely (emotionally and physically) until you meet your future spouse. (Ludy and Ludy)

These examples probably sound familiar to those whose moral sense about sex has been formed by the church—even if that education never happened in explicit, formal ways. One reason for the familiarity is that establishing sexual boundaries is a long tradition in Christian sexual ethics and that if Christians have learned anything about sexual ethics, it's probably come in the form of a boundary ethic.

Three Defining Characteristics of a Boundary Ethic

First, a boundary ethic is *rule-oriented*. Rules define the boundary and at the same time establish the "oughtness" of the boundary. There are lines not to be crossed, usually in the form of actions to be avoided. Sometimes there are also thoughts and feelings to be resisted. The rules might be a means of reaching positive moral goals (sexual "purity") or avoiding things like sexual temptation or lust. Or they might help people identify in very specific ways when people should feel guilty. The rules might also be understood as guidelines that help us put our convictions into practice.

When people advocate a set of rules for guiding one's sexual life, or when someone chooses to adopt a set of rules to define their own sexual ethic, there are several legitimate questions to consider: Where do the boundaries actually come from? What exactly *are* the rules? What status do they have—are they moral absolutes, or simply guidelines? And what reasons explain why they make sense or ought to be followed? Writers who propose a boundary ethic sometimes treat some of these questions while ignoring others, and the answers they give vary from one advocate to the next.

Second, a boundary ethic is *obedience-oriented*. It places primary importance on keeping oneself on the right side of the line, and this is often accomplished by obeying the rule that defines the line. Obedience is a pervasive element of morality. In the Christian tradition, if one knows nothing else about Christian morality, it's likely one could at least summarize the requirement to obey the Ten Commandments. Obeying parents, authorities, or simply obeying the law is so fundamental in our human experience that we aren't surprised when we find it as a common feature in sexual ethics. A somewhat simplistic reminder of an ethic of obedience is summarized by the bumper sticker "God said it, I believe it, that settles it." Still, if one truly believes that a moral rule is God-given (however one understands that idea), then obeying the rule is serious business.

The tradition of Christian sexual ethics has a more developed understanding of the motive for obeying the rules, and in contemporary sexual ethics, we find several typical reasons for obedience.

- Obedience is evidence of *faithfulness to God*. Both the Jewish and Christian traditions have underscored this motivation to keep God's commandments. Loving God and obeying God are often closely identified; God's people were taught to see them as inseparable. "You shall love the LORD your God . . . and keep his commandments always" (Deut 11:1). Jesus told his disciples, "If you love me, you will keep my commandments" (John 14:15). In the biblical tradition, obedience is motivated by love and is a sign of that love.

- Obedience *acknowledges the truth of the commandments*. Of course, not all obedience is authentic. In real life, people don't always obey the rules for the best of reasons, even though the motivations might be very powerful. As one of my students said, "I maintained my boundary ethic out of an oppressive fear of displeasing God, my church, and my family." In contrast, authentic obedience implies a confession of faith. It is a way of saying that one believes the rules have a real claim on us, because they are valid, true, and worthy of being obeyed.

- Obedience is also understood as *a way to experience God's blessing*. In the Old Testament, Israel is promised God's blessing when the people obey God, and they find themselves thriving when they keep God's law (see Deut 28). The writer of Proverbs celebrates the wisdom of God's commandments—in chapter 4 we read, "Keep my commandments and live," "The path of righteousness is like the light of dawn," and "My words are life to those who find them." In the context of a boundary ethic, people thrive when they observe the boundaries because God's law reflects what is essential for human well-being. Josh McDowell puts it this way: "God's motivation behind every command in the Bible is to provide for us and protect us."[2]

- Finally, obedience is sometimes also recommended as a *means for avoiding negative consequences*. One of my favorite summaries of a traditional Christian sexual ethic (also quoted in chapter 1) focuses clearly on averting unwanted results. It goes like this:

> There was a young woman named Wilde,
> who kept herself quite undefiled;
> by thinking of Jesus,

---

2. McDowell, *Why True Love Waits*, 201.

infectious diseases,
and having an unwanted child.
[Source unknown]

In the context of a boundary ethic, the limerick calls attention to the dangers we'd want to avoid and the implied boundaries that exist to protect us from these harms. In the popular sexual morality of contemporary culture, as in many areas of the moral life, the principle "Do no harm" functions as a primary moral norm. Actions that harm people are seen as wrong; actions that don't hurt anyone are considered a matter of personal preference but morally neutral. Avoiding harm is a powerful motivator, especially when accompanied by fear—like the fear of an "unwanted pregnancy" or of contracting a fatal sexually transmitted disease. When the rules keep us safe, common sense and self-interest provide a strong incentive to observe the boundaries. McDowell's *Why True Love Waits* provides one of the most exhaustive catalogues of negative consequences one can avoid by observing the boundary of reserving sexual intercourse for marriage. A long list of physical, emotional, relational and spiritual dangers fills more than one hundred pages.[3]

Third, a boundary ethic is *act-oriented*. This means that its primary focus is on our actions—what we actually do—rather than our motives or intentions, or on the consequences. Most models of a sexual boundary ethic explain which actions are appropriate within a specific context. The least complex and most common version says "sex belongs only in marriage." But since it is act-centered, a boundary ethic requires some clarity about which actions "count" as violations. As a result, as we saw in chapter 1, this is where one must address the question, What counts as sex? When my students wrestle with that question, they begin with a list of potential *acts* that might count:

- Gazing into each other's eyes
- Holding hands
- Hugging
- Kissing
- Caressing intimate body parts
- Genital stimulation to orgasm
- Oral genital stimulation

3. McDowell, *Why True Love Waits*, especially chapters 10–15.

- Sexual intercourse

As you might imagine, the first four are rarely considered "sex" even though they may be romantic gestures of love. The last four seem a bit less clear and it's harder to gain any consensus about what should count as "sex." It's generally assumed that when people say "sex" they mean sexual intercourse. That's simply a fact about how we use language. So when people say something like "sex only belongs in marriage" they are likewise often referring to sexual intercourse. If that's the case, the boundary seems clear, and all that's left is to provide the biblical and theological rationale for why the line is drawn there and why it should be obeyed. But this doesn't yet provide a workable boundary ethic.

In real life, since boundary ethics are act-oriented, a functioning boundary ethic appears to require much more! One of the most common questions I encounter among college students who have been taught this boundary ethic is the question, How far is too far? In other words, they know where one line is drawn, but no one has been very clear about any other lines. (We'll come back to this question again in a few pages.) While this question is often criticized,[4] it seems natural and understandable when sexual ethics is taught in a way that focuses on boundaries. If the boundary really is the dividing line between actions considered sinful and those that aren't, someone who sincerely does want to avoid sin seems justified in asking where the line actually is. "OK, so no sexual intercourse prior to marriage. That's clear." Do other boundaries exist? Are all other sexual acts morally irrelevant when it comes to establishing a sexual ethic? Is everything else a matter of personal preference and mutual consent? A sexual ethic focused on sexual acts will only be complete when it pays attention to the full range of sexual activity about which people wonder.

When Christian writers address these additional questions, the discussion often turns to consider whether other forms of sexual activity should also count as sex, and thus be included on the prohibited side of the line. For example, commenting on the list of sample boundaries above, one writer has said, "Oral sex is sex and belongs in the intimacy of a marriage, not in the explorations of physical intimacy outside of marriage." This writer clearly says that oral sex is also an act that counts as sex, along with sexual intercourse. But the statement also implies that there are other acts of physical intimacy that do not count as sex. Some suggest that any form of sexual activity resulting in orgasm counts as sex, while some claim that any sexual activity that "leads to intercourse" counts as sex. In all of these

---

4. A common critique is that people who ask this question are simply seeking to get as close to the line as possible and aren't really concerned with the spirit of the rule.

discussions, you will notice that in order to make a boundary ethic usable, one must decide which acts get included on one side of the line or the other.

There is one more possible complication arising from an act-orientation. If marriage is the line that determines whether actions are right or wrong, might one also ask, What counts as marriage? A person seeking to do the right thing, in this ethical model, will be asking, When am I on the right side of the line? While that may seem easy to answer, people sometimes feel that engagement is so close to marriage (there is already a public declaration of one's intention to live in a lifelong covenant of love) that it is *morally equivalent* to marriage. Others who choose to live in a committed relationship without a wedding or without a marriage license might think that their relationship counts as marriage—being more loving, committed, and healthy, perhaps, than many legally recognized marriages they know. So it seems that even the marriage line is sometimes fuzzy! Fuzzy boundaries lead to confusion, and the sense that one might have crossed a fuzzy boundary has the capacity to create an ill-defined sense of guilt.

TWO MODELS OF A BOUNDARY ETHIC

There are several ways to develop a boundary ethic as a way to guide sexual choices and behaviors. Lewis Smedes and Dennis Hollinger provide two good examples of this approach. Both are clearly grounded in a biblical and theological framework. Smedes based his boundary approach on a theological understanding of God's law, while Hollinger's boundary is based on the meaning of sex, as determined by a theological reading of God's creation intent. While the emphasis varies, the approaches overlap in a way that would allow one to combine them. However, the emphasis in each one is distinct enough that each needs to be highlighted on its own merit. On what authority is the boundary based? What would it mean to say that it's wrong to cross the line? Where is the line? And what goals is one likely to seek in obeying these boundaries?

Model One: A Moral Boundary to Designate Sin—Lewis Smedes' Ethic of Law

Perhaps the most common way to think about a boundary is to see it as the line between appropriate behavior, on the one side, and sinful behavior, on the other. It's the line you should not cross if you want to act in ways that honor God and if you want to avoid sinful actions. Boundaries are a way of *naming sin.* And if that word is too full of baggage, boundaries are the lines we draw to avoid the kinds of harmful, destructive, demeaning, or dehumanizing actions that a loving creator prohibits so that we can experience the fullness and joy in life that God intends.

How does anyone know where to draw such a line? Clearly, if someone tells us that crossing a particular line means we are engaging in sinful actions, we need to know with a relatively high degree of certainty that this line is reliably drawn! Getting the lines in the wrong place would mean either treating sinful behavior as if it's healthy and good or treating behavior that's healthy and good as if it's sinful.

For Lewis Smedes, author of the long-popular book *Sex for Christians,*[5] the boundary line that prohibits sex outside marriage is justified because it reflects God's moral law. Smedes distinguished a morality of law from a morality of consequences.[6] It is important to consider the consequences of our actions. Do they harm people or relationships? Actions that we may expect to have harmful consequences should be avoided. For Smedes, this is a basic moral requirement. But while morality is concerned with consequences, it is not *only* concerned with consequences, he argues. To understand the prohibition of sex outside marriage as moral law means that there is an absoluteness grounded in the inner reality of the act of intercourse. Intercourse outside marriage is wrong independent of external factors. Whether or not is has good or bad consequences matters, but that is not what ultimately makes it right or wrong. What motivates people to engage in sex and the moral qualities they bring to the relationship matters too, but again, it's not ultimately what counts. Many of us have been taught to evaluate the moral character of behaviors on the basis of motives and consequences, so the claim that something else matters even more sounds a little out of the ordinary. Here's how Smedes approaches it:

First, he identifies Pauline writings in the New Testament as the primary basis for the unqualified prohibition. Sexual intercourse between unmarried people is included in the New Testament condemnations of *porneia.* The Greek word is translated as fornication, or more commonly today as *sexual immorality.* The term is obviously vague and begs the

5. The following includes some closely paraphrased sections from chapter 5 of Smedes, *Sex for Christians.*

6. Smedes does acknowledge several consequentialist reasons that are likely to impact one's sexual practices: Will such behavior hurt you, the other person, or the relationship? If so, these alone might be reason to abstain from sexual activity. These kinds of considerations fit another form of boundary ethic that I call a "morality of caution" (see below). Smedes says that such an approach ultimately misses the fact that it is the moral quality of the act of intercourse itself that makes it a moral good within marriage and a distortion of the meaning of sex outside marriage.

question what really counts as sexual immorality. Smedes explains why sexual intercourse is among its clear meanings:

> Paul makes it clear that [porneia] also means sexual intercourse for unmarried people. In I Corinthians 7 he concedes that to be both unmarried and a virgin is, under the circumstances, the best life. But "because of the temptation to immorality, each man should have his own wife and each woman her own husband" (I Cor. 7:2). Better to marry, he said, than to be ravished with unfulfilled desires. So he must have meant that "immorality" included sexual intercourse outside marriage.[7]

His summary affirms the long-standing and widespread tradition of interpretation that has undergirded Christian prohibitions of intercourse outside marriage.

While people have been told for a long time not to engage in sex outside marriage, Smedes says the crucial question is, what makes it morally improper? The moral law, Smedes argues, is grounded in a positive insight about the inner reality of the act of sexual intercourse. In other words, the "no" to sex outside marriage is based on a positive view of sex. It's even a very high view! It isn't a case of saying "sex is bad, don't do it." Instead, Smedes argues that because it is very good, it should be reserved for the context that honors its goodness. The Pauline insight draws on the idea in Genesis 2 that in sexual intercourse, two people become one. In Smedes' words, "Sexual intercourse involves two people in a life union; it is a life uniting act."[8] He goes on to say that Paul sees sexual intercourse

> as an act that signifies and seeks the intrinsic unity—the unbreakable, total, personal unity that we call marriage.
>
> It does not matter what the two people have in mind . . . The *reality* of the act . . . is this: it unites them—body and *soul*—to each other. It unites them in that strange, impossible to pinpoint sense of "one flesh."[9]

So, for Smedes, sexual intercourse is wrong for people who are unmarried because

> it violates the inner reality of the act; it is wrong because unmarried people thereby engage in a life-uniting act without a

---

7. Smedes, *Sex for Christians*, 108.
8. Smedes, *Sex for Christians*, 109.
9. Smedes, *Sex for Christians*, 110.

> life-uniting intent . . . Sexual intercourse for unmarried people
> . . . is a contradiction of reality.[10]

In order to avoid any confusion about what Smedes means by a life-uniting *intent*, it's necessary to distinguish two meanings of the word. Smedes doesn't mean that sex is appropriate as long as people *intend* to get married. In that sense, an intention is like a plan. For Smedes, what one intends is more like what one means by what one does. Think about it this way: sexual intercourse says something. It says, in essence, the same thing that marriage or marriage vows say: I take you, and you alone, unconditionally and forever as my husband or wife. Being married means living that intention as it's expressed in the traditional words of the marriage covenant. Engaging in sexual intercourse means the same thing: it says what one intends or means in marriage. Thus, to be truthful, one must only engage in the act of intercourse when one is living this intention in marriage. To say what intercourse means in any other context is the moral equivalent of telling a lie. A couple might soon plan to be married. But for Smedes, planning to live the intention isn't the same thing. Marriage is a meaningful boundary because the marriage covenant itself is a meaningful change of status. It establishes the intentions stated in the vows.

Model Two: The Meaning of Sex and Sexual Boundaries

Ethicist Dennis Hollinger is another proponent of a boundary that prohibits sex outside marriage.[11] Hollinger's way of explaining the boundary emphasizes a biblically based theology of the meaning of sexual intercourse that can be seen in the purposes for sex. To observe the boundary is to live in a way that reflects God's intention for sex as seen in God's creation-intent. Hollinger states the boundary (no sex outside marriage) very clearly in these summary comments:

> Pre-marital and all non-marital sex is morally wrong because it does not fit with God's intended purposes for this good but finite and now fallen gift . . . Both Genesis and Jesus state that in sex we become one flesh with another person. This is the consummating act of marriage.[12]

10. Smedes, *Sex for Christians*, 110.

11. Hollinger, *The Meaning of Sex*. See especially chapter 4 for his more complete explanation of the purposes of sex.

12. Hollinger, *Meaning of Sex*, 134–35.

While Hollinger's account of sexual intercourse is consistent with Smedes' (Hollinger quotes Smedes approvingly at several points), Hollinger's *boundary* for sexual intercourse is based on the combined *purposes* for sexual intercourse. Here's a brief summary of Hollinger's presentation of those four purposes:[13] The first purpose of sexual intercourse is the consummation of marriage. In becoming one flesh, the relationship between two people is now different. The paradigm for understanding sexual union as the consummation of marital union is Genesis 2:24–25:

> Therefore a man leaves his father and his mother and clings to
> his wife, and they become one flesh. The man and his wife were
> both naked, and they were not ashamed.

Hollinger describes the close connection between the oneness that is part of marriage and the oneness that is expressed in the physical union of intercourse. Two people "merge their deepest longings and commitments into a shared reality"; they experience a "striking vulnerability" and give themselves "physically and emotionally to one another [in] an act of trust . . ."[14] One might ask, "Is he talking about sex or marriage in those descriptions?" The point seems to be that sex and marriage are merged in an experience of this one-flesh union, and in a way that God never intended them to be separated. So Hollinger can say that sexual intercourse, "by its very nature and God's design," is "intimately bound up with marriage."[15]

Procreation is the second purpose of sexual intercourse. "God's intention from creation is that children be born out of a sexual union that is covenantal, permanent, loving, enjoyable, and responsible."[16] This doesn't mean that in every sexual act a couple must intend to have a child. Both the Roman Catholic and Protestant traditions recognize that sexual intercourse is both procreative and unitive—it has the God-given capacity to produce a child *and* to create a deeper sense of unity and love between husband and wife. Yet, since these capacities can never be absolutely separated, a man and woman who engage in sexual intercourse should be "willing to receive the potential fruit of their love."[17]

The third purpose of sexual intercourse is to express love. Love is understood here as a combination of *eros* (a love that responds to something

13. See *The Meaning of Sex*, chapter 5, for the complete explanations. I have summarized key points drawn from that chapter in a way that, I hope, represents Hollinger's argument fairly and accurately.

14. Hollinger, *Meaning of Sex*, 100–101.

15. Hollinger, *Meaning of Sex*, 100.

16. Hollinger, *Meaning of Sex*, 102.

17. Hollinger, *Meaning of Sex*, 105.

lovable, or the love we might simply call "romantic love") and *agape* (the love described in 1 Cor 13). Hollinger echoes the oft-made claim that "sexual intimacy is the most intimate, physical, and expressive way of saying 'I love you.'"[18] This purpose is one that we often find standing alone as the single justification for appropriate sex. Since the term *love* is vague, Hollinger claims that it is necessary to say more clearly what kind of love is ready for sex:

> I suggest that it must be a covenantal love that's for keeps and a love that is willing to bear the potential offspring that comes from sexual intercourse. Such love is found in the marriage of a man and a woman.[19]

With this proviso, even though one purpose of sex is to express love, the marriage boundary is still maintained.

The fourth purpose of sexual intercourse is to experience pleasure. In contrast to the long tradition within Christianity of denigrating pleasure, and while aware of the fact that human sinfulness can turn pleasure into an idol, Hollinger affirms that one purpose of "God's good gift of physical intimacy is pleasure. God designed it that way, building it into the very fabric of our bodies."[20] The pleasure associated with sexual intercourse is certainly physical, since both the male and female anatomy were designed for sexual pleasure. But the fullness of sexual pleasure, as Hollinger points out, goes well beyond the physical realm. It is also emotional and spiritual and is experienced in "the joy of commitment, security, fidelity, and the deep consolation that this is God's doing."[21]

Hollinger's holistic understanding of sexual pleasure leads to another important moral insight related to the purposes of sex. *They are themselves part of a whole*:

> One of the purposes of his good gift of sex is pleasure. But true and lasting sexual pleasure is found only in a consummated one-flesh relationship, with covenant love and commitment, and an ability and willingness to bear the potential fruit that comes from such unions.[22]

---

18. Hollinger, *Meaning of Sex*, 106. Hollinger is quick to point out that there are other important ways to express love as well, including "listening, caring, laughing, giving, waiting, initiating, and the many everyday cues that say 'I love you'" (ibid., 110).

19. Hollinger, *Meaning of Sex*, 107.

20. Hollinger, *Meaning of Sex*, 111.

21. Hollinger, *Meaning of Sex*, 114.

22. Hollinger, *Meaning of Sex*, 115.

Thus for Hollinger, the boundary that restricts sexual intercourse to marriage is supported not only by the purposes of sex but also by the belief that these purposes cannot be separated.

> When we isolate only one or several of the purposes, we distort God's intentions and fall short of his designs and hence his joy. These four purposes are found only in one location, the marriage of a man and a woman. This is where God designed sexual intimacy to be.[23]

Ethicists Lewis Smedes and Dennis Hollinger both provide biblical and theological explanations for the sexual boundaries they recommend. While their supporting arguments might leave some questions unanswered or be open to critique, each is a serious attempt not only to state the boundaries but also to show why the traditional Christian sexual boundary makes sense.

HOW FAR IS TOO FAR? ARE THERE BOUNDARIES FOR OTHER FORMS OF SEXUAL ACTIVITY?

By now you are probably noticing that while a boundary ethic is very clear about where to draw the line on sexual intercourse, there is a big question still looming. It is one already raised earlier in the chapter: How far is too far? Can a boundary ethic help us decide whether there are any forms of physical expressions of love appropriate in romantic relationships prior to marriage? If so, where are we to draw the moral line?

First, let's set aside the criticism that asking how far is too far is only a way to push the limits. There are obviously many ways people push the limits when it comes to moral obligations, and sometimes those get justified by rationalizing our behavior. Some people might use this question as a way to push the limits. But let's assume the best here: if moral boundaries really are a way to honor God by avoiding some behaviors that threaten God's intentions for human flourishing, it's important to distinguish those harmful behaviors from others that aren't harmful. Asking where this line is drawn can be a way of seeking to take the boundary seriously as an expression of God's will.

If we simply ignore the question "How far is too far?" and remain silent on "everything else," couples sometimes interpret the silence as a permissive "everything but sex" approach, sometimes known as "technical chastity." One student's testimony captures what I have heard many times:

---

23. Hollinger, *Meaning of Sex*, 115.

> When the only moral guideline I was given told me not to have
> sex, there didn't seem to be any reason to avoid everything else.
> So in one relationship after another I went as far as I could with-
> out having sex, and thought that I was doing the right thing.
> Now I'm not so sure.

Can a boundary ethic help Christians decide where to draw the line
that tells us what kinds of sexual actions (not including intercourse) are
morally permissible as healthy ways of expressing love? My own view here
is that a boundary ethic becomes less helpful as the boundaries become less
well established. One option that will become clear in the following two
chapters is that a relational ethic and an ethic of sexual integrity can be used
to supplement a boundary ethic, especially in areas where biblical boundaries are fuzzy or simply not to be found.

In Lewis Smedes' boundary ethic, the boundary established by God's
law is the one that reserves sexual intercourse for marriage. But there are
no equally clear biblical boundaries for physical expressions of love like
hugging and kissing, intimate caressing, or oral sex. While it is possible to
infer a boundary line that applies to these, it is very difficult to point to rules,
laws, or boundaries that establish lines as clear as those Smedes draws for
intercourse and marriage. Smedes himself does not turn to boundaries when
he discusses sexual activities that don't include intercourse. Instead, he calls
on a concept of *responsibility* to guide these forms of behavior. Responsibility
serves more as a *guideline* (wise moral advice) than a boundary. Because
there is a wide range of sexual behaviors that aren't explicitly addressed in
the Bible or in the historical tradition of boundary ethics, we usually see
those who take a boundary-ethics approach to sexual intercourse shift to
guidelines and advice when they address the question, How far is too far?

Sexual Activity Guidelines Rooted in Boundary Ethics

1. Be Responsible (Lewis Smedes)[24]

When Christians can't turn to God's law for moral guidance, Lewis Smedes
urges dependence on another important moral guideline. He calls it *responsibility*. Unlike the clarity offered by obeying the moral law, responsibility does not have a simple yes or no built into it. Smedes understands

---

24. This section summarizes chapter 7, "Responsible Petting," in Smedes, *Sex for
Christians*.

responsibility as the quality that arises from the kind of character people bring to their behavior. What it looks like to be responsible depends on the sort of person one is, and Smedes gives content to the principle of responsibility by pointing to some of the fundamental questions and commitments that form one's character. He invites each of us to ask, What values do I prize? What do I most deeply want? What are my goals and priorities? Do I regard others highly? Do I love myself? What kinds of expectations do I have for my future?

The bottom line for Smedes seems to be this: a person of good character will bring good things to a romantic relationship and can be trusted to treat both the other person and sexual actions in caring ways that nurture deep love and respect for God and for his romantic partner. Smedes considers several issues as he thinks through what responsibility means in the context of sexual activities that exclude intercourse.

CAN INTIMATE CARESSING BE AN END IN ITSELF?

We sometimes refer to hugging, kissing, and intimate caressing as foreplay, implying that they are activities leading to sexual intercourse. But can these activities stand alone as meaningful and fulfilling expressions of love, even if sexual intercourse isn't intended? Smedes says they can. Sexual activities can have the meanings we intend, even though they may remind us that there are other meanings, desires, and activities that naturally lie beyond them. Intimate caressing, he says, communicates "personal closeness and sharing, with flexible but recognizable limits."[25] Caressing is a way of expressing love, even when it is not a step toward intercourse. It might be a reminder, too, when we realize that it doesn't feel complete, that there is even more one might intend or mean. The covenant of marriage professes a love that is exclusive, unconditional, and life-lasting—even if that covenant is not yet a couple's reality. When it becomes their shared covenant, a more complete sexual union will be an expression of the union of marriage. The fact that caressing does not say everything that might be said isn't a problem. Its moral value comes from the fact that it says only what it means.

25. Smedes, *Sex for Christians*, 130.

HOW DOES A RESPONSIBLE PERSON DECIDE HOW FAR IS TOO FAR?

Smedes' claim that intimate caressing can be an end in itself implies the principle that he believes ought to guide a couple's level of sexual activity outside marriage: "The deeper and closer to commitment the personal relationship is, the more heavy the petting properly becomes."[26] (Smedes used the term "petting" to designate the range of physical intimacy that could include anything between cuddling and genital stimulation to orgasm.) Guided by this principle, Smedes claims that when done "freely and responsibly," petting "can be an experience of growth in understanding and loving."[27]

Setting limits that our bodily desires might fight against obviously requires a high degree of control and discipline, along with the ability to evaluate the quality and depth of the relationship and level of commitment. Not everyone will possess the self-control, self-awareness, or honesty that responsible petting calls for. Part of being responsible is having the capacity to make this assessment.

WHAT DANGERS ARE ASSOCIATED WITH THIS WAY OF BEING RESPONSIBLE?

To put it bluntly, we can be pretty good at fooling ourselves when it gets us what we want. So Smedes points out that phony disguises often present themselves as thoughtful and well-informed moral discernment. Without the ability to distinguish one from the other, responsibility can easily degenerate into promiscuity. Without the maturity and ability to honestly critique our motives and intentions, it becomes easy and more likely that we will find ways to justify behavior that falls far short of what Smedes means by responsible sexual activity.

2. Focus on the Purposes of Dating (Stanley Grenz)[28]

Stanley Grenz poses the question of sexual boundaries in the stage of life he calls *singleness*. He's not thinking here of singleness as a life commitment or as a calling to celibacy but as a prelude to possible marriage. It's the time of life we often call "dating." For teens and young adults this is the stage of life

26. Smedes, *Sex for Christians*, 131.

27. Smedes, *Sex for Christians*, 134.

28. Grenz, *Sexual Ethics*, chapter 10, "Singleness and Sexual Expression," is the source of the summary of Grenz's way of answering, How far is too far?

when people are exploring relationships and romantic love. In an era when divorce is common, we could also think of singleness as the time following the dissolution of a marriage and leading perhaps to another marriage. A particular challenge of singleness is the time gap that exists between the development or presence of the *readiness* for sex and the traditional social and religious recognition of its *appropriateness*.

One contemporary solution, of course, is to simply cast aside the traditional barriers that disapprove of sex outside marriage. Peer influence is likely to support that idea. According to the Guttmacher Institute's 2011 Fact Sheet, "By their 19th birthday, seven in 10 teens of both sexes have had intercourse."[29] The media portrays sex as acceptable, and the hookup culture embodies that approval. Even aside from these influences, Grenz points out that the modern practice of dating "encourages the coupling of young people into a series of semi-permanent relationships, allows teens to spend time alone as couples, and fosters experimentation with sex."[30]

Grenz's approach to sexual intercourse prior to marriage is very similar to what we've already seen in Smedes and Hollinger. The act of sexual intercourse has meanings that aren't consistent with being unmarried. What sexual intercourse means can only be fully realized within a marriage. There are practical advantages of abstinence, too, giving the boundary additional support. Grenz names three: Sex forms a strong bond, and the marriage bond is best established when this bond hasn't occurred with other partners prior to marriage. If sex is truly a unitive act, it makes sense to experience that unity only in the context of covenanted love. Waiting until marriage also avoids the psychological dangers associated with comparisons and past memories. Finally, abstinence protects one from sexually transmitted diseases.

Grenz clearly makes a case for avoiding intercourse during singleness. But what about everything else? How does he help us answer the question, How far is too far? Grenz answers this question by providing guiding principles that do not draw distinct boundaries but instead call a couple to make decisions about sexual activity by focusing on the purposes of dating.

Dating has three purposes, according to Grenz: it is a social activity that allows teens and young adults to enjoy the company of people their own age; it provides an opportunity to learn how to relate to and respect other people as sexual beings; and it provides an opportunity to learn what qualities make for a good marriage.[31] Because dating behavior is to be guided

29. Guttmacher Institute, "American Teens' Sexual and Reproductive Health."

30. Grenz, *Sexual Ethics*, 203.

31. Grenz, *Sexual Ethics*, 211.

by the purposes of dating, Grenz says that a primary consideration ought to be whether one's conduct is "conducive to building a [healthy] relationship that will foster each person's growth."[32]

Sexual activity in dating is guided by goals and principles rather than specific boundaries, but there are a few further pieces of advice to support these goals and purposes:

- Physical activities in dating should always show respect for the other person, and one should never engage in conduct that will cause a loss of respect.

- One should not engage in dating behaviors that will lead to regret in the future—especially if the relationship ends.

- One should not engage in physical activity that can no longer be controlled, and to insure that control, Grenz advises couples to "draw the line of activity well below the point at which the passion of the moment could blur their vision of their own ultimate good."[33]

Grenz calls these pieces of advice "boundaries," but it is important to notice that they are boundaries that Grenz (and others) recommend that a couple set for themselves. They are not the kinds of boundaries that tell us where to draw the line. Single people set these boundaries based on their own careful discernment of how to best live out principles like those that Grenz believes ought to guide dating practices.

BE CAREFUL! BOUNDARY ETHICS AND AN ETHIC OF CAUTION[34]

Sometimes a boundary ethic takes the form of an approach to the moral life that I call an "ethic of caution." A boundary is created to draw a line at a point where sexual activity becomes dangerous—but not where it is actually wrong. Consider an analogy: Let's say there's a dangerous precipice and many people have fallen over it to their death. So we decide to put up a fence to keep people at a safe distance from this danger. We add a sign that says, "Dangerous Precipice. Do Not Enter!" Now, it's the fence that is the

32. Grenz, *Sexual Ethics*, 212. Grenz adds the word "healthy" when he introduces this principle earlier.

33. Grenz, *Sexual Ethics*, 212.

34. While this description borrows from a variety of sources, it is not an attempt to accurately describe any *single* author's sexual ethic. I have omitted references even while paraphrasing a few authors in order to create this overall illustration.

boundary rather than the edge of the cliff. It protects people from danger on the other side by drawing a cautionary line.

If we connect the analogy to sex, falling off the precipice is engaging in sexual intercourse in a context where it's wrong to do so. But experience tells us that when people get too close to sexual intercourse, they sometimes "fall" into it even when they didn't intend to. So to keep them safe, we draw a line somewhere before this—perhaps at nudity or genital stimulation—to fence off the dangerous territory. Where one draws the line of caution is somewhat arbitrary. It's not hard to imagine someone building a barrier at the beginning of the road leading to the precipice as a way of saying one shouldn't even begin venturing down this path. That's like saying it's safest to stay a long way from sexual intercourse, and it's best not even to think about how close you could get before being in danger of crossing the fatal line. But other cautionary boundaries are more permissive. They recommend that couples stop engaging in sexual activity when it would seriously tempt them to go further.

An ethic of caution presumes three lines. One is the moral line that shouldn't be crossed. A second is a line that keeps one at a safe distance from the moral line. The third line distinguishes safe activity from dangerous activity. Here's a way of illustrating the distinctions:

- Non-problematic physical expressions of love
    » actions not prohibited by the Bible or Christian tradition
    » actions that are not likely to encourage inappropriate desires or sinful behaviors
- Danger Zone (Boundary of Caution)
    » actions that encourage inappropriate feelings (lust)
    » actions that increase the likelihood of engaging in sinful activity
- Sinful Sexual Activity
    » actions expressly prohibited by the Bible and/or Christian tradition and that cross the line into the arena of sinful behavior

A boundary of caution shares many of the insights seen in Smedes' and Hollinger's approaches. Those recommending a boundary of caution affirm that sex is a gift of God through which we can experience an intensely joyous sharing of love, as long as it occurs in the proper context. At the same time, it is a powerful drive that is easily abused and misused. Since there is such great potential toward distortion, sex must be treated with great care. In other words, one must be very careful when it comes to sex.

This combined insight that sex is very good and also liable to distortion and abuse has led many Christian writers to advocate an ethic of caution, and it is an approach that is reflected in the personal ethic of many young Christians I've encountered. In fact, an ethic of caution might be the most common contemporary Christian expression of a boundary ethic. Writers rarely label their own approach this way, since it would imply a less authoritative approach than most would want to claim. In an ethic of caution, the boundary draws its rationale primarily from the conviction that there are some seriously negative consequences out there that are important to avoid and that staying a safe distance from them is the best means to do that. The boundary is a line between what is safe and what isn't. The consequences one seeks to avoid might be physical (e.g., an STD), emotional (e.g., feeling used by someone), or spiritual (e.g., engaging in sinful behavior).

At the same time, lines that protect people from dangerous negative consequences also protect positive values, and an ethic of caution is likely to include this goal as well. The boundary says, in effect, "If it's important (for example) to protect your purity, to live a Christlike life, to keep your virginity, or to guard your heart, it's best not to cross this line."

Cautionary guidelines are intended to keep us far from violating God's commands. Here's an example: the danger might arise from the notion that "one thing leads to another." So, while the "one thing" (kissing, let's say) might not be wrong, if the behaviors it may "lead to" are wrong, an ethic of caution might have a "no kissing boundary." It wouldn't be *wrong* to kiss— just *dangerous*. A sixteen-year-old female who draws her boundary just past kissing explains her sexual ethic this way: "I think it's unsafe to do anything, like, past kissing, because then you want to do more." Commenting on this quotation from interviews examined in his research, Mark Regnerus says, "Boundaries are necessary to protect her from doing anything she believes she would come to regret."[35] It's not the kissing she would regret but the sexual activities designated by "wanting to do more."

Someone else has suggested this cautionary advice: draw a firm line just below the physical action you'd consider sinful. This implies that anything below that line isn't. Then ask yourself, Would God be pleased seeing me engaged in the physical activity directly below that firm line? Since the implied answer is "probably not," you should then draw a line at a level of physical activity at least one step lower.[36] While this might be good advice, at least if one adopts a boundary-of-caution approach, it clearly demonstrates

35. Regnerus, *Forbidden Fruit*, 113.
36. Gresh, *And the Bride Wore White*, 90–91.

that boundaries are apt to become much more subjective within the gray area that doesn't quite count as sex.

Where someone draws the boundary will vary from person to person, since there's no easily justified absolute to call on. In fact, one advocate of an ethic of caution suggests his own guidelines for consideration but goes on to say that others might be able to do some of these things with a clear conscience. His boundary prohibits caressing (for example: back rubs, playing with hair), cuddling, being alone late at night, etc. He concludes that everyone needs to come up with his or her own guidelines based on sincere convictions drawn from the Bible. Yet, while the specific boundaries are difficult to justify broadly, advocates of caution typically believe that being cautious about sex is something a loving God wants for us. As another author puts it, one can imagine God saying, "For your own safety and well-being, stay within the bounds of my provision and protection."[37] In order to develop a careful, thoughtful ethic of caution, one would need to have a very clear sense of what needs to be protected, as well as a high level of honest, personal awareness of one's own limits, intentions, and self-control.

AVOIDING TEMPTATION AND SEXUAL SIN

A boundary of caution not only proposes to protect one's body from sin, but in a sense to protect one's soul (inner self) as well. Boundaries are often proposed as a way to avoid temptation and lust and to keep people from falling into sexual sin. This approach to caution is sometimes clearly influenced by the image presented in this paraphrase of 1 Corinthians 6:18: *Flee from any kind of sexual immorality.* Temptation is not to be treated lightly, and when you know that something tempts you toward sin, it is not only safe but wise to avoid it.

How is this version of an ethic of caution expressed in contemporary Christian boundary ethics? The first step is to warn against engaging in anything that could arouse inappropriate feelings, thoughts, or desires. Visual stimulation such as pornography falls into this category, but so does looking longingly at people who arouse sexual desires or fantasies. There are also warnings against flirting or getting too close emotionally, since these things might have the same effect on some people.

It's important to notice that when certain kinds of behaviors are labeled as temptations, there usually isn't a precise definition of what is tempting and what isn't. That often depends on the individual involved and how she is personally affected. It depends on whether the person risking temptation

37. McDowell, *Why True Love Waits*, 205.

has a high level of self-awareness about how the potentially tempting activity might influence her. It depends on whether she has enough self-control.

Temptations aren't identified in an ethic of caution as being sinful in themselves. Here the boundary gets tricky because sometimes temptations are discussed in ways that make them sound like the temptation itself is the sin! In fact, it's most common for advocates of caution to say a resounding "No!" even to things that aren't wrong but that might be temptations. They are a potential step in the direction of sin, and getting too close is clearly *dangerous*, at least, and something to be avoided if you value staying on the right side of the line that defines God-honoring behavior. In the context of the dangers of temptation in male-female friendships, one author advises, "When in doubt, run as fast as you can in the opposite direction of the temptation coming your way."[38]

Warnings against visual temptation presume another line that defines what counts as lust. It isn't necessarily the admiring gaze that's wrong. Acknowledging a person's beauty might simply be a form a gratitude to the creator. But the boundary of caution that tells us to "bounce our eyes" away from an attractive person is designed to protect us from the temptation to cross a boundary—one that is defined by those warning us about the dangers of our gaze.

If things like friendship, visual beauty, or less intimate forms of physical romantic contact *actually do* tempt people to act in ways they shouldn't, the ethic of caution might be an effective way to resist levels of physical sexual activity that one believes are wrong. When we listen to personal stories, we discover that people typically do find themselves engaging in increasing levels of physical sexual activity over time and as a relationship develops. They also find themselves desiring increasing levels of physical activity, even if they decide to say no to those desires. Experientially, one thing does seem to lead to another—in the sense that there's a natural, internal progression that draws us toward sexual intercourse. An ethic of caution is designed to protect us from being tempted by our natural urges to engage in more sexual activity than we ought to. The goal is to eliminate even the temptation to sin.

ASSESSING A BOUNDARY ETHIC

Rules and Reasons: Boundaries Don't Always Come with Sufficient Justification

If there is a rule against something, that alone might serve as an effective reason not to do it. If someone says it's God's rule, the stakes are even higher.

38. Gushee, "Sexual Ethic for College Students," 11.

When there are negative consequences for disobedience, we have yet another reason to comply. But rules and the pressures we feel to obey them don't necessarily count as reasons. And the fact that a rule exists doesn't mean it's necessarily a good rule. We often ask for the reason behind the rule. *Why* can't I? *Why* shouldn't I? A boundary ethic, by definition, gives us the rule that defines the boundary—for example, unless you are married, don't cross this line! In the two models I have summarized in this chapter, the advocates of a boundary ethic are careful to explain the reasons behind the boundary lines. Smedes and Hollinger even argue that since the reasons are grounded in God's intentions for sexual intercourse, the boundary (no sex outside marriage) has the status of a moral absolute. This is at least the case for Christians who accept the authority of the biblical text and these authors' interpretations of it.

Drawing lines that function as moral rules is one of the clearest and simplest approaches to morality. If the line is clearly drawn and carefully explained, it doesn't necessarily make it easy to obey, but it does make the boundary accessible as a moral framework. You can use it—even if you don't necessarily understand the reasons behind it. Clearly drawn lines don't require high levels of moral reasoning or advanced moral maturity. In a matter-of-fact way, they simply invite (or even demand) obedience.

In everyday life, the boundaries don't always come with clear explanations. Most Christians have been taught that they "aren't supposed to have sex outside marriage." They have learned the boundary. But in repeated testimonies from Christian young adults over the years, most didn't learn (or don't remember hearing) any reasons why. They have learned an "ought" without the reasons for it. It should be no surprise that sexual boundaries unaccompanied by compelling reasons are often crossed. Both our bodies and our emotions are sources of powerful urges that tell us to do one thing, while the rule is telling us to do another. The unexplained rule is easily overwhelmed by sexual desire.

Guilt, Shame, Forgiveness, and Healing

These issues are so prominent in people's efforts to figure out and then live out their sexual morality that they deserve their own chapter, which comes just a bit later. For now we can identify the relationship between these human experiences and a boundary approach to sexual ethics.

A boundary ethic defines a violation, and if it draws the line clearly, it also tells us (intentionally or not) when to feel guilty. Legitimate guilt is a recognition that a valid rule has been violated. In theological terms, and consistent with Smedes' boundary ethic, it is a recognition that one has violated God's law. Shame, a closely related concept, adds the dimension that one has also violated one's own sense of *wanting to* honor God. So one could feel ashamed of being guilty.

In spite of its negative reputation, guilt isn't always a bad thing. Within a boundary ethic one is likely to find a theological framework in which appropriate guilt can be identified. But forgiveness, renewed commitment, and healing can also take place. A boundary ethic provides not only a way to name guilt but also a way to deal with it. If a legitimate boundary is crossed, guilt is simply our subjective recognition that we have done something we believe and know is wrong. If some behaviors are categorized as violations of God's will, for example, and if people sometimes actually do violate God's will, guilt is just a fact of human existence. Sometimes guilt is simply the truth that must be faced. It signals us that we need to repent, receive God's generous forgiveness, and recommit ourselves to doing what we believe is right.

The simple anticipation of guilt and shame is sometimes enough to keep people on the right side of the line. But not always. When it doesn't, violators (like the student who told her story at the beginning of this chapter) can be eaten up by a sense of guilt and shame that destroys their sense of self-worth. The violation can even create a veil of shame that makes it difficult to sustain a relationship with God.

A boundary ethic does not, however, always generate appropriate guilt. Sometimes the boundaries are too vague. The boundary that calls for "purity" can be an example of this. If purity is a vague notion that includes the exclusion of sexual thoughts, the repression of sexual urges, and the refusal of virtually all physical expressions of love, people are left with a large, amorphous cluster of "sin" that typically offers few helpful guidelines but gives many reasons to feel guilty! (More on this later in my critique of a purity ethic.)

Inappropriate guilt is even more likely when normal, God-given emotions and desires are loosely associated with terms like "lust" or "sexual immorality." As I argue elsewhere, lust is only a useful notion for identifying sin if we are able to distinguish it from sexual desires that are human but not sinful. Lust is a distortion of sexual desire, not the feelings or acknowledgment of it. Without clear distinctions, people don't know when they should feel guilty or when they should simply rejoice in their God-given capacity to experience and enjoy sexual feelings and longings. Likewise, admonitions to "avoid sexual immorality" are hard to argue with, but they presume that one already knows what is "sexually immoral." The term presumes a boundary or set of boundaries, but to preach avoidance of sexual immorality without explaining what would count as a violation is not only unhelpful but will almost certainly engender false guilt.

Unanswered Questions?

Boundary approaches to Christian sexual ethics have often left many questions unanswered. This observation alone does not mean that the articulated boundaries aren't valid. It might simply mean they are insufficient, or that the Christian community needs to do a better job teaching the boundaries. On the other hand, perhaps some boundary ethics have inherent shortcomings and need to be supplemented by a more robust morality. In order to illustrate the problem, consider some questions a boundary ethic often leaves unanswered.

First, take the common boundary "Don't have sex until marriage." After hearing this boundary, the next question is usually some version of this: But what do you *mean* by *sex*? It might sound like a question that should be easy to answer, but in my experience, students have found it very difficult! What counts as sex? Sexual intercourse (penetration of the vagina by the penis)? Oral sex (oral stimulation of the penis or the clitoris)? Intimate touching that leads to orgasm? Sexual fantasy accompanied by masturbation? All of these—and maybe even more?

It's helpful to distinguish two basic ways people answer the question, even though it's an oversimplification. The narrow (and potentially *overly* narrow) answer is that what one means by "sex" is sexual intercourse. That's the way we use the term today, and it is the sexual act that boundary ethics identifies when describing the biblical prohibition against "sex" outside marriage. The broad answer (which is also potentially *overly* broad) is that sex includes the whole range of physical actions that excite sexual desire and lead up to sexual intercourse.

If the narrow answer is accepted, the boundary is clear when it comes to sexual intercourse, but it leaves uncertainty about all the other ways people use their bodies to express love. Hence, the unanswered question is the familiar one already examined above: How far is too far?

If the broad answer is accepted and a wide range of physical expressions of love are included, the boundary that applies to sexual intercourse is expanded to apply to most everything else as well. The wide range of ways we express affection physically are painted with a broad brush that makes them all suspect. But why? If one wants to know why kissing or other forms of physical intimacy ought to be saved for marriage, the reasons once again start to look more like subjective guidelines rather than firmly grounded rules.

A second unanswered question can also plague a boundary ethic. Once again, consider the "no sex before marriage" boundary. The line speaks clearly about premarital sex but fails to address the question of what makes sex morally appropriate *within marriage*. Obviously one is now on the right side of the line, so the boundary no longer exercises its power to prohibit sex. Now a new boundary tells married people that their sexual union is exclusive. They may only engage in sexual intercourse with each other. Sex outside the marriage covenant is now the boundary violation to avoid.

Marriage doesn't provide blanket sexual license, however. Being on the right side of the boundary may permit sexual intercourse when it was previously prohibited, but the traditional boundary doesn't help those now on the marriage side of the line develop a positive sexual ethic for their marriage. This boundary approach has been aptly characterized by one author this way: it pays attention to the who and when of sex, not so much the what or how.[39] But these later questions are important ones! Is sex within marriage *always* appropriate? If not, what makes it sometimes inappropriate? What kind of moral qualities make married sex morally good? If a boundary ethic is the whole of one's moral instruction, it's easy to find oneself encountering a huge void once the boundary no longer applies. As we'll see in a subsequent chapter, a relational ethic could fill that void, since it focuses not on boundaries to determine what's right but on the meaning of sexual actions and on the quality and character of the persons involved and the quality and character of their relationship.

CHAPTER SUMMARY

When Christian sexual ethics takes the form of an ethic grounded in an interpretation of the Bible's boundaries for sexual activity, we can find clear lines that identify when sexual expressions of love become sinful. Carefully articulated boundary ethics such as those explained by Smedes and Hollinger go beyond simply drawing lines to providing clear explanations for why these lines make sense and legitimately demand being observed. In short, the meaning of sexual intercourse coincides with both the meaning and purposes of marriage, leading to the conclusion that sexual intercourse is only an appropriate expression of marital love, which is proclaimed most clearly in the covenant of marriage.

39. Regnerus, *Forbidden Fruit*, 22.

A boundary ethic acknowledges that God's boundaries are intended to protect sex, marriage, and the health and well-being of people in relationships of romantic love. The barriers exist primarily to protect the goodness of God's gift of love, not to keep us from doing something bad. The "badness" involved in crossing the line is that it distorts the meaning and purpose of the goodness of sex. Because sex is valuable, boundaries protect it from the potential to distort, abuse, and cheapen it. Author Rob Bell expresses this positive motive well when he writes, "Life is not about toning down and repressing your God-given life force. It's about channeling it and focusing it and turning it loose on something beautiful, something pure and true and good, something that connects you with God, with others, with the world."[40]

We've also seen that a boundary ethic is often accompanied by what I've called an "ethic of caution." Guidelines that encourage us to be careful when it comes to sex often recommend against actions that may not be wrong in themselves but that could encourage temptation or behaviors that are wrong. When protecting something valuable, an ethic of caution provides a buffer zone that functions a lot like surrounding a fragile item with protective packing. An ethic of caution, I've suggested, functions best when it's clear where the real moral line exists and what it is we are actually trying to protect. But I've also suggested that a boundary ethic could benefit from additional moral considerations, such as those found in a relational ethic and an ethic of sexual integrity. The following chapters provide an overview of these distinct approaches to Christian sexual ethics.

40. Bell, *Sex God*, 83.

4

Some Ways to Think about Sexual Ethics
A Relational Ethic

A RELATIONAL ETHIC IS another way to embody the kinds of things God cares about in our relationships and sexual practices. We've already seen how a boundary ethic can be a way to do this. That approach identifies rules that establish clear boundaries Christians should observe, because to obey God-given boundaries is to honor God. Taking a somewhat different approach to sexual morality, a relational ethic begins with an acknowledgment that there are no timeless biblical rules that establish clear and specific boundaries across the whole range of sexual activity. As a result, it attempts to answer the question, How can Christians make moral decisions about sex in the absence of precise rules of conduct?

In order to answer that question, we can begin by examining four central affirmations that combine to form a relational approach to sexual ethics. These affirmations point toward the ways that sexual activity can be lived out so that our behaviors correspond to the kinds of things that matter to God. The four affirmations are as follows:

1. Sexual behavior is an expression of Christian discipleship.

2. The "quality" of the relationship matters.

3. Sexual activities mean something—they communicate the kinds of love that are present in a relationship.

4. Physical expressions of love may appropriately increase gradually, as do the emotional, social, and spiritual dimensions of love.

Let's examine in some detail what these mean and how they might form a way to discern the appropriateness of sexual activity in relationships of romantic love.

CENTRAL AFFIRMATION #1: SEXUAL BEHAVIOR IS AN EXPRESSION OF CHRISTIAN DISCIPLESHIP

Even though a relational ethic focuses on the qualitative dimensions of a relationship rather than on physical boundaries, as traditional approaches typically do, this approach to morality is intentionally grounded in Christian discipleship. A relational ethic is a way of explaining why and how our sexual practices matter and how they can be conducted in ways that show serious devotion to God. Or, to put it differently, a relational ethic is a way to answer the question, If you are trying to live your sexual life in a way that responds to Jesus' call to "follow me," what would that look like?

Many of us are accustomed to a way of answering that question that simply draws lines we aren't supposed to cross. And in some cases, there aren't any good reasons given—we're simply told that the reason not to cross the line is that we're violating a God-given boundary. Or perhaps it is a pragmatic boundary (to avoid certain harms or dangers) or a boundary based on personal preferences (I wouldn't want *my* future husband to have done *that* with anyone else).[1] Whether there are such boundaries is a long and complicated debate, and we've already looked at ways to draw wisdom from a boundary ethic and also seen how such an approach may fail to give satisfactory answers to some very important questions.

How does a relational approach attempt to directly connect our sexual behavior to Christian discipleship? In general, it does this by imagining what it would mean to apply the orienting convictions drawn from Scripture to the day-to-day lived experience of *eros*—the love we experience as romantic love. We have to do the same thing in many areas of the moral life. Jesus teaches us to love our neighbor, but we are the ones who have to figure out what that looks like when we encounter our actual neighbors.

---

1. I call this a *personal preference boundary* because there seems to be no clearly universal line that might be drawn. You may wish your future spouse had never said "I love you" to anyone else, or kissed another person, or seen anyone else naked, or . . . To live with integrity, it makes sense that you would live your life in the way you wish you future spouse would. But so far as I can tell, there is no way to universalize the line that shouldn't be crossed.

But imagining what neighbor love or sexual activity looks like in actual relationships isn't simply fanciful imagination. It's an imagination shaped by a well-formed understanding, expressed in those deep convictions that give us direction and guidance.

A relational ethic places high demands on us, because it holds people and sexual activity in very high esteem. Both are part of God's creation and are intended to honor the creator. Christians are expected to do that in every area of life, and sexual expressions are just one example.

CENTRAL AFFIRMATION #2: THE "QUALITY" OF THE RELATIONSHIP MATTERS

When thinking about sex relationally, the morality of our actions arises out of the quality and characteristics of the love present in a relationship. What makes a sexual act good is that it reflects the deeper goodness of the relationship in which it occurs, and the depth and character of the love it communicates. If that sounds exceptionally permissive or liberal, don't jump to any conclusions yet! A relational ethic has *very* high expectations for romantic relationships and demands a well-developed capacity for careful discernment and for honest, self-critical assessment.

In a relational approach to sexual ethics, *the qualities that characterize a relationship provide criteria by which to discern and assess the appropriateness of sexual activity*. Physical expressions of love—like touching, caressing, hugging, kissing—are ways people communicate how they care for each other, what they mean to each other, and how they love each other. So in a relational ethic, we'd expect the meaning of physical actions to correspond to social, emotional, and spiritual dimensions of the love present in a relationship. We'd expect physical actions to correspond to relational realities that can be put into words. There is no scientific way to measure the "depth" of a romantic relationship. But there are some reliable qualities and characteristics that can explain what is meant by talking about the "qualitative dimension" of a romantic relationship. The following list is not meant to be exhaustive or definitive, but illustrative. I begin with a more detailed explanation of four relationship characteristics and end with a summary of qualities others have listed in their own approaches to what I would call a relational ethic. Hopefully, you will recognize in these descriptions a way to assess the character of a real-life relationship. When relationships lack these qualities we can work to develop them.

A. Respect for Each Other's Value and Worth

Every person was created by God in God's own image. You'll recall that this is one of the convictions that orient a Christian's ways of thinking about sex. Our sexual behaviors begin with a way of seeing people for who they are: creatures of great worth, who matter supremely because they matter to God. Both you and your romantic partner (present or future) are people God loves and cares for, and people for whom Jesus died. A relational ethic invites a "way of seeing" through a lens of faith.

A good example of what is meant here can be seen in another context: Mother Teresa's way of teaching Missionaries of Charity how to "see" the destitute and dying people they were learning to care for. She commonly emphasized the importance of seeing any human person in the way described in Matthew 25: as Jesus himself, in the guise of a common human person. In the parable Jesus tells, those who feed the hungry are taught that their acts of compassion should be seen as if they were caring for Jesus himself. Conversely, their disregard for people in need can be seen as a disregard for Jesus. In Jesus' concluding words: just as you did it to one of the least of these who are members of my family, you did it to me. It's a metaphor for a way of seeing and respecting someone's worth and is just as appropriate in the context of romance.

There are a variety of other ways to describe how respect might look in a relationship. For example, we can think of it as welcoming acceptance. In early stages of a relationship we can choose to extend a kind of relational hospitality that receives the other as a guest and allows her to come into our lives with a minimum of judgment. Respect for a person's created worth might also include a deep appreciation for her unique characteristics and gifts or admiration for the specific traits she displays. It will likely include generous affirmation as well as encouragement to live, think, and feel in ways that are consistent with being a person of great worth.

The word *autonomy* has often been used when writing about a relational approach to ethics. *Autonomy* refers to the capacity we have as rational humans to think about and make our own moral decisions and also the freedom to choose to implement them. To recognize someone's autonomy typically means to respect them by granting them the freedom to think for themselves, decide for themselves, and make their own choices.

While there are some ways of emphasizing autonomy that lead to excessive forms of individualism, there is also a dimension to autonomy that makes sense in a Christian context. Recognizing and respecting your personal autonomy means to respect that God created you to be your own person, free to respond to others in love, free to make choices, free to give your heart and your allegiance to another. While it's a modern term, we could think of autonomy as the responsive freedom Jesus recognized in others when he offered them the invitation to "follow me."

Lovers recognize and respect each other's personal autonomy when they show a deep regard for each other's ideas, choices, hesitancies, doubts, and fears. If you respect someone's autonomy, you will encourage their thoughtful consideration of important moral choices and will avoid trying to manipulate them to do what *you* want. Respect for autonomy encourages discussion and makes space for disagreement. It always allows partners to express their own thoughts and feelings and it honors the decisions that arise from those—even if you might wish otherwise.

Respect for a person's value and worth prohibits ways of seeing and treating others that are common today. Perhaps you've heard the reductionist language that refers to a person (often a woman) in terms of a body part: "Piece of . . ." comes to mind. Sadly, such language betrays a way of seeing someone that denies and distorts their value. In fact, any portrayal of a person that demeans their God-given worth, their image of themselves as God's beloved, or that ridicules or attempts to overpower their values and choices is a violation of the respect that is central to a relational ethic.

B. Mutuality

Two liberties meet, two bodies meet, two hearts come together.[2]

Physical ways of communicating love involve a mutual giving and receiving. A kiss is not only given but received. In a relational ethic, a kiss that is not received is understood like a verbal offer that is refused or like a gift that is rejected. In the right context, there might be nothing wrong with offering a gift that someone ends up rejecting, but to offer it again and again would be a sign that something's wrong. Sexual expressions of love, since they are (at least in part) a form of communication, are two-way expressions. Ideally, both partners are saying something approximately equivalent and are hearing something more or less equivalent.

This dimension of mutuality also places an emphasis on the equality of each partner's participation in a relationship—in this case, equality in the physical dimension of the relationship. But a relational ethic is holistic, so physical mutuality would be a reflection of broader mutuality in other dimensions of the relationship as well. In order to understand what mutuality means, it might be helpful to contrast it with a question that

2. Farley, *Just Love*, 222.

would be very *inappropriate* in the context of a relational ethic. The question might be asked by an acquaintance inquiring about what transpired on a date: "Did you *get* anything?" Sexual expressions are not about "getting" or about "doing things" to people. They are about giving and receiving, about saying something through touch that another person hears and says back— or receives with understanding. Each person gives and each person receives.

One place we'd expect to see mutuality is in a couple's understanding of the nature of their commitment to each other. Romantic relationships are covenantal agreements. When mutuality is present, there is less mystery in a relationship than one sometimes finds in new or immature romances. That's not to say romance is ever devoid of mystery! But in a relational ethic, partners aren't guessing about the other person's feelings toward them, about the level of commitment present in the relationship, or about their level of comfort. There may not be an easy-to-explain precision about such things, but without a degree of clarity on important questions, this dimension of mutuality is lacking something important.

C. Commitment

Every relationship has some level of commitment present—or a lack of it. A random hookup is one kind of relationship . . . but by definition it's a way of relating to someone without any kind of commitment except for the agreements of the moment. Engagement is another kind of commitment: it's a public announcement of a couple's readiness and intention to move toward exchanging the vows that constitute the exclusive, unconditional, lifelong covenant of marriage.

As relationships mature, we'd expect the types and levels of commitment present to grow as well. Initially, people make a commitment to spend time together so they can get to know each other. At that early stage the commitment is conditional. It says (though perhaps unspoken) "If I like you, this might continue" or "If we seem compatible, this might get serious" or "If we have fun on this date, I might ask you out again!" That's not much of a commitment, of course, and when people are at the lower end of the commitment scale, they tend not to voice their commitments (or the lack thereof) at all.

Eventually, people sometimes move to higher levels of commitment. They decide to reserve expressions of romantic love (*eros*) for each other only; their romance is now exclusive. Again, there is no template for describing or assessing the level of commitment at any particular point, but there *are* many relevant indicators. People become willing to commit more of their time to each other—but also to give each other greater freedom, because with increased commitment comes increased security. People develop a greater willingness to make sacrifices for each other, to take care of each other, to make decisions in light of the other's values and goals.

They eventually reach a point where they can look back to a shared history and look forward to a shared future. They begin to say, "You can count on me for anything" and to believe that this is true. "Anything" might be a bit vague, and for a while might be an overstatement. But as the level of commitment increases, they know with greater clarity what that honestly means.

What's happening here is that their commitment is turning into a covenant—one that expresses a shared understanding of the nature and meaning of the relationship. And the covenant is moving away from conditional love toward unconditional love; it is moving toward a commitment that says "I will love you no matter what." In other words: for better or worse. In the Christian tradition, marriage is typically the name we give to the final level of commitment in romantic relationships.

D. Shared Life

Many qualities of a romantic relationship develop out of a couple's shared life: the level of honesty they are willing to risk and the corresponding trust they place in each other; the knowledge that they are safe; a sense of belonging that allows them to be themselves while knowing that their identity includes choosing to be part of someone else's life . . . and a sense of belonging that comes from having been chosen. You've probably noticed that these aren't exclusive to romance. Friendship is likely to include many of the same things. But that's no coincidence, since sharing your life with someone you feel romantically attracted to will likely include another kind of love at the same time: the love called friendship.[3]

When a relationship is at a stage that allows people to say "we have a shared life," it means that some measure of time has passed. This is more likely to be the case after many months or years. It is probably an illusion if a relationship is only a few weeks or months old. Why does time matter? As in physical maturity, the passing of time is what has given opportunity

---

3. I have found C. S. Lewis' distinctions between four types of love to be a helpful way of designating the qualitative differences that usually get lost when we use only the single word "love." *Philia* is the Greek word for the love we call friendship. In modern Western culture, "lovers" often also expect that friendship-love will be a dimension of their relationship.

for growth. The qualities that make up relational maturity take time to develop because they are based on shared experiences, shared activities, and shared conversations. If you assure me that you can trust someone, I might ask you what makes you so certain. Perhaps she came through the one time you were counting on her. But that trust naturally deepens when you have placed trust in someone over and over again, and she has never let you down. Maybe you felt like you could trust her from the beginning. But with the passing of much experience, trust has come to mean something deeper as it shifts from a prediction or a hope to a multifaceted story full of a preponderance of evidence.

The quality of a relationship gets deeper and broader when people have a chance to share more and more of their lives. Out of that shared experience they develop the characteristics that define a mature romance—things like trust, honesty, a sense of safety and belonging.

REPRESENTATIVES OF A RELATIONAL APPROACH TO CHRISTIAN SEXUAL ETHICS

In developing their approaches to sexual ethics, other Christians who have thought about these issues have enumerated their own lists of relational characteristics. There is considerable overlap in their approaches, so I have chosen to briefly summarize an early representative of this approach and a more contemporary one. Each overview provides my digested summary of the kinds of relational qualities that need to be present for sexual activity to be morally good, and therefore also good for our emotional, spiritual, and relational health. Think of these lists of relational characteristics as illustrations of what I mean when claiming that "the quality of the relationship matters" in a relational approach to sexual ethics.

Harvey Cox

In the 1960s and 1970s, Harvard theologian Harvey Cox[4] contributed the voice of Christian theological ethics to the emerging conversation about the

4. Harvey Cox would be considered a "situational ethicist" especially by those for whom specific rules or boundaries are the best (or only) approach to Christian sexual ethics. A relational ethic could be understood as situational in this sense: the specific characteristics of the relationship and the specific character of the people involved are central to whether sexual activity can be understood as morally *good*. In a relational approach, God-honoring sexual practices are the expression of real people who experience real, loving relationships.

"sexual revolution." Addressing the question, What is it that makes sexual activity good?, Cox provides a list of characteristics that *humanize* sexual activity—or, in other words, help it attain the human ends that are consistent with what God intends. The "goodness" of sexual activity in a relationship is achieved by aiming toward seven characteristics, and Cox posed a set of questions to help people assess the sexual dimension of their relationship:

1. Is the sexual relationship *self-liberating?*

   This means that the relationship frees us to live and love ourselves and others more fully.

2. Is the sexual relationship mutually *other-affirming?*

   Sex should not be exclusively self-serving, one-sided, or destructive; it builds up participants' sense of self and their relationship.

3. Is the sexual relationship characterized by *honesty?*

   A humanizing sexual relationship means that individuals are honest with themselves and with each other, and their relationship is characterized by high levels of trust and disclosure.

4. Is the sexual relationship characterized by *faithfulness?*

   Individuals commit themselves exclusively to each other in a relationship to which they remain faithful.

5. Are participants in the relationship *socially responsible?*

   Individuals in a humanizing sexual relationship consider the impact of their behavior on others and on social institutions.

6. Is the sexual relationship *life-serving?*

   Does it enhance life and the kind of well-being we seek for ourselves and for others?

7. Is the sexual relationship *joyous?*

   The relationship and its sexual dimension are experienced as joyous and not merely pleasurable. This is in contrast with sexual relationships that are guilt-producing, burdensome, dutiful, and/or demeaning.

Margaret Farley[5]

A more recent sexual ethic that also exemplifies a relational approach comes from another prominent moral theologian, Sister Margaret Farley, who spent

5. See especially chapter 6 in Farley, *Just Love.*

her long teaching career at Yale University. Farley's criteria are summarized as obligations that arise from the combined norms of justice and love, which she believes ought to be present in every sexual relationship. Farley explains that her use of the term *justice* begins with the classical definition: "to render to each her or his due." Her norms provide a more precise way to understand what people are actually "due" in sexual relationships. She goes on to remind us that when we use love as a moral norm, it is necessary to ask what a good, just, or true love is. Her book *Just Love: A Framework for Christian Sexual Ethics* explores these issues.

Here is a summary of the characteristics that she believes will be embodied in sexual relationships that are an expression of just love. Each characteristic is grounded in what she calls the fundamental relationality of sex.

1. Just love *does no harm.* This characteristic recognizes the vulnerability and intimacy involved in sexual activity and seeks to protect people from the ways our desire for pleasure and power can lead to harm. In relationships of just love we would not expect to find behaviors that harm others, such as exploitation, deceit, and betrayal.

2. People in relationships guided by just love *respect the autonomy of persons.* This means one's partner is free to consent to sexual contact, and in order to make that freedom meaningful, each person ought to tell the truth and keep their promises. Respecting the right to consent that arises from human autonomy prohibits rape, manipulation, and any other form of coercion.

3. Just love values the *mutuality of participation.* Recognizing that sexual activity is fundamentally relational, this means that activity and receptivity must be part of both persons' participation. It prohibits the traditional understanding that one partner is always active and the other always passive in sexual encounters and also refuses to see sex as simply the satisfaction of physical desire.

4. There will be *equality between partners* in sexual encounters. This ensures that consent arises out of freedom and makes mutuality possible by removing the power differentials that can often get in the way. When there are elements of dependence, we would expect that dependence to be mutual (lovers need each other and meet each other's needs). When equality is present, people in relationships of just love do not see or treat their partner as property.

5. A *covenant/commitment* will characterize the relationship in which sexual activity occurs. At a minimum this means that the relationship has a history and a future. The Christian tradition has defined

the ultimate covenant as marriage. Prior to marriage, couples make covenantal commitments that usually deepen as relationships mature. The presence of a covenant helps rule out sexual activity that separates the physical act from the wider meaning of committed relationships.

6. Sexual relationships should be *fruitful*. Sometimes fruitfulness is experienced when new life comes into the world as a consequence of sexual relationships. But interpersonal love is fruitful in other ways too: it brings new life to those who share their love and nourishes the lives of family, friends, and neighbors who are touched by the healthy joy of healthy sexual love.

7. Sexual relationships of just love will reflect forms of *justice*. In the relationship itself this means that people will always seek to protect third parties from harm: future lovers for those not yet married, children who might be born, and the wider network of loved ones affected by the relationship. Beyond the relationship, the norm of justice is a reminder to nurture social justice in order to protect the broader environment in which sexual relationships occur, seeking gender equality, for example, and rejecting sexual and domestic violence.

Summary: Relational Criteria

Thinking about sexual activity in terms of relational characteristics such as those outlined above is an alternative to models of moral reflection that invite us to apply rules and regulations to sexual behavior. It shifts the focus away from boundaries marking what is forbidden and redirects attention to the qualities of actual relationships as a key component in discerning what is good. Relational criteria are not provided in order to tell people precisely what kinds of sexual activity they may engage in or where to draw the line. The criteria give us a way to think about what characteristics must be present in order for a wide range of sexual practices to serve the kinds of relational goals that lead to healthy and flourishing human relationships—in other words, the kinds of sexual relationships that would honor God's gift of sexuality.

Even though criteria used to assess the quality of a relationship don't provide a systematic way to make decisions about sexual practices, they do imply limits—boundaries of a different kind, we might say—that are intended to help us see why sex doesn't belong at all in some relationships, and why it might not yet be appropriate in others.

CENTRAL AFFIRMATION #3: SEXUAL ACTIVITIES MEAN SOMETHING: THEY COMMUNICATE THE CHARACTERISTICS OF LOVE PRESENT IN A RELATIONSHIP

The third affirmation that grounds a relational ethic is the claim that sexual activity means something. Sexual activities communicate the nature and depth of love that is present in a relationship. This idea that "sex means something" needs some clarification, so we'll start by sorting out what I mean by this claim. I'll then illustrate some ways to think about what sexual activity communicates.

A relational ethic sees the whole spectrum of sexual activity (for example, from holding hands to sexual intercourse) as physical actions filled with meaning. If someone asks, "What did you mean when you did that?" you ought to be able to explain in some reasonable way (although it's not always easy to put it into words) what the physical action meant. Sometimes people excuse their sexual permissiveness with the dismissive expression "Well, it didn't really mean anything." But in a relational ethic, if it doesn't mean anything, it shouldn't be done. It's the same with words, isn't it? We don't go around saying things to people and claim that the words don't really mean anything, so they don't matter. Words and actions do matter, precisely because they are meaning-filled. We use words with care to say what it's appropriate to say. Sexual activities aren't done only for fun or only because they feel good. They aren't part of a game of conquest. They are God-given gifts that serve as a language of love, and they are meant to express love in ways that tell the truth.

We can also understand the idea that sex means something by considering the alternative: sexual activity can be undertaken in ways that "de-mean" sex too. This implies that it is *supposed to* mean something, but due to the intentions and context of the act, the meaning has been distorted or disrespected. It doesn't end up meaning what it is supposed to mean. For example, if someone has been the victim of sexual activity undertaken on the basis of manipulative lies, we'd agree with his regretful reflection that "it didn't really mean anything." What would be sad here is that it was *supposed to* mean something. We give sex meaning by our intentions and our love, but when there is dishonesty, the meaningfulness of sex is distorted.

Premarital sexual activity is sometimes justified by young lovers with the claim that it is necessary in order to express a depth of love that cannot be put into words. Does sex communicate a love that words cannot convey? Do actions speak for themselves? In a relational ethic, the claim that sex means something doesn't need to go so far. Meaning isn't "built in" so that it is always automatic, clear and discernible. The meaning of sexual activity comes from two sources: the meaning God intends and the meanings carried by the intentions and understandings of the individuals involved. I have already summarized Dennis Hollinger's argument that sex means something because God has given it a meaning. The meaning of sexual intercourse can be understood in terms of the four God-given purposes: the consummation of marriage, procreation, love, and pleasure. Hollinger also argues that sex means what God intends only when these four purposes are held in unity.[6] Hollinger sees the meaning of sex as inherent and therefore independent from our intentions, since it is God-given.

We don't need to see God-given meanings and human-given meanings as being in conflict. The human meanings that arise from our intentions, hopes, and the nature of our love add another important layer of meaning to our sexual activity, and the meaning of our sexual actions is incomplete without it. In the scholarly debate about this issue, it is easy to take an either/or approach: either sexual meanings are built into sexual activity or they are given to sexual activities by our intentions, which differ from time to time and place to place.

What kinds of human meanings do we bring to sexual activity? Consider Lisa Fullam's examples of the broad range of meanings (both positive and negative) that might be embodied in sexual activity:

> Sex can be everything from a momentary transaction without emotional meaning, to a profound experience of loving union between partners. Sex can be celebratory or can be solace in sadness. Sex can help us develop a deeper understanding of ourselves, our partners, and God. Sex can be tender or violently abusive; it can heal and can deeply wound. It can be solitary, shared, or abstained from altogether. Sex can signify acceptance and mutuality, or it can be a competition to demonstrate prowess and to gain one's own pleasure unconnected to that of our partner.[7]

It's clear that not all human meanings are consistent with the God-given purposes of sex or with human health and happiness. This human layer of meaning depends on what people bring to sexual activity. What sex means and what sex communicates at this level is tied to what we intend sex to mean. But it is not only our intentions that create and communicate

---

6. Hollinger, *Meaning of Sex*, 95. See above, chapter 3, for an extended summary of Hollinger's explanation.

7. Fullam, "Sex in 3-D," 151.

meaning. Meaning is taught by community and by culture. It is also our shared, lived experience. Thus meaning can never be disconnected from qualities of a relationship like respect, mutuality, and commitment. The meanings we create in sexual activity are products of the lives we share.

This brings us back to the earlier question whether sex says what words cannot say. In a relational ethic, I'm proposing that sex says what words have already said and will say. Sex enacts our professions of love, care, loyalty, and forgiveness. It also enacts what we have *done* to demonstrate love, care, loyalty, forgiveness, and all the other dimensions of love a couple shares. In a relational ethic, what sex means and what the relationship means come together in sexual activity.

Embodied Meanings of Sexual Activity

In order to make the claim that *sexual actions mean something* a credible one, it makes sense to give some examples of what we may be saying with our bodies that could also be expressed in corresponding words. The distinctions might be more important than the actual descriptions, since readers might have much better ways of explaining these connections than my attempts below. What is especially noteworthy, however, is that in this approach to sexual ethics, different levels of physical intimacy express different levels of relational intimacy. What we say to each other helps create the quality of our relationships, but at the same time it is meant to tell the truth about the quality and character of the relationship. And there is a progression that is identifiable, even if it is imprecise.

Holding Hands

The meaningfulness of holding someone's hand is already apparent in non-romantic contexts. Sometimes people who pray in a group hold hands to say that they are connected by shared beliefs or by mutual caring. They are symbolizing a oneness that unites them. Holding someone's hand in greeting (a handshake) is another way we use the touch of hands to express meaning. A handshake affirms someone by saying with our bodies what we sometimes simultaneously say with our voices: I'm glad to meet you! It says I acknowledge your presence and I recognize you as a fellow human person. We are united at a basic level, as our hands are united. Handshakes are very meaningful! Perhaps that becomes especially apparent if someone refuses the offer of our extended hand.

Holding hands is also an expression of *eros*, of romantic love, and in a context where other words and deeds say the same thing, taking someone's hand is an act of reaching out and a symbol of being connected. If a partner asked, "What does it mean when you hold my hand like that?" there would be words to explain it. Perhaps "I'm glad you're part of my life," or "We belong to each other," or "I don't want to let you go," or (your own words). But if someone holds your hand who has no business doing so, because there is nothing in the relationship to suggest that words could be said to correspond to this form of intimate touch, then even a simple act like hand-holding can easily be seen as inappropriate.

Hugging

A hug can also express meaning outside the context of romance. Family members and friends express their affection with an embrace. In that act we say with our bodies that we are glad to be part of each other, that we belong to each other, that we hold the relationship to be of special importance. Hugging symbolizes feelings of closeness and caring that go beyond our everyday encounters with people.

In a romantic context, a hug might mean what we'd mean in friendship, since *eros* (romantic love) and *philia* (friendship-love) have considerable overlap. A hug means we hold the other person close emotionally and reflects a sharing and merging of two lives. It might express comfort, gladness, and security in someone's presence. Romantic hugs also express a physical desire to be close to someone for whom we have a romantic attraction.

Now perhaps you're thinking that these descriptions take simple physical actions far too seriously. Maybe you're thinking, "I just hug because it feels good!" Well, of course it does. In the right context, touch gives us pleasure. Knowing that someone wants to hug us affirms our sense of personal worth and perhaps our body image as well. Being close to someone is an experience of human community. There's nothing wrong with any of that. But a hug isn't just about you, so part of its meaning is that you enjoy your own pleasure and also the pleasure you are bringing to someone else. You like what's being said to you in the hug, but you also mean to say the same thing to someone else.

By inviting you to think about hugging (or any other form of sexual activity) as more than merely a pleasurable action, I'm encouraging you to deepen its meaning by seeing it in the context of a meaningful relationship. In other words, hugs aren't all the same. When you know what you mean by the hug you give and what someone means when they return it, the physical touch is supplemented by emotional satisfaction. A holistic hug feels better. A relational ethic might seem to permit more sexual activity, but because it insists that physical actions correspond to relationships that are meaningful in ways that go beyond physicality, a relational ethic will most likely place stricter limits on sexual activity than we see in most of contemporary culture.

Kissing

A kiss can express meaning in relationships characterized by non-erotic forms of love, and in some cultures (or subcultures) a kiss is a simple form of greeting. Romantic partners might use kisses the same way, kissing as a way of saying hello or goodbye.

Surprisingly, kissing seems to have little meaning among many of my relatively conservative Christian students. It's become such a common practice in early romantic encounters before the relationship has come to mean anything. In fact, it's sometimes justified with the words "it doesn't really mean anything." I usually call that into question. Of course, given my approach to the meaning of our physical actions, people can choose not to mean anything by a kiss, a caress, or even by sexual intercourse. But as someone who wants a kiss to be meaningful, I'm always somewhat baffled by this alleged practice of meaningless kissing.

When a kiss *is* meaningful, I suspect that it conveys an exclusive sense of intimacy. Meaningful kissing doesn't usually take place with more than one person at a time, and kisses celebrate a level of vulnerability and connection that bring a couple mutual joy and pleasure. Kissing is usually perceived as more invasive than hugging and communicates the willingness to let someone into our lives at a deeper, more personal, and more private level. And the pleasure of kissing is a symbol of the pleasure lovers find in each other's company and in sharing each other's lives. That's why one would feel betrayed if one's partner kissed someone else in this romantic and meaningful way.

Intimate Caressing

Human touch is a powerful form of communication. A gentle touch by the right person at the right time can convey a deep sense of love, concern, and care. But touch is usually uncomfortable when it is out of place. We have an intuitive or culturally trained sense that it should mean something, so if the wrong person touches us in the wrong place, a violation has taken place;

the touch fails to respect what such touching is supposed to mean, and as a result, it disrespects us as persons. Inappropriate touch, like inappropriate words, makes us embarrassed and uncomfortable—or even upset and angry.

Among lovers, the same touch that would make us uneasy in other contexts can be a meaningful communication of love. Intimate touching, by which I mean the range of touching that includes caressing intimate body parts and genital stimulation, is an inherently vulnerable activity. It allows another person to be close enough to invade what we would define as very private space. This requires a deeper level of trust, since we are literally putting private parts of ourselves in another's hands. Intimate touch says that we are willing to do this, not only with secret body places but also with many of our secrets, hidden feelings, hopes, and dreams. It says that we want to share these, that we take pleasure in revealing and in knowing another so intimately. More intimate touching corresponds with greater depth in other parts of a relationship, and it both symbolizes and celebrates the realities of the love that people experience in the whole of their shared life.

There's a fear that is often expressed when people consider the prospect of intimate touch in relationships that still fall short of the ultimate commitment that comes with a covenant of marriage. Even in the absence of any other critiques of a relational ethic, this approach is often rejected because "one thing leads to another." Intimate touching, even if theoretically appropriate at one stage in a relationship, is seen as a slippery slope leading to even greater intimacy (sexual intercourse) before a relationship has reached that stage of meaning.

A relational approach to sexual ethics rejects the slippery slope idea as a matter of principle, even though we can't avoid the fact that people do sometimes lack the self-control or self-discipline to match physical expressions of love with the meanings and realities embodied in their relationship. (For more on this, see below, "A Relational Ethic and the Character of the Person.") Lewis Smedes, from whom I have learned much, expresses an alternative to the slippery slope assumption. Smedes says that intimate caressing can be a delicately tuned means of mutual discovery that is an end in itself, with no intention of having sexual intercourse. It conveys personal closeness and sharing, with flexible but recognizable limits.[8]

8. My summary paraphrases Smedes' discussion in *Sex for Christians*, 130.

Sexual Intercourse

Sexual intercourse is normally seen as the most intimate of sexual expressions. If we could translate this act of love into words, what is it that we may be expressing with our bodies? Keep in mind that whatever words we use are the same words we would use and hear outside the context of sexual intimacy. They are spoken in the kitchen or while taking a walk, and because they are, one knows that this is what's meant when two bodies are joined. Consider some examples that intentionally contain double meanings. Sexual intercourse means

- I love you and you alone, unconditionally, for life. In other words, sex means what we say in marriage vows.

- I trust you with all the parts of me that are most intimate. In the same way that I trust you with intimate parts of my body, I trust you with my hopes and fears, my viewpoints and values, my deepest joys and sorrows.

- I give myself to you completely. My love for you, at its best, is generous and holds nothing back.

- Your love for me gives me intense pleasure, and I hope that my love for you does the same.

- I join my life together with yours with the intention that we are and will always be one. Sexual unity is a symbol of the covenantal unity present in the whole of a relationship.

- I am secure in your love and make myself vulnerable to you.

- I am safe with you, even in the abandon of ecstasy.

- I will love a child that results from our union.

These confessions of love make profound claims. The examples are not meant to be prescriptive or exhaustive; they are meant to illustrate ways in which we convey meaning in and through the activity of sexual intercourse. The meanings are intended, and in order to be understood, they must be expressed in the daily lives of lovers who say these things with their bodies but also embody the meaning in other spoken words and concrete actions.

Summary: Sex Means Something

In a relational approach to Christian sexual ethics, sexual acts should never be separated from their meaning. And in this approach, there is a moral difference between physical expressions of love because there is a connection between what we mean and the reality of the relationship. The meaning of the sexual act must tell the truth in a way that corresponds to the real relationship.

One of the main differences between this approach and a boundary ethic is that it provides a way to see a progression of sexual activity in ways that are morally meaningful. Every sexual act can have its own meaning, and it becomes morally responsible when that meaning is a truthful reflection of the maturing love that is actually embodied in the day-to-day lives of a couple. Sexual activity isn't an inevitable path to intercourse but a truthful communication that corresponds to what can truthfully be said and seen and experienced. This affirmation provides a basis for the final one.

CENTRAL AFFIRMATION #4: PHYSICAL EXPRESSIONS OF LOVE MAY GRADUALLY INCREASE, AS DO THE EMOTIONAL, SOCIAL, AND SPIRITUAL DIMENSIONS OF LOVE

Relationships develop. They grow and change and mature. Sometimes they meander, leaving us a little unclear about where they are going. The trajectory of growth isn't always an evenly ascending line; sometimes it goes up and down like the stock market. Sometimes relationships end. At other times, they deepen and flourish. A relational ethic presumes that the level of sexual activity—how we use our bodies to express our love—changes and grows in ways that roughly mirror the growth and development of a romantic relationship. It's not easy to draw a chart to illustrate how this looks precisely, but it's essential in a relational ethic to depict the progression in a way that can shape our sexual lives.

In the diagram below, a ladder depicts a relational ethic, and while no diagram is perfect, this one does give a general picture that helps explain what it means to think of the various dimensions of a romantic relationship as a journey toward increased love, intimacy, communication, trust, and other important relational characteristics. I find the ladder image helpful not because it depicts a climb but because the rungs depict *correspondence* between the two sides.

Relational Ethic Diagram

Sexual Intercourse		Relationship Designations	Relational Characteristics	Qualities of Character	Meanings - Communicated
		•Marriage	•Honesty	•Maturity	"I take you, for better or worse, for life."
		•Engagement	•Trust	•Critical self-assessment	
		•Pre-engagement	•Commitment		•Unconditional commitment
Intimate Caressing		•Serious and Steady	•Stability	•Honest self-awareness	•Deep love, concern care
		•Exclusive dating	•Mutual Respect	•(add your own)	•Comfort, closeness, emerging love
		•Exploring Possibilities	•Shared History		
			•(add your own)		•Mutual romantic interest
		•New and uncertain			
Hugging and Kissing					•(add your own)

On the right side of the ladder are examples of the qualitative dimensions of a relationship. Their (1) presence and (2) depth help us discern, for example, what we would mean by calling a relationship "serious" or "mature." In other words, these characteristics will emerge as a romantic relationship develops and grows, and individually, each will take on greater depth as time and circumstances nurture these qualities.

On the left side of the ladder are examples of sexual activities that express the meanings of love in ways that approximate the kinds of explanations provided in the previous section. This list probably resembles what most people would see as a progression from less significant to more significant levels in terms of both physical and emotional intimacy and vulnerability. Even though the levels of physical engagement might be culturally recognized, there are also individual factors that affect the way we see and experience physical contact, so from one person to the next there might be some minor modifications in this progression.

Interspersed among the rungs of the ladder are some of the qualities of character that are necessary components of a relational ethic. These will be explained in the section that follows. Taking note of them now, however, sounds an important warning. Using a relational ethic places stringent demands on moral agents, and without attentiveness to those demands, this approach would become badly distorted.

But here's an important warning: a picture freezes in time what is dynamic in real life. Consider an example: trust isn't just trust. Trust sprouts and grows and changes. It isn't simply present or not. It's present in different ways and to different degrees and at different times. It differs even between individuals within a relationship. It is affected not only by one's partner but also by one's past. So within any given couple, learning to trust is a journey in which trust develops and grows, but that journey might not look quite the same for each person. Complicated? Definitely! If we lose sight of the complexity, we oversimplify the way a relational ethic works.

A relational ethic says that sexual activity is an expression of Christian discipleship (affirmation #1) when we bring the qualities present in a relationship (affirmation #2) and the meanings of sexual activity (affirmation #3) into what I'd call an "inexact but recognizable correspondence." Another way to say this is that the gradual progression of meaningful physical expressions of love is morally permissible because the level of physical involvement is a truthful expression of the qualities and character of the whole relationship. Forms of physical sexual intimacy short of intercourse can be meaningful, appropriate means of mutual discovery and communication. They can be an experience of growth in understanding and love.[9]

In contrast with a boundary ethic, a relational ethic grants such permission because it affirms that these are the kinds of factors that matter to God. Sexual expressions of love find their goodness and meaning in relationality. We live that relationality through body, heart, and mind—all parts of the whole person God created. People and their relationships matter deeply. Physical touch matters deeply too, and finds its value and meaningfulness in the lived reality of a loving relationship. But progressing gradually toward deeper levels of physical intimacy implies a few important things that are either missed or rejected by some other approaches to Christian sexual ethics.

Meaningful sexual acts cover a broad range of behaviors.

Sexual intercourse is only one of those, and it has its own unique place in the progression of sexual activity. Can it be separated from other forms of intimate touch in a way that sees those activities not as foreplay inevitably leading to intercourse but as ways of gradually expressing a growing relationship of love? Yes. That affirmation is at the heart of a relational approach. It only makes sense to say that sexual activity gradually increases

9. My way of rephrasing a relational ethic is loosely borrowed from Lewis Smedes' explanation of what he called "responsible petting," or the range of physical sexual activity that comes between intimate caressing and intercourse. See chapter 7 of his *Sex for Christians*.

to match the gradual progression of the growth of the relationship if those physical expressions can be complete in themselves.

The sexual side is a matter of intentional choice. People are able to ignore the progression and have sex on the first date or hookup. But the relational side isn't simply a matter of choice. Relationships take time and effort to grow, and the progress is gradual. Attempts to rush it accomplish little. A relational ethic invites people to choose to restrain sexual activity voluntarily so that its progression matches the quality and character of their whole relationship. An imbalance would be reflected by rungs on the ladder that move toward sharper diagonals. Since we can't create a precise correspondence between sexual acts and relational stages, we can't expect precision. But it becomes easier to recognize distortions when we see sexual activity far outpacing relational maturity. "Going too far too fast" is the name sometimes given to that distortion.

One thing does not necessarily lead to another.

The slippery slope toward sexual intercourse isn't inevitable because sexual activity isn't "all or nothing." Each level of sexual activity, the great variety of ways people show and share their love through physical touch—each has its own meaning and integrity. A kiss is a complete form of sexual activity. Things need go no further for a kiss to say what it means. The same is true in other forms of human interaction. Sharing a secret or revealing a viewpoint not often made public creates a connection with someone. We give them a part of ourselves that has value; they receive it with gratitude and care. It's a meaningful exchange even if you don't tell all your secrets or reveal all your thoughts. Those can be saved for another time. It's the same with sexual activity—except that restraint is almost always an exercise of mind over body. It means that we decide to observe limits that honor the meaningfulness of sexual practices. It also means that we decide to honor the depth and character of the relationship we have with another person. Discerning the right time to share our emotional or sexual selves is part of mature restraint.

Intimate touch is not a mistake to regret, as long as it was truthful.

When caution dominates a sexual ethic, it's often advised that we avoid behaviors that we might someday regret. There's wisdom in that warning.

Regret can be painful and long-lived. It's often easier to avoid it than to get over it. Anyone who really wants to have kissed only the person he marries will have to engage in the level of self-discipline that saves the first kiss for the wedding. But a relational ethic provides a way to see why engaging in intimate touch isn't morally wrong, even though one might someday wish things had been different if the relationship ends. According to a relational approach, intimate caressing can be a truthful expression of the love that actually exists between two people. It says what is true at the time if it is an honest expression of love—even if that love doesn't last.

A RELATIONAL ETHIC AND THE CHARACTER OF THE PERSON

A relational ethic is far from permissive. In fact, it might appear to demand more than seems possible. You might ask, Why does sex have to be so complicated? Can't I just relax and enjoy it? Do I really have to be concerned about what it means and do all this relationship analysis? What happened to romance and spontaneity? Christian approaches to sex do include constraints to unlimited sexual freedom, and in every approach to sexual ethics presented here, there's an assumption that discipleship (embodying Christian convictions in every aspect of life) requires intentionality and diligence. But I hope you can also recognize that embodying a God-honoring ethic also honors people and sexuality in ways that enhance joyful sexual practices and healthy relationships.

In a relational approach to sexual ethics, the character of the people involved in a relationship is crucial. Lewis Smedes poses several questions that point to the importance of the "sort of person one is," convinced that *who* comes to a sexual encounter determines in large measure what makes it morally good. Have the people involved created a relationship in which sexual activity fits into the overall meaning of their love? Do they have well-grounded values that lead them to respect sexuality and each other? Do they know what they want for their relationship and for their lives? Do they have a clear sense of priorities and goals, both individually and for their relationship? Are they consciously aware of the narrative they are writing with their lives, and can they honestly affirm that it is the story they want their lives to tell?[10]

---

10. These questions are my paraphrased version of those Smedes asks in *Sex for Christians*, 135–36.

Maturity

The fact that those are hard questions to answer points to an important dimension of personal character required for a relational approach to sexuality: maturity. The ability to give thoughtful responses to such questions obviously presupposes a level of maturity well beyond what we'd normally see among teens beginning their first experiments with sexual activity. Unfortunately, I've observed that people often begin their sexual encounters well before they are mature enough to assess their behavior morally. Only later do they gain the capacity to do this, and then often they look back in regret on a past sexual history that doesn't reflect the approach to sex that they'd want to consciously adopt.

Maturity is a vague character trait, and we're inclined to think we have it even when those around us are still watching us grow into it. For the purposes of a relational ethic, there are a couple of ways to assess maturity. The first is to ask oneself whether questions like the ones posed above have ever been consciously mulled over or, if not, whether they could be addressed in meaningful ways. Second, have the traits described below— critical self-assessment and honest self-awareness—developed as somewhat stable dimensions of one's character? Can important people in our lives see and affirm them?

While it might sound a little harsh, it's hard to imagine how a relational ethic could function with integrity in the absence of a mature sense of self, honest critical assessment of one's motives and goals, a high level of self-awareness, and self-control. None of us are perfect in these ways, but without these personal capacities, a relational ethic too easily turns into a method for self-justification and the rationalization of sexual activity.

Critical Self-Assessment

We don't usually like to talk about sin or to be reminded of its presence in our own thoughts and desires. A *boundary ethic* acknowledges the reality of sin by clearly naming the boundaries that keep us on the right side of a line that distinguishes sinful sexual practices from those that honor God's intentions for sexuality. A *relational ethic* respects the reality of sin by providing a way to carefully and intentionally discern how our sexual practices express and reflect the love present in our romantic relationship. But even human discernment cannot escape sinful tendencies. We can't fully trust ourselves. But rather than being paralyzed by that fact, we have to figure out how to be responsive to God's call to bring our sexuality and spirituality into a healthy union. Sin makes discernment essential, even though we know it might sometimes be flawed.

The day before I sat down to write these pages, a former student who is studying off campus for the semester wrote these words in a note to me: "I get frustrated with myself when I realize that I can't just follow my own morals every day and then start to feel guilty. These constant feelings of frustration and guilt are wearing away at me and sometimes I feel over-whelmed and tired of it all." She was engaging in critical self-assessment, and in this case used it confessionally. Confession is one key contribution of critical self-assessment because it functions to keep us honest and oriented.

Another contribution of critical self-assessment is the capacity for self-critique. A relational ethic requires that people assess the qualitative dimensions of their relationship. This can be difficult, since "falling in love" isn't a fully rational experience. Infatuation sometimes parades as an impostor for mature love, creating illusions of perfection, compatibility, and permanence that sometimes fade away when reality finds its way in.

In order to use a relational ethic, people need to discern and critically assess several important things about themselves and their relationship. Here are a few of the questions implied by what has already been said in this chapter and that would need to be assessed critically by anyone who wants to use a relational ethic with integrity.

- How do we integrate our faith with our romantic love and sexual activity?
- What level of respect, honesty, mutuality and commitment are present in the relationship?
- Can we answer questions similar to those posed by Harvey Cox and Margaret Farley earlier in this chapter?
- Can we say clearly to ourselves and each other what we mean by our sexual activity? Are those meanings embodied in the rest of our relationship?
- Is the level of our sexual relationship progressing in ways that generally correspond to the growth in the rest of the relationship?

Honest Self-Awareness

Critical self-assessment presumes honesty. This might seem to go without saying. The reason it is important to mention is because I presume that honesty is easily compromised when sexual desires threaten to overpower it.

We know how readily we engage in self-justification when we find ourselves wanting to do or explain actions that we realize are wrong. In fact, we are probably dishonest with *ourselves* as often as we explicitly mislead others.

Are we able to be honest about our motives and the quality of romantic relationships when passion threatens to interfere with careful discernment? A relational ethic quickly becomes a sham when it is used dishonestly to rationalize sexual activity that doesn't truthfully meet relational criteria.

In the Christian tradition there is a spiritual exercise of *self-examination*. In my own Reformed tradition, there is a long tradition of inviting people to examine themselves prior to participating in the Lord's Supper. This practice helps enrich the sacrament. Honestly acknowledging our sin prior to the sacrament helps make the proclamation of the forgiveness of sins even more meaningful. Recommitting ourselves to following the way of Jesus more faithfully gains even greater clarity in light of honest confession. Self-examination is an honest, inward look at our passions and practices that seeks to bring them into ever-greater conformity to the goodness and well-being God intends.

Self-Discipline and Self-Control

The exercise of self-control is essential in a relational ethic, since sexual activities are chosen on the basis of morality rather than being determined by biological drives. As is often the case, what we desire isn't always what's good, so the ability to control our actions is a central feature of morality. That's why self-control is one of the fruits of the Spirit (Gal 5:22–23) and is held up as an important part of sexual morality:

> For this is the will of God, your sanctification: that you abstain
> from fornication; that each one of you know how to control
> your own body in holiness and honor . . . (1 Thess 4:3–4 NRSV)

The possibility of self-control creates the conditions for an ethic that includes freedom within constraint. It is not necessary to say no to everything, out of fear that to say yes to one thing leads inevitably down the slippery slope to every form of sexual sin. It's always *possible* that self-control will fail—in our sexual lives as in any part of life. This is likely behind the lament in Romans 7:15: "I do not understand my own actions. For I do not do what I want, but I do the very thing that I hate" (NRSV).

It's also possible that we can learn self-control, so that we need not always live out of the fear that sin will enslave us. Just a few chapters later, in his letter to the Christians in Rome, Paul acknowledges the power of grace to transform us, making it possible for our love to be genuine and for us to hold fast to what is good (see Rom 12).

Christians always live in the tension between the power of sin and the power of grace. A relational ethic acknowledges the power of sin but in the face of that reality calls Christians to let grace transform them. A relational ethic strives to embody sexual lives transformed by grace.

IN CONCLUSION: A RELATIONAL ETHIC IN BRIEF

I am a person of worth. God created me with a body, heart, and mind; I am a physical, emotional, and intellectual person, loved by God in all the fullness of my being, and worthy of being loved by others in the same way. This is true not only of me but of all God's creatures.

My sexual ethic reflects my belief that sexual health and wholeness are part of my overall health and wholeness. Sexuality cannot be compartmentalized and separated from the rest of my life. It is among the things that really matter, and I intend to treat my sexuality and sexual practices with consideration and care.

All forms of sexual activity mean something. They are ways to express love. Physical expressions of love should match the reality of the relationship in which they are performed. It follows from this that

- What I say with my words should correspond to what I say with my body.
- The level of physical vulnerability should match the level of honesty, trust, and vulnerability present in the relationship.
- There should be a correspondence between my commitment to a person and the level of sexual activity I engage in.
- While it is not easy to explain the way that specific physical actions correspond to the quality and characteristics of a relationship, there is a progression through stages of a relationship. Lower levels are the building blocks of a foundation upon which higher levels of the relationship are built. Sexual expressions of love should correspond to this fact.

Sexual intercourse is the ultimate act of sexual relating and ought to be reserved for relationships of ultimate seriousness. Marriage is an example of a relationship of ultimate seriousness. In the vows of marriage, I promise to love one person exclusively and unconditionally, for as long as I live. Sexual intercourse, as the ultimate physical expression of love, says the same thing.

In being committed to this sexual ethic, I do not imply that I will always live it perfectly. But in calling it my ethic, I do intend to live it out and I will strive to act in ways that are consistent with it. I will ask others who know of it to help hold me accountable—especially the person who is my partner in romantic love. If I fail, I will try to forgive myself and will ask God to forgive me; then I will set out again to live in a way that is consistent with what I have said I believe.

Other people may have different moral commitments and may choose to act in ways that look different. Even if I do not believe that what they think or do is right, I will strive to treat them as neighbors who deserve the same kind of love and respect that I desire and deserve

5

Some Ways to Think about Sexual Ethics

An Ethic of Sexual Integrity

INTEGRITY IS ONE OF my favorite virtues. It would be a great honor to be recognized by others as a person of integrity. Striving for it is a lifelong pursuit, and even those who seem to us to have reached it know that the journey toward integrity remains incomplete.

It is also a rich term. At its root integrity is about wholeness, and it invites us to see sexuality as part of the whole of life. In thinking about integrity as it applies to people in general, Stephen Carter says,

> A person of integrity . . . is a whole person, a person somehow undivided. The word conveys not so much a single-mindedness as a completeness . . . the serenity of a person who is confident in the knowledge that he or she is living rightly.[1]

In the Christian tradition, Carter suggests, the idea of integrity is captured in the Beatitudes with the phrase "pure of heart."[2] While the term *pure* is often used in a sexual context to indicate a level of perfection or sinlessness, integrity as purity of heart intends something different. It means seeing sexuality as a dimension of the whole person, and one that needs to be *integrated* into the other parts of life in ways that consistently reflect how we see ourselves and others in relationship to God.

1. Carter, *Integrity*, 7.
2. Carter, *Integrity*, 8.

An ethic of sexual integrity invitesw us to focus not only on the rules or the quality of relationships we seek but also on the heart of our moral identity. Acting with integrity means acting in ways that are consistent with the commitments we make across each part of our life. It means creating a consistent whole. While we are often taught to think that sex is private, this should not mean that it is somehow isolated from who we are in public. Sex isn't publicly displayed, and sexual relationships treat partners with respect by observing confidentiality. But as a popular aphorism has it, integrity is about who we are, even when no one is looking.

People who act with integrity are apt to elicit observations like "I'm not surprised at all; that's exactly what I would have expected him to do!" Or, in cases of surprising (and perhaps untrue) revelations, "I'm shocked. I can't believe she would ever do anything like that!" People who live with integrity live out of a stable set of values and virtues. They are predicable, morally reliable. We often hear the terms *centered* or *grounded* applied to people of integrity.

I'm also using the term *sexual integrity* to name a content-rich way of thinking about sexual ethics, by saying what I think it means to live with sexual integrity. The ten components of sexual integrity I will describe are meant to do two things. First, they illustrate dimensions of the wholeness that can characterize a Christian sexual ethic. In addition, they suggest ways to move beyond a simple description of integrity as a concept to indicate what living with integrity can mean in the sexual arena of life. Each reader may choose to describe his or her own content-rich meaning of sexual integrity in ways that differ from what is offered here. In that case my own list can simply serve as a source of ideas to consider.

MORAL VISION AND INTEGRITY

Integrity arises from the way we have been taught to *see* things. Sometimes this has been referred to as a worldview. Sexual integrity is a reflection of the way we answer at least four basic worldview questions.

The first question we might ask ourselves is, How do I see myself? Am I part of God's wondrous creation, and therefore a person of great worth? Am I someone who deserves to be treated (by myself and others) with care and respect? When I look in the mirror, who do I see? Who do I want others to see?

Integrity also leads us to ask another question: How do I see persons who are potential or actual romantic partners? Are they people with whom I seek meaningful friendships? Can I be comfortable and safe in their presence? Do they encourage me to be the best I can be? Do they seek to lead their own lives with integrity?

A third integrity question is, How do I see relationships? Do I expect them to be God-honoring above all else? Do I expect them to be characterized by mutual giving and receiving? Do they focus on the multifaceted dimensions of each person, so that they are not just about physical or emotional fulfillment but also about shared interests, a wider circle of friends, activities that matter to both people?

A fourth integrity question is, How do I see God? Is God a relational being who has created us to love and be loved in a variety of ways—as family members, friends, romantic partners, neighbors near and far? Does God seek our well-being, forgive our shortcomings? Does God call us to live as followers of Jesus in every aspect of our lives?

Taken together, the way we answer questions like these creates a moral vision. It's a vision that both describes what we see and calls us to be or become what we see. It's a vision we live *toward*. Integrity doesn't imply perfection; instead, it provides direction.

INTEGRITY OR COMPARTMENTALIZATION?

Integrity can be pictured as the conjunction of three things:

- Knowing what's right (moral vision)
- Saying what's right (honesty)
- Doing what's right (courage)

When these overlap and are basically in harmony with each other, three separate and important dimensions of the moral life are integrated into a whole self. We do not always live out this ideal.

Integrity is the opposite of a compartmentalized morality. When people profess one thing and do another, or adopt one set of moral guidelines for one situation and act like someone else in another context, they can be said to lack integrity. We may compartmentalize morality for one of the following reasons:

1. We ad-lib our moral commitments when we haven't learned how to integrate our basic convictions in a new life context. Moral uncertainty can lead to morality-on-the-fly, and like a kite in the wind, we're apt to go in whichever way the breeze is blowing. If we haven't figured out what kind of person we want to be in our sexual lives, we might live as

sexual beings in a compartment that doesn't fit so well with the rest of our more settled morality.

2. Social cues are confusing. We don't live in just one social environment. Differing and even conflicting moral messages come from different places: family, church, school, team, workplace, television, news sources, celebrities, and print media. The wide array of sources for sexual messages is dizzying. In a homogeneous society, the messages would tell us similar things and would be mutually supportive. But most people's experience is the opposite, since American culture is wildly heterogeneous. Messages reflect a diversity of worldviews, values, and practices. Many of these are in conflict with each other, and this is especially confusing when we live in several of these moral "worlds" at the same time.

3. Peer pressure: If we are uncertain about our own morality, it can become easy to fill in the gaps by adopting the values and practices we observe around us—especially among influential peers like classmates, coworkers, and friends. "Everyone is doing it" has a familiar ring. And that's natural, because morality is communal.

We potentially live in many different "compartments" where our ideas and behaviors can be determined by a variety of diverse norms. Keeping the different areas of our lives in separate compartments is sometimes the easiest way to negotiate a complicated world. Rather than trying to integrate all the areas of our lives (along with the activities and roles specific to each) into a coherent whole, it is simpler to live out each area of life according to the norms that culture provides for it. This might lead to a considerable inconsistency from one area of life to the next. Compartmentalizing several areas of life may feel whole as long as we can separate each one from the others. A common example is the person who lives in the religious area only when in sacred space (church) or sacred time (Sunday morning). But once we begin to let our religious lives, our political lives, our social lives and our consumer lives intersect, we often find inconsistencies or incongruencies that create an uncomfortable dissonance. Integrity is the ideal that helps us bring each area of life into harmony with the others.

WHAT MAKES AN INTEGRITY MODEL OF SEXUAL ETHICS DISTINCTIVE?

Talking about integrity is using virtue language. Christian ethics is often divided into three basic approaches:

- An *ethic of law* (deontological ethics) focuses on the rules or commands that are taught and enforced by the communities that shape Christian morality. Doing what is good means acting in ways that obediently enact the rules or commands that Christianity teaches. A boundary ethic is an example of this approach.

- An *ethic of ends* (teleological ethics) focuses on the goals that one should seek in living morally. Actions that seek and achieve goals that are deemed worthy are good. A relational ethic is an example of this approach.

- An *ethic of integrity* focuses on the virtues and values that have become part of who we are. The stories we have lived in our families, faith communities, and other formative communities merge to form a cluster of embodied habits of heart and mind. As this occurs, a moral identity takes shape. If we think about morality in this way, what we do is an expression of who we are and often the result of a formative process we aren't always consciously aware of. In a mysterious but also comfortable way, the moral commitments we've soaked up while going about daily life just seem to course through our veins like our moral lifeblood.

INTEGRITY, IDENTITY, AND EMBODIMENT

Integrity emphasizes embodiment. It is a way of embodying the kind of person we want to be. And since integrity is about wholeness, it means that our sexual selves reflect the kind of people we want to be in all of life. Sexual morality is not simply something out there, needing to be observed, obeyed, and applied. It is *me* living out my own moral identity. It is *you* being what you care about. It is people enacting the commitments that have become central to their self-understanding. It is Christians reflecting the story of God's love, forgiveness, righteousness and justice in their sexual lives as well as in the rest of life.

Integrity is rooted in one's *moral identity*. You can't live with integrity if you don't have a moral center. My own description of moral integrity is inseparable from the convictions discussed in chapter 2. If someone's core convictions about sexuality and sexual practices differ, their embodied integrity and sexual identity would reflect those differences. Integrity is fully compatible with a belief that the Christian tradition recognizes a set of sexual rules as truthful reflections of what God expects from us. And it's also compatible with the belief that in God's creation, certain goals are consistent with what sex was intended to mean and to accomplish in healthy human living.

WHAT DOES IT MEAN TO BE A PERSON OF SEXUAL INTEGRITY?

1. Sexual integrity means that partners respect each other's sexual limits.

Acts of sexual intimacy have meanings and comfort levels that are often socially inscribed and deeply personal. Respect for these limits means that we will not attempt to physically or psychologically override another's limits in order to satisfy our own desires.

Part of our comfort level is deeply personal but also seemingly automatic and bodily. It's not unlike individual comfort levels with personal space or with being (or not being) a "touchy-feely" person. We don't choose it; we simply recognize it. When you say "that really makes me uncomfortable," it's not always easy to say exactly why. It just does. Or perhaps there are negative associations that have been deeply ingrained and are kept hidden in a private place deep inside of us. Whatever the reason, especially in early stages of a relationship, our discomforts don't need to be defended or explained. They simply need to be recognized and respected.

You may rightfully insist that others do this for you, and you should be equally willing to do the same for anyone else.

Sexual limits are also implied by moral commitments. Many people have adopted sexual boundaries, sometimes even before they have stopped to examine the basis for those boundaries. Many people have relational goals they seek, and they want to make choices that are consistent with those goals. It makes things a bit easier when someone can explain their moral choices and the reasons behind them. But even when they can't, those moral commitments and choices are part of who they are.

When we have moral reasons to say no to certain kinds of sexual activity, violations create a sense of moral discomfort. When someone comes too close to our moral limits, it feels a bit like being too close to the edge of a cliff when you're afraid of heights. Whether or not your moral commitments are carefully thought out or defensible isn't the issue at first. The fact that they are your moral commitments is enough. This is the insight behind the maxim "No means no."

Not all of our moral limits reflect moral absolutes. After closer and more careful reflection we may adopt a revised set of moral boundaries or require far more from a partner prior to sexually intimate acts. What we say yes or no to today may not be the same in the future, with increased moral maturity. Or, intimate touch that feels uncomfortable at first can eventually become a means of communicating deep trust and love. We can develop enough trust in someone to give her permission to accompany us on a slightly uncomfortable journey of mutual love and discovery. So no may eventually become yes.

You can insist that other people recognize and respect your moral commitments even if they do not share them or agree with them, and you should do the same for others.

Respecting each other's sexual limits clearly means that sexual integrity involves regarding another person's morality and the choices it leads them to make as having a claim on one's own behavior. This claim clearly implies the applicability of the golden rule: doing unto others as we would have them do unto us. The result is that the most conservative or most restrictive morality prevails. In order to sustain this first principle of sexual integrity, some other virtues are foundational.

Patience

The first principle of sexual integrity acknowledges that there's a lot of variation in people's sexual comfort levels, personal desires, and sexual morality. And the even darker truth is that people sometimes simply seek to take advantage of others for their own personal satisfaction.

In the best-case scenarios, when a healthy mutual friendship-romance is developing, patience is a virtue that serves sexual integrity. Learning to be patient means learning to set aside immediate satisfactions in the name of a greater good. Patience affirms that the whole person matters and that one is willing to build the foundations of trust and commitment that are necessary for increased levels of sexual activity. Patience affirms that a relationship is a whole made up of at least two individual parts, and that each person's values and goals matter.

When a romantic partner isn't willing to exercise patience, there's reason for concern. The hard work of building a healthy romance makes patience an essential ingredient, even apart from matters of sex. Respecting another person's discomfort or their refusal requires the patience to set aside one's own desires in favor of a whole person who matters. Patience doesn't come easy in any area of life but is a virtue that enhances much in life that is valuable.

Self-Control and Self-Restraint

When a romantic partner's sexual boundaries or sexual desires don't match our own, the moral obligation to respect and honor their moral and personal choices makes the exercise of self-control and self-restraint of paramount importance. Especially when we accept the presupposition that sexual activity is only appropriate in a context of love, a romantic partner should be able to count on the fact that her moral limits will be both respected and supported. One who values and even nurtures the ability to exercise self-control creates a safe and comfortable place for a partner to know that she is loved not as a means to an end but as herself.

Saying yes to someone else's limits sometimes requires saying no to our own desires. Put this way, self-control is an expression of love—or even sacrificial love. But it's not always easy to express love if you're feeling like you have been rejected. As an exercise of sexual integrity, self-control is rooted in the fact that we see our partner's choices as part of what we care about deeply. As a result, we are able to set aside what we want (self-restraint). In an ethic of sexual integrity, self-control replaces any form of manipulative pressure aimed at getting someone to do what we want them to do.

2. Sexual integrity means that we have a holistic regard for each other.

Love includes a person's ideas, interests, skills, personality, traits, and commitments, among other things. A relationship characterized by sexual integrity will keep these in balance. Sexual integrity recognizes that people are far more than a means to sexual satisfaction, even though sexual pleasure can be one dimension of a healthy human relationship.

To illustrate this principle of sexual integrity, I have sometimes asked students to imagine a scenario in which a romantic partner asked, "What would you rather do: spend quality time with family and friends, perform meaningful service to others, explore the beauty of art or nature, hold a deep conversation about our hopes and dreams, or engage in sexual activity?"

In the right context, sexual activity might be an appropriate option. But if it was the only choice you ever made, the relationship would soon become distorted, narrow, fragmented. It would no longer treat the person as a whole self but instead reduce them (and you) to a sex toy. In other words, it would lead to a serious kind of dehumanization. Romantic love can become unbalanced, especially in a culture that skews love toward sexual attractiveness and sexual fulfillment. Learning to think from a perspective of sexual integrity resists any efforts to reduce a person to less than he is.

Healthy human relationships require *seeing* people the right way. They require a lens that sees truthfully in the face of cultural myths that sometimes reduce people to sex objects. One of the things this integrity lens can do is expand our understanding of intimacy—or nakedness. Rob Bell suggests that the affirmation in Genesis 2—"And the man and his wife were both naked and they were not ashamed"—reflects this holistic way of seeing each other. It is about "whole persons coming together. All of him being given to all of her. All of her being given to all of him."[3] But this is not simply giving someone all of our *physical* being. It isn't simply "going all the way." Bell describes this wholeness as the mingling of all the ways of their souls:

> It is easy to take off your clothes and have sex. People do it all the time. But opening up your soul to someone, letting them into your spirit and thoughts and fears and future and hopes and dreams . . . that is being naked.[4]

When relationships are built on this kind of holistic regard for one another, sex is integrated into the whole of a life and a relationship. Sex finds meaning in this whole and is full of meaning when the fullness of each component of the person is brought together in physical expressions of love. At the same time, this wider array of nonphysical dimensions of love will be adequate to sustain the relationship during periods of abstinence from sexual expressions of love.

3. Sexual integrity means sharing a high level of openness and honesty across a broad range of relational intimacy.

Sexual activity will not be a substitute for other sincere expressions of love. Sharing our bodies is an intimate form of sharing, but it is not sharing everything. We are more than our bodies. Sexual integrity calls us to match forms of physical expression with other forms of expression.

For some people, sexual intimacy might be a difficult way to be open to another person. We're not all equally comfortable with physical touch and personal intimacy. This might be one of the most challenging ways we make ourselves vulnerable to someone. But it's not always that way. Sometimes sexual acts, especially when they have become commonplace, can become an easy substitute for other significant forms of deep sharing.

3. Bell, *Sex God*, 156.
4. Bell, *Sex God*, 156–57.

Physical nakedness literally means that our bodies, in all of their beauty and in all of their imperfection, are revealed fully. What is usually hidden is now shown. But physical nakedness really only reveals a small part of a person. Beneath our skin we are a complex mix of hopes and fears, life experiences and ways of understanding them, viewpoints and beliefs. Sexual openness doesn't touch this depth of a person. It's possible to be *sexually* open and honest, yet still hide the deepest and most personal dimensions of ourselves.

Revealing the story of our lives to someone may actually be much harder than revealing our bodies. In any form of human sharing we can never know for sure how someone will receive what we offer. Will she disagree or disapprove? Will he take me seriously, continue to love me even if I tell a deep truth about something that matters to me? Do I feel safe enough to reveal my doubts, confusions, frustrations?

I have often read in student papers the claim that sexual intercourse is the deepest kind of sharing that can take place between two people. I always wonder if the claim is overstated. It isn't usually stated as a form of self-reporting but as a learned idea, yet to be experienced. I think I know where it comes from: it is part of a narrative that holds sexual intercourse in very high esteem, seeking to protect it from casualness or recreational intent. The goal of the claim is to reserve this act of physical ultimacy for relationships matched by equal emotional and social ultimacy—namely, marriage.

But, like "Better Than Sex Cake," there are other contenders for the deepest kind of sharing. Acts of sacrificial love come to mind. Or acts of selfless generosity. Being trusted with someone's secret is a deep act of love, and being loved in spite of one's own rarely shared dark side is another strong contender. Of course, each of these can also be a component that undergirds sexual expressions of love. Perhaps it's unhelpful or even impossible to nominate any single way of expressing love to the ultimate status implied in my students' claims. Since people and love are both multidimensional, maybe it's more accurate to say that we express the depth of love in a wide variety of ways.

Still, it's easy to be fooled by sexual intimacy, because it is a powerful way to express our love and to merge our emotional and bodily selves in union with another. Sexual integrity involves seeing sexual expressions as one among many ways of being honest and open with another.

4. Sexual integrity means that we know our sexual limits, understand the reasons for them, and can articulate these.

Sexual integrity involves acting on the basis of values and reasons so that passion is channeled in ways that contribute to human well-being. A romantic relationship gains depth and satisfaction from knowing and respecting each other's values—which in turn intensifies the meaning of physical forms of love.

What we do with our bodies is integrally related to what we think with our minds, what we feel, and how we see ourselves in relationship to God. We are body/mind/heart/soul beings, and to separate or ignore any of these dimensions of the human person is to deny the holism God built into our created nature. Physical expressions of love are therefore inseparable from our reasons to say yes or no to certain kinds of sexual acts. Our sexual limits are inseparable from the way we understand ourselves as sexual beings, and the way we see ourselves is inseparable from the way we understand ourselves in relationship to God. It's all one big entangled cluster of the human self.

Spontaneity is sometimes characterized as "just doing it"—which implies that thinking about it first is an unnecessary interference. Even more, the extra step of also talking about it might make things seem just way too complicated. Sexual integrity begs to differ. A person who embodies sexual integrity doesn't act first and think about it later. Integrity *integrates* reasons, meanings, choices, and behaviors into a coherent whole.

How does understanding your sexual limits and being able to explain the reasons for them enhance sexual expressions of love? The reasons for our sexual activities (and for saying no to some things) give them meaning. A kiss may be pleasurable, but knowing what you mean by it and what someone intends to say to you when he does it enfolds a physical action in a constellation of intentions, commitments, and affirmations. If you can tell someone what you mean by your intimate touch (not every time or in the moment), your touches are enriched because they are no longer simply something that you do but something that you say.

Refusals can have positive meanings too. In early stages of a relationship, saying no to a new level of sexual activity, when accompanied by reasons, may actually convey the deep value one places on the relationship *and* the deep meaning one attributes to sexual activity. A simple no, while valid, can feel like nothing more than rejection. But the reasons for that no may increase one's respect for the person who refuses, enhance one's own understanding of the meaning attached to physical actions, and foster admiration for someone who takes you seriously enough to explain!

5. Sexual integrity means that we consider potential harms that may come to ourselves, the other person, or the relationship, as important constraints on personal desires.

Persons of sexual integrity value others as highly as they regard themselves. They will not engage in sexual activity that threatens to harm others physically, emotionally, or spiritually.

The moral requirement that we do no harm to others is nearly a universal moral rule. It's used to justify personal morality, public legislation, and informal social rules. The obligation to do no harm to others transcends religion, politics, and social class. Of course, in spite of its nearly universal recognition as a moral norm, people often hurt others. Moral norms don't always translate into moral practices.

While it is always somewhat of a mystery why it happens, even people who profess to love us can hurt us—sometimes more deeply *because* they claim to love us. Sometimes the hurt is intentional, sometimes it is subconscious, and sometimes unintended. A romantic partner can cause physical harm, destroy one's self-confidence, instill self-doubt, inflict emotional pain, or undermine one's religious or moral convictions.

Ethicist Margaret Farley, a Catholic moral theologian, has articulated several norms for sexual morality that are clearly focused on the avoidance of harm but also on respect for the person and the relationality involved in sexual activity. We avoid harm not simply because it's wrong but because we see others through the lens of God's justice and love.

Farley reminds us that there are several forms that harm can take, including "physical, psychological, spiritual, relational. It can also take the form of failure to support, to assist, to care for, to honor, in ways that are required by reason of context and relationship."[5] The likelihood of harm in the sexual sphere is heightened by the fact that in our sexual relationships we are especially vulnerable. This vulnerability is part of what gives sexual expressions of love the power to touch us deeply and to communicate love in profoundly intimate ways. But vulnerability also opens us to the abuse of power and exploitation. As Karen Lebacqz states, "Any exercise of sexuality that violates appropriate vulnerability is wrong."[6]

Consider a common sexual norm: that in any sexual exchange, both partners give their free consent. The positive requirement that consent be present guards against a wide range of sexual harms. Rape and violence used against unwilling victims is clearly prohibited by the requirement

5. Farley, *Just Love*, 216–17.
6. Lebacqz, "Appropriate Vulnerability," 435–38.

of consent. Likewise, taking advantage of people with limited capacity, or who are immature, or those over whom one has power, are all prohibited, since no real consent can be present in such cases. Gaining sex through manipulation that depends on lies or deceit are other examples of sex that violates the respect shown by gaining free consent.[7]

Sexual integrity means seeing persons as God's wondrous creation but also as fragile beings who can be easily injured. This is equally true for both men and women, in spite of stereotypes. Fragility is not weakness but an element of the human condition, fully compatible with our strength and resilience. Wondrous, fragile creatures are to be handled with care.

Caring for romantic partners involves both advocacy and restraint. As an advocate, we seek to protect the person we love from harm and do what is necessary to enhance her well-being. We take care of people we love. Advocacy can be demanding. It takes time and energy and may require significant personal sacrifice under some circumstances. Caring also sometimes demands personal constraints. It sometimes requires saying no to what we want in order to honor what someone else wants. Balancing the needs of self and other, battling selfishness, and being willing to compromise are part of the burden of caring.

6. Sexual integrity means that in sexual activity there is mutual giving and receiving.

Sexual activity involves the mutual sharing of oneself with another and the sharing of mutual pleasure. Sexual behavior that is only "giving" or "getting" lacks this kind of integrity.

Mutuality is part of the wholeness of any sexual exchange, at any level of sexual activity. It means that we don't simply *do things to people*, as if there is an active and a passive participant. A sexual act is a form of giving, and the companion act is a form of receiving. Or a sexual act is a form of communication, and the companion act is understanding. Even when we think about a sexual act as initiated by one partner, and in that sense one-sided, it is never really one-sided. Sexual actions have integrity when they are mutual.

This doesn't deny that there is individuality and difference involved in sexual practices. When we give ourselves to someone in any relationship, we don't necessarily give or receive in precisely the same ways. We give something of our uniqueness. In friendship, for example, where there is also mutual giving and receiving, friends give themselves to each other in ways

7. Farley, *Just Love*, 218–19.

that reflect their particular personalities and personal characteristics. The exchange isn't measurably identical, even though it is happening from both sides. This is true in sexual activity too.

When people share their sexual selves, a complex interaction takes place. There is desire, intention, pleasure, meaning, the union of two selves. What each person desires and intends, the ways they experience emotional and physical pleasure, and the meaning of their union will obviously differ somewhat. But sexual activity has integrity when desire is present in each partner, when intentions are similar and when they are understood.

There's been much discussion among philosophers[8] about the *communicative or expressive function* of sex. Sexual actions are not just physical. Their purpose, while it includes physical pleasure, is more than orgasm. Communication is taking place. One partner is saying something to the other, and the other is both receiving and responding.

This sexual communication has been referred to as a form of body language. Robert Solomon gives examples of several interpersonal attitudes and feelings we might express through this body language—such things as shyness, domination, fear, submissiveness and dependence, love, indifference, lack of confidence and embarrassment, shame, jealousy, possessiveness.

We express meaningful messages with our bodies, and these messages are both given and received. When sexual activity is embedded in this context of expressiveness, it becomes more than the physical pleasure that can be experienced alone through masturbation. Masturbation isn't mutual. Compared to the expressiveness of a meaning-filled mutual sexual exchange, masturbation is analogous to talking to oneself.

There is even more happening in a healthy sexual relationship than the exchange of meaningful messages. Messages tend to be primarily cognitive, producing mutual understanding. But sexual activity also produces emotion. It makes us *feel* accepted, loved, connected, cared for, and at the same time, given the ideal of mutuality, produces the same feelings in one's partner.

Sexual integrity recognizes that there is reciprocity at the core of sexual actions because they always involve two whole persons who infuse their actions with meaning and history and intentionality. Again, quoting Margaret Farley, the sexual encounter involves "two sides of one shared reality" coming together: two liberties meet, two bodies meet, two hearts come together—metaphorical and real descriptions of sexual mutuality.[9]

8. Jean-Paul Sartre, Thomas Nagel, Robert Solomon, and Janice Moulton are among those who have written on the communicative nature of sexual acts. This section draws broadly on their descriptions and discussion.

9. Farley, *Just Love*, 222.

7. Sexual integrity means that choices regarding sexual behavior are made as part of the fabric of one's whole life.

Because we are the product of a variety of communities and relationships, our sexual practices will arise out of serious engagement with family, friends, our religious community, and other important formative communities. To allow the whole fabric of our lives to shape our sexual behavior is to acknowledge that while we are individuals, we also value and respect our relatedness to others.

In contrast to this communal view of our sexual morality, the familiar script of individualism provides a tempting alternative. Lauren Winner describes individualism as "two consenting adults, unmoored from any community or society, free to make their own decisions. So long as they don't violate the other's consent, they can do as they please."[10] Contrary to the popular idea that we are isolated individuals who should make our own moral decisions, unaffected by those around us (radical autonomous freedom), an ethic of sexual integrity places an intentionally high value on the formative communities in which we participate by choice, chance, or necessity.

What makes us want to isolate ourselves from the world around us? Do we find it oppressive, burdensome, and uncaring? Perhaps at times each one of these factors helps account for our reaction. But what if the communities that surround us seek what's best for us, invite us into meaningful dialogue, provide us with resources to think and act wisely, and give us the grace to learn and fail and do our best?

I agree with Winner's claims that the body of Christ is a basic unit of ethical meaning, and we find ourselves in that body when we find ourselves in dialogue with the communities that seek to shape our lives, such as church and family and friends. "Speaking to one another about our sexual selves is just one (admittedly risky) instance of a larger piece of Christian discipleship: being in community with each other."[11] It's not always easy to find a community that is authentically committed to serious conversation about sexuality—or to serious issues of Christian discipleship in other areas. Still, we are communal beings, even though our communities are affected by the sin and imperfections we all struggle with. And whether we like to admit

10. Winner, *Real Sex*, 50. Winner does make an important clarification. She says that while sex is communal rather than private, it is still personal rather than public (ibid., 59). This means that while our sexual morality is part of the fabric of communal life, our sexual practices in relationships of love are deeply personal and not normally a matter for public display or discussion.

11. Winner, *Real Sex*, 53.

it or not, we are shaped by these communities in conscious and unconscious ways, even when we pretend that we aren't.

We can't avoid hearing the moral messages of those who surround us, and it would be a difficult task to sort out who teaches us what. Some messages are overlapping and some are contradictory. Some of the moral communities that shape us are silent about sex, while others speak loudly and often. In the experience of my students, families are notoriously quiet about sexual ethics, except for simple and often only implied messages. Church communities, based on many years of anecdotal reporting, often have little more to offer. Sometimes we find ourselves wishing that people would just leave us alone so we could make up our own minds. But at other times, realizing that our own minds lack the resources to decide what's best, what most honors God or enhances life, we wish that the communities we value would provide us with more information and wisdom!

The notion that we are isolated individuals is simply a myth. Believing it can give an advantage to those who know they have formative influence (advertisers or peddlers of propaganda, for example) because it may create the illusion that I am the one deciding something all on my own. In reality, I'm deciding on the basis of what others have fed me. Life is inescapably social, and moral messages abound. We can only pretend that we aren't influenced by them.

Recognizing the impact of the communities that shape us gives us some power to be intentional about which voices to heed. We could choose to exercise this power by trying to listen to no one at all. But where do the voices in my head come from? Or, we could choose to exercise this power by listening with intention to the communities who care about us and who stand with us. Sexual integrity moves us in this direction, encouraging us to see our wholeness not just in ourselves but in community with others.

8. Sexual integrity means that in sexual activity, we avoid separating our bodily selves, our emotional selves, and our spiritual selves into separate parts, but instead acknowledge that they are inextricably entwined.

Persons of sexual integrity seek to correlate their sexual activity with their spiritual journey and to integrate sexuality into the whole of their lives. This principle serves as a challenge to the dualisms we sometimes experience or encounter. One such dualism is the separation of sex and love. Another is the separation of sexuality and spirituality.

We've often been taught to think about sex and love in ways that are dualistic. Dualism in this sense divides what ought to be united. Consider this example: The notion and practice of "casual sex" is a familiar way of separating sex and love. Casual sex is recreational. It seeks pleasure and perhaps also a surface level of personal affirmation. It wouldn't be surprising to hear someone explain afterward that "it didn't really *mean* anything." In fact, if a consenting partner in a casual sexual encounter found out that it *did* mean something to the other person, she may feel betrayed! It wasn't supposed to mean anything, and it isn't supposed to be complicated by meaningfulness.

In her book *Sex and the Soul*, Donna Freitas tells the story of a student who struggles with the response of "dateable" girls: "They want you to call back and to call them up and hang out, and it's not just after a party and that sort of thing. Like, *during the day!*" It was a shocking revelation to this student that the girl he had sex with might want to hang out *during the day*, revealing a serious disconnect, according to Freitas, between women who see hooking up as the surest way to a boyfriend and males who "just forget about the emotional stuff."[12]

Approaching sex from the perspective of sexual integrity, sex and love can be separated but they shouldn't be. As bodily selves, we seek to express romantic love in physical ways, and as emotional selves we say with our bodies what we feel. But these aren't two parts of us that can ever be separated without engaging in a form of human reductionism. We can pretend that our bodies and "hearts" aren't connected, but they are inextricably entwined.

There is another common form of dualism in our ways of thinking about sex. It's the dualism of *sexuality* and *spirituality*. Donna Freitas reports that in her conversations with college students on several campuses, it was common to find that students had trouble even conceiving of ways to integrate their sexual and spiritual lives.[13] Minimally, this means that even many Christians have learned to divorce sex and bodily pleasure from spirituality. God is good and sex is good, but it's not always clear that they have anything to do with each other—especially when it comes to saying anything affirming that celebrates our God-given sexual dimension.

Dualistic thinking about sex isn't surprising. Western culture has been separating sex and love for a long time, and it's hard to grow up in that environment without learning to internalize dualistic ways of thinking. When we learn the language ("casual sex" or "friends with benefits" or "hooking

12. Freitas, *Sex and the Soul*, 130–31.
13. Freitas, *Sex and the Soul*, 212–16.

up," for example), we learn not only the words but the concepts that go along with them. We learn to think that sex and meaningfulness can be separated.

Christianity hasn't provided many resources for thinking about how sexuality and spirituality are appropriately intertwined, either. Over the past generation we've learned instead to compartmentalize our sex lives and our faith lives, perhaps with the exception of a guilt-producing moral norm. But rather than helping create a healthy linkage, negative religious attitudes toward sex seem to drive sexuality and spirituality further apart. Sexual integrity strives to bring them together.

9. Sexual integrity means that sex is not used to create love but to communicate a love that is already present.

Sexual integrity recognizes that we thrive best as persons when sexual activity is undergirded by mature love. While sexual activity may create an illusion of love or emotional intimacy, it is only mature love that provides the wide range of qualities that undergird the physical and emotional vulnerability associated with sexual activity. Persons of sexual integrity recognize that what makes "good sex" good is that is an expression of the goodness of deeply shared love.

A curious contradiction is that sex is often used as an attempt to create love. Several years ago, in one of my first efforts to understand why some of my students hooked up with virtual strangers at parties, I bluntly asked a student I knew well, "Why do people do this?" Her response, which has been affirmed many times since, is that they are hoping the sexual exchange will create a stable relationship of romance. Sex can easily become a means we use to accomplish a variety of ends we value and seek: We want others to see us as beautiful and desirable. We want others to affirm our masculinity or femininity, and we want to be chosen, prized, valued. We want to be loved and to be seen as lovable. While these are legitimate human desires, the real danger here is that sex gets used to bolster our own self-love, when it is meant to be a relational practice in which we express love to another.

Using sex to create a healthier self-love easily backfires. Sex outside a relationship of committed love usually ends as one partner's interests wander or simply wane. Abandonment or rejection becomes our reality, and now there's a new barrier to self-love. If sex had been a hopeful investment in a meaningful relationship, it now becomes a failed investment, and that can easily lead to seeing oneself as a failure too.

Sex is no more likely to create love in a relationship where love is lacking than it is to create love between initial strangers. As a stand-alone activity, sex is capable of creating two things: physical pleasure and the illusion of love. Because of the first, recreational sex that aims only at an isolated experience of pleasure is at least honest. It pretends to be nothing more than it is. But the fact that sex can easily create an illusion of love is more dangerous. Where love does not exist, sex can mimic love in some powerful ways. It calls for a level of vulnerability, involves a high degree of physical intimacy, creates a physical union, and enables two people to find deep pleasure in each other. All of these things can be said of love as well. And in the absence of love, these may feel like a satisfying substitute.

Sexual integrity integrates love and sex in a way that makes each mutually enhancing and that creates a healthy whole. Love enfolds sex in a commitment that has a history and a future. The person with whom one is vulnerable has already responded to a wide range of one's vulnerabilities and demonstrated trustworthiness and care. The one who brings you physical pleasure has already been the source of many forms of joy, laughter, and happiness. A loving partner has already shared the union of friendship, service to one another, and the hard work of merging two lives together.

10. Sexual integrity means that we reserve ultimate forms of physical expression for relationships of ultimate commitment.

Sexual integrity values each stage of intimacy in a relationship. In so doing, it places great value on sexual intercourse as the most final, complete form of physical union with another, typically reserving it for a relationship that is characterized by an equivalent form of unity.

Context, intentions, and meaning all fit into an integrative way of sharing sexual intimacy with another, because they are part of what gives sex its wholeness. This isn't the case, however, when sex is separated from commitment.

- Sex outside the context of commitment doesn't have integrity. It can't express the same meaning and intentions that it could in the context where those meanings and intentions exist. Adultery, for example, may feed one's self-esteem and meet one's desire for attention and pleasure, but it is fundamentally incomplete and therefore ends up telling a series of lies. Out of context, sex lacks integrity.

- Sex apart from appropriate intentions lacks integrity too. If sex expresses an intention to give oneself fully and unconditionally to another, it tells a lie in circumstances where one chooses to hold back giving oneself, or when love is still conditional and uncertain.

- Sex is dishonest when it pretends to convey a meaning that is not embodied in a relationship in nonsexual ways. High levels of sexual activity might imply a high level of relational commitment, but relational commitment only becomes real when it is supported by other life practices that embody commitment. These include things like a history of forgiveness and reconciliation, actions that sacrifice one's own desires for the sake of the other, and being there "for better or for worse." Sex alone can't substitute for the practices of commitment.

Reserving sexual intercourse for relationships of ultimate commitment brings together insights and norms from each of the other models of sexual ethics already discussed. Boundary ethics excludes sexual intercourse from relationships in which sex doesn't yet mean what marriage means: an unconditional, exclusive, and permanent union of love. A relational ethic sees sexual intercourse as a stage in one's physical expression of love that corresponds to very high levels of social, emotional, and spiritual union. In each case, wholeness (or integrity) is at the core of the argument. Sexual activity, and especially sexual intercourse, has integrity when it embodies and expresses commitments, meanings, and intentions that express the kind of ultimacy we hear in vows like those in the covenant of marriage: I will love you and take you and you alone, unconditionally, for life.

6

Evaluating Popularized Approaches to Christian Sexual Ethics

A VARIETY OF POPULAR approaches to Christian sexual ethics have been expressed by young college students over the years. They are often the result of high school youth group education. Students espouse these ideas in class and recommend their favorite book. I've noted a common feature in many of the ones that have been recommended to me. The author often frames his or her approach to sexual ethics in the context of a personal account of the struggle to find a Christian sexual ethic during the time in life when dating becomes serious. Honest storytelling is followed by wisdom and advice the author has gained through this sometimes difficult journey. They write now from a place in life where they have reached a more complete state of sexual health and wholeness.

There are many positive insights in the approaches recommended in this body of literature. In the examples I've chosen to examine, I've tried to identify some of these insights—even when I have also gone on to express some misgivings. As you will see, I can't recommend a whole-hearted adoption of any of these approaches. However, parts of any one of them might make good sense if complemented by another approach. For example, several of these ways of seeing sexual ethics seem to presume a boundary ethic, at least in the background. So, in conjunction with a carefully articulated boundary ethic, some of the positive insights expressed in this popular literature would provide a more complete package.

When one Christian writer discusses another's ideas—even when doing so in a critical manner—we have what I call "in-house conversations." Each response should be seen as a thoughtful engagement with another Christian perspective that is the result of different people grappling seriously but differently with an important topic.

1. WHAT YOU'RE "COMFORTABLE WITH"

If you ask a few people you know how they think someone should decide "how far is too far," it won't be too long before you'll hear a popular, commonsense approach to sexual ethics. It will go something like this: "I guess it depends on what people are comfortable with," or "You shouldn't ever do something you're not comfortable with." There isn't anything uniquely Christian about this approach, though I have heard it countless times from Christians who are struggling to find some standard from a personal faith tradition that has given them little to work with.

I suspect that its popularity also comes from the fact that "what you're comfortable with" has the advantage of being generally acceptable even to people who don't share the same faith or moral convictions. The standard is relativistic: what you're comfortable with depends on what your moral standards, experiences, and personal comfort levels happen to be. The standard implies that as long as you're doing what you're comfortable with, that's OK. It's a very subjective and permissive approach that is easily tolerant of other people's varying sexual morality. It doesn't put people off and fits easily into our individualistic culture.

There are some positive insights in this approach to sexual ethics, even though I think that it's insufficient and even problematic. Let's begin with the positives. In its best light, being comfortable with a behavior is a reflection of conscience. We're comfortable when we're acting in ways that our underlying conscience approves of. The most obvious claim being made by this approach is that you should only engage in sexual activity that you don't find morally problematic—which isn't such a profound insight. Of course, this already indicates one of the problems with using "comfort" as a measure of morality. It begs the question. If being uncomfortable means you are doing something morally objectionable, the deeper question is, What is it that actually makes the act morally objectionable? We would need to look outside the ethic of comfort to find that answer. Whether something's comfortable or not is an important clue, though, and one worth paying attention to.

Another positive insight is that when we refuse to do what is uncomfortable and refrain from making others uncomfortable, we are showing respect to ourselves and to others. We are respecting our and their moral freedom, feelings, and fears. Respect, one of the orienting convictions informing a Christian sexual ethic, demands that we honor feelings of discomfort. But there is also an exception to this that requires careful negotiation. New sexual experiences might actually be uncomfortable—morally, emotionally, or physically. Morally, we sometimes find ourselves doing what is right (e.g., sex in the context of marriage) when for a long time it was considered wrong (sex with the same person, but *prior* to marriage). The moral and emotional baggage doesn't always magically disappear. When we find ourselves feeling uncomfortable about sexual activity that is morally permissible, we need to be exploring these behaviors in a stable, loving, trusting relationship where we can be comfortable (secure) being temporarily uncomfortable.

A final positive insight is that if sex is a way to show and express love, its being comfortable (or gradually becoming more and more comfortable) could be seen as an intrinsically important component of loving sexual activity. In addition, sex is pleasurable, both actually and symbolically. It symbolizes the pleasure we experience in loving and being loved by one particular person, just as it gives us pleasure in the physical expression and sharing of that love. Good sex, in this context, is an experience of comfortable pleasure. If there is something about sex that is uncomfortable (morally, emotionally, or physically), then there is a barrier to sex fulfilling one of its purposes in a holistic way.

These positive insights allow us to say that sex being comfortable is an important component of sex that is *good*. In the ways that I have described, comfortableness is a necessary condition, and if it isn't present, it's a red flag that at least needs attention. Most likely there is something wrong that must be addressed.

But sex being comfortable isn't enough. It doesn't say all that needs to be said about sex. Aside from what I've implied above by way of critique, there are at least two related concerns about this moral standard that make it problematic.

First, a standard of comfort is too subjective to qualify as a moral standard. While it may tell us *why* someone engages in a certain level of sexual activity, it doesn't tell us whether it's right to do so. Not everyone will agree that in order to serve as a moral standard, a standard must have a higher degree of objectivity, so I am importing my own conviction here. What's wrong with a subjective assessment of personal comfort? Being comfortable with a behavior is a function of multiple influences. First, it's partially related to another underlying moral standard that is actually the morality at work, at least behind the scenes. This is the moral standard we really ought to be claiming and the one we ought to be thinking about critically and carefully. We are comfortable when we are acting in ways that are consistent with that standard and uncomfortable when we are violating it.

The standard hiding behind our claim of comfort might have many sources. Maybe it's the one parents taught either explicitly or implicitly. Perhaps it's the common cultural standard that people pick up rather automatically from social expectations, peer conversations, media portrayals, and cultural institutions (like school sex education classes). Whatever this standard says, it's the morality people are using, often without realizing it, to generate feelings of comfort or discomfort.

Having an unexamined morality in the background leads to a serious problem: we are often comfortable with personal or social practices that we really ought to find very troubling. And we are sometimes troubled by actions that, upon more careful reflection, we might decide aren't really wrong at all. In the first case, societies gradually come to accept actions for a variety of reasons that do not always stand up to moral scrutiny. If a majority of people find something acceptable, there is social pressure to conform. If a powerful minority has the ability to define the norms through propaganda, perhaps promulgated through popular media, there is also social pressure to conform. People can be made to feel comfortable about slavery and racism, or they can learn to be comfortable with racial equality and with living in diverse communities. We can be comfortable wasting scarce resources and polluting our environment—or we can be taught to feel very guilty and uncomfortable about doing that. I've encountered students who are comfortable with weekly sexual escapades that involve getting females drunk so they can take sexual advantage of them. And I've encountered others who find such behavior disgusting. The fact that someone is comfortable with something doesn't tell us it's good. That's why, on its own, it isn't a sufficient moral standard.

Second, a standard of comfort is a shifting line that is based more on a person's actual practices than on his or her moral convictions. People can be taught to feel comfortable. We often get more comfortable with activities that once made us nervous, uneasy, or afraid. Speaking in public is a good example. In the realm of sexual activities, a first kiss might be very uncomfortable, but with time and experience, the discomfort usually disappears. The same is true with other forms of sexual activity. The process of incrementalism comes into play here. If you're asked to do something well beyond your moral limit, it's not likely you will do it. Taking that kind of leap causes far too much moral discomfort. But what if you take a tiny step in that direction instead of a giant leap? Then you take another small step, and then another, until you eventually reach that point well beyond your moral limit. But it's not so noticeable now, because you have become slowly accustomed to being at this new place, one small step at a time. By taking small, incremental steps, you've become comfortable with something that your morality might still say ought to make you very uncomfortable. Comfort is relative to personal experience, and comfort levels move over time without necessarily being connected to morality.

That's one reason why people often report that in new romantic relationships, they move much more quickly to the same level of sexual activity they had reached in their previous relationship. The time it takes to "get comfortable" is greatly reduced. Does that mean that this level of sexual activity is good? The fact that you're comfortable with it doesn't tell us enough to say yes or no. Perhaps (based on a particular version of a boundary ethic) you shouldn't be comfortable doing what's wrong. If you are, it's because you have become morally desensitized by repeated sexual experiences.

If you are uncomfortable with your level of sexual activity, you might be violating your moral convictions. Discomfort is an invitation to careful moral discernment. The key questions are, Should you really be feeling uncomfortable, and if so, why? But if you are comfortable with your current level of sexual activity, there's also good reason to stop and think about it. Why are you comfortable? Is it because you're acting in ways that reflect your deepest moral convictions? Is it because you've become accustomed to doing what everyone else is doing, even though you can't really say why it's good to be doing that? Being comfortable doesn't generate much dissonance and therefore doesn't serve as a very effective motivator to assess our behavior. But comfort demands to be interrogated by thinking about morality too, in order to ensure that we're feeling comfortable with actions that we (morally) ought to be comfortable with.

2. PURITY

The term *purity* occurs in a variety of contemporary approaches to Christian sexual ethics. One popular attempt to articulate a "purity ethic" in a systematic way can be found in Dannah Gresh's *And the Bride Wore White: Seven Secrets to Sexual Purity*.[1] The language of sexual purity occurs in several other popular Christian sexual ethics books that give advice to single Christians, and many young Christians seem to have absorbed at

1. Gresh, *And the Bride Wore White*.

least a vague purity ethic from their formal and informal instruction. When purity is set forth as a goal for Christian sex, it usually takes the form of a boundary ethic, where *purity* names the state of living within the boundaries, whatever they happen to be. Advocates of a purity ethic, however, aren't always upfront about the boundary ethic lurking in the background.

The term *purity* has always seemed a bit mysterious to me. It's never been clear exactly what one needs to avoid in order to attain purity. On its own, the term *purity* is vague and leaves us wondering exactly what kinds of thoughts, desires, or behaviors may contaminate us, and what concrete, lived alternatives qualify as marks of purity. Its commonsense association with a state of perfection adds to the mystery. Purity isn't a self-sufficient standard.

What do people mean when they advocate sexual purity? In her book *Passion and Purity*, Elisabeth Elliot defines the concept of purity like this:

> Purity means freedom from contamination, from anything that would spoil the taste or pleasure, reduce the power, or in any way adulterate what was meant to be. It means cleanness, clearness . . . "all natural" in the sense the Original Designer designed it to be.[2]

If we think about purity this way, it seems to function primarily as a lofty goal that calls Christians to the highest possible standard. It even sounds like an impossible one to reach. In order to understand what kinds of attitudes and behaviors will enable people to attain the standard as it's understood by purity advocates, some additional moral guidance is necessary. Here's a brief summary of two examples of a purity approach.

If we look more closely at a couple of examples of a purity ethic it's clear that in spite of the commonsense association with a state of moral perfection, purity does not actually mean perfection. This gets one problem out of the way quickly. But it does still clearly imply that a life of purity is a life lived in accordance with God's will. But what God actually expects isn't always clear.

Eric and Leslie Ludy, the husband-and-wife team who authored *When God Writes Your Love Story*, see purity as a goal to strive for during romantic relationships prior to marriage. In an imaginary conversation, God poses as a friend and asks Eric,

> "You desire purity in your wife, don't you?"

> "You better believe it, I do! . . . I want my wife to be *pure!*"

---

2. Elliot, *Passion and Purity*.

"If you desire purity in your wife, how much more do you think she desires purity . . . *in you?*"[3]

We learn more about the actual requirements for purity when Leslie Ludy writes,

Each time I was involved with someone, I poured my heart, my emotions, my affection, my time, and all my attention into that person. Not to mention the fact that, though I may have been technically a virgin, I wasn't keeping myself physically pure.[4]

There are clearly overtones of virginity in the term *purity*, and sometimes it might mean little more than that. Often, however, it includes more than simple virginity. This becomes clear when we listen to warnings about impurity. Impurity is associated with going "too far," beyond an imprecise line, but one determined primarily by what a person would wish his or her spouse hadn't shared emotionally or physically with another in a prior relationship. The boundary could be stated like this: don't engage in romantic activities of an emotional or physical nature that you'd want to save for the person you marry. This line is also presumed to be divinely sanctioned, though the basis for this divine guideline is far less clear than in the approaches to a boundary ethic already examined in a previous chapter. The Ludys seem to think you can know whether your romantic partner is the person you'll marry and implicitly suggest that it's best not to date until you've found that person. Since many people guess wrongly about having found "the one," this would leave many Christians unintentionally in the state of impurity they seek to avoid. But since the authors themselves were in such a state of impurity during their dating years, the idea of purity does indeed function more as an ideal than a realizable goal.

Positive Insight: Purity as "Sanctified Sex"

A purity ethic clearly intends to bring sexual practice and Christian faith into unity with each other, seeking to bridge the common divide between sexuality and spirituality. There is often a tension between the religious narrative we live in one segment of life and another narrative that doesn't quite fit. An ethic of "sexual integrity" (see chapter 5) describes a unified wholeness that intends to bring sexual life into the realm of religious convictions, but without resorting to a notion of purity. The idea that

3. Ludy and Ludy, *When God Writes Your Love Story*, 100.
4. Ludy and Ludy, *When God Writes Your Love Story*, 94.

"God writes one's love story" means that romance is practiced in ways that conform to an understanding of God's intentions for the sexual side of life, and in that sense, it is a call to sexual integrity.

In the New Testament, the letter to the Ephesians (especially chapters 4 and 5) exhorts Christians to live in ways that are consistent with their confession of faith. This includes rejecting some of the ways they have lived before and some of the ways they see others around them living. Within the picture of Christian living described there we find this admonition about the way Christians should conduct their sexual lives: "But fornication and impurity of any kind, or greed, must not even be mentioned among you, as is proper among saints" (Eph 5:3).

The notion of purity can be understood in a very general way to describe the sexual lifestyle that the letter to the Ephesians prescribes for people who strive to "lead a life worthy of the calling they have received" (Eph 4:1; my paraphrase). Another way to think about this is captured in the phrase "sanctified sex." In its best sense, the word *purity* is used by the authors summarized above to point to a goal that has elsewhere been described as *sanctity*—or if we think about it developmentally, a process of *sanctification*. The overtones of holiness here are not meant to describe an achieved perfection. A sanctified life *reflects* the holiness of God. In the language of Ephesians, it is "to be made new in the spirit of your minds; and to be clothed in the likeness of God in righteousness and holiness" (4:23–24; my paraphrase). The goal is a lofty one, and there is much one would need to learn to know what this means in each arena of human life. The idea of sexual purity seems to take this lofty goal seriously, believing that in the area of sex, like all other areas of life, one can and should reflect the characteristics of Christian discipleship.

A Critique of Purity Ethics

Purity is too broad and imprecise to provide concrete moral guidance. It can only work as a sexual ethic if it imports another standard. But in doing so, a purity ethic functions more like a "cloaking term." Rather than cloaking an underlying morality with the term *purity*, Christians would be better served by a more forthright explanation of the moral guidelines, rules, or divine commands that must be obeyed in order to be "pure." In that case, purity is the end or goal being sought by another means—obeying God's rules, for example. A purity ethic usually clearly implies a rather straightforward obedience ethic, in which one attains purity by obeying the rules for Christian sex. What a purity ethic lacks is a careful articulation of and justification for these rules.

Purity rules that lie in the background of a purity ethic are often simply the conventional morality of the recent Christian tradition. To claim that purity is required by God is to claim that obeying these rules is required by God. Perhaps this is true, but without careful articulation and explanation, the claim hardly qualifies as a sexual ethic. Let me give an example: in Ephesians 5, impurity is equated with sexual immorality. Christians should clearly avoid sexual immorality. To say this is the equivalent of saying that Christians should avoid impurity and seek purity. Being told to avoid immorality isn't very helpful, however, until one knows what is immoral and what is not. The term *immorality* is also cloaking a more specific moral code that is being assumed.

It isn't always easy to determine what is being assumed. As a result, beyond simply being a cloak that hides another assumed morality, the term *purity* ends up functioning like a code word, but it's supposed to be a code that Christians will already know. Is it possible to decode the term with any sense of certainty? Perhaps purity is a code word for virginity? In that case, to be pure is to be a virgin—a male or female who has not yet had sexual intercourse. If so, it designates a state of being. But purity might also designate obedience to a wider range of sexual rules. Being pure is being obedient. But purity might also designate motives and intentions. It might be code for "trying hard to obey, even if not always perfect." Purity in this case would mean that one has pure motives, or a "pure heart." Purity might also designate certain kinds of limits on human desires. To be pure is to keep oneself from having desires that it would be wrong to satisfy. In this regard, purity is often associated with avoiding lust. (See chapter 9 for a detailed discussion of the concept of lust.) For some advocates of purity, all of these meanings are probably intended!

The cloaking or codelike language of a purity ethic highlights a central problem with this approach. Purity is simply a concept that is too vague to be helpful, even though it reminds Christians of a worthy goal. If the term has value, it needs to be supplemented by a full-bodied ethic that helps people think and act in ways that qualify as "pure" or that help one attain the goal of sanctified sex.

There is a second problem that arises in a purity approach. Is purity as it's described in popular approaches ever attainable? If the concept remains vague, the answer is almost certainly no. Unless one has a clear sense of what purity is, it would be hard to determine that one is on the right path. I worry that a purity ethic, rather than helping shape and empower a life of sexual discipleship, is more likely to produce unavoidable guilt and a sense of failure. For example, a group of women who recently attended a seminar on Christian sexuality returned to tell me that it left them feeling like spoiled goods (most of them had been sexually active at levels far beyond what was implied to be allowable for Christians) but without any sense of what to do about it. They had already failed to live a Christian sexual ethic of purity, and now that they were impure, it was too late to do anything about it. Impurity was a state of being that couldn't be reversed. Unfortunately, I don't see this as an isolated example but as a typical and logical response to popularized versions of a purity ethic.

The goal of purity can clearly inspire faithful living as well, but since purity is questionably attainable, placing it at the heart of a Christian sexual ethic has the potential to create an attitude of resignation. One may be forced to conclude, "It just can't be done, so I might as well give up trying."

Christian self-identity is more appropriately understood as living in a state of grace than living in a state of purity. Forgiveness and healing need to be emphasized as much as purity, since our human journeys toward sanctity in any area of life are fraught with missteps, detours, and rebellious alternatives. Forgiveness is empowering. It enables people who have fallen to be restored and re-energized. It gives people hope they can do what they are called to do and the security of knowing that grace follows them even through their missteps, or when the path ahead becomes unclear or hard to follow.

3. COMMITMENTS AND PROMISE RINGS

Abstinence commitments are a popular way for Christian youth ministries to introduce a boundary ethic and gain adherence to it through education and symbolic events. These approaches and ceremonies take many forms, and I'll make no attempt to provide a complete account of the organizations, literature, or ceremonial events involved. Instead, a summary characterization (and hopefully an accurate one) will serve to illustrate how this approach to Christian sexual ethics works and what it means.

If you are unfamiliar with this phenomenon, here's how the process works: around the time that Christian youth reach dating age, they are given a ring or some other piece of jewelry, usually by their parent(s), that symbolizes their commitment not to engage in sexual intercourse until they are married. Several organizations sponsor events or provide a framework for taking a pledge of abstinence, including Unaltered Ministries and True Love Waits (TLW).[5] Ring ceremonies typically take place either at large regional

5. For more information on these organizations, see their websites. True Love

events or within local congregations or youth groups. The ring symbolizes a pledge taken by the person receiving it. One version of the True Love Waits pledge (2011) reads this way: "Believing that true love waits, I make a commitment to God, myself, my family, my friends, my future mate, and my future children to a lifetime of purity including sexual abstinence from this day until the day I enter a biblical marriage relationship." A more recent revision ties this approach to a purity ethic. It says, "In light of who God is, what Christ has done for me, and who I am in Him, from this day forward I commit myself to Him in the lifelong pursuit of purity. By his grace I will continually present myself to Him as a living sacrifice, holy and pleasing to God."

The biblical text inscribed on rings used in the Silver Ring Thing is often 1 Thessalonians 4:3–4: "God wants you to be holy, so you should keep clear of all sexual sin. Then each of you will control your body and live in holiness and honor" (my paraphrase). True Love Waits says that its abstinence approach

> challenges teenagers and college students to make a commitment to sexual abstinence until marriage. True Love Waits encourages moral purity by adhering to biblical principles . . . [utilizing] positive peer pressure by encouraging those who make a commitment to refrain from pre-marital sex to challenge their peers to do the same.[6]

The language of sexual purity (discussed above) is used throughout the literature on abstinence pledges. The rings symbolizing the promise to wait are even sometimes called "purity rings." Waiting for sex establishes purity in this approach primarily because unmarried Christians are resisting Satan (impurity) and obeying God when they flee from temptation and abide by the moral requirement to save sex for marriage. The moral requirement to save sex for marriage seems to be more presumed than argued, most likely on the basis of the long tradition that identified premarital sex with sin. Ephesians 5:3 is used in the True Love Waits commitment service to establish a biblical foundation: "But fornication and impurity of any kind, or greed, must not even be mentioned among you, as is proper among saints." This text doesn't actually say what kinds of behaviors constitute sexual immorality. The author of the text (like the authors of the True Love Waits

---

Waits, a ministry of Lifeway: https://www.lifeway.com/en/product-family/true-love-waits. Silver Ring Thing, now called Unaltered Ministries, has been re-envisioned in a way that responds to the critique of its earlier approach; see http://silverringthing.com.

6. True Love Waits, https://www.lifeway.com, accessed August 24, 2016.

pledge) presumes that the reader already knows the answer to this question on the basis of traditional morality.

Supporting the central requirement to wait (save sex for marriage), abstinence pledges are often accompanied by other admonitions that encourage unmarried Christians to stay far away from sexual intercourse. Implementing an ethic of caution (see chapter 3), abstinence is understood to be best accomplished when other boundaries are also observed. This makes abstinence not only a decision in the heat of the moment but a more holistic lifestyle.

True Love Waits reflects a worldview in which there is a constant battle between good and evil. *Good* means sexual abstinence and the lifestyle that supports it; *evil* includes the worldly activities that encourage sex outside of marriage. Good and evil are personified in God and Satan in the language of True Love Waits. One finds in the TLW commitment ceremony sermon outline a clear tension between alternate loyalties. Satan creates a web of destruction and desires to entangle us in it. That web is said to include such things as parties and drinking, pornography, sexual sin, music contrary to the truth of the Gospel, mental sexual images, and falling into "flesh patterns." The alternative is to follow a spiritual path of purity, characterized by love, humility, and a focus on God.

Positive Insights: Why Pledges Have Value

I find two important positive insights reflected in the familiar virginity pledges. These insights can be affirmed even though, as my critique below makes clear, abstinence programs don't deliver everything necessary to achieve the positive dimensions implied and fail to provide a full-bodied sexual morality. Unless one imports abstinence guidelines from an already established moral framework, one may wonder exactly what's being prohibited by the notion of "waiting."

The first important insight contained in this approach, though not unique to it, is the recognition that a lived *Christian counterculture* is essential if one is to effectively contest the sexual practices of popular culture. If Christian morality calls Christians to say no to what most people are doing, practicing abstinence is more likely when it is supported by a group of people who are living out this alternative vision of sexuality. A Christian counterculture includes both an alternative moral commitment (true love waits to have sex until marriage) and a community that supports its embodiment in our lives.

A second important insight is the acknowledgment that living out a commitment to sexual abstinence before marriage requires an entire *lifestyle*. It would be helpful if the pledge programs gave a clearer picture of that lifestyle and avoided the generalities contained in pious phrases and admonitions. Still, it is essential to recognize that abstinence from sexual intercourse is part of a larger pattern of behavior. It involves attitudes about one's self-worth, the nature of romantic love, the meaning and purpose of sexual activities, etc. It also involves a network of alternative practices in the wider arena of romance and sexuality. While we might sometimes make decisions isolated from a wider network of lived commitments, most of our decisions are embedded in a lifestyle. This is especially true of those that reflect our underlying faith and character. Abstinence programs recognize that decisions about sex can't be isolated from the formation of character, embedded in lived practices. Whether such ideals are met is another question.

A Critique of Abstinence Pledges

1. Vague Boundaries

One of the most common sexual ethics questions I have heard in the last twenty years is, How far is too far? The question sometimes reflects a narrow moral framework and may be motivated by a desire to push as close to a moral boundary as possible. However, most often it is expressed as a responsible and sincere question: Are there any physical ways to express love in a romantic relationship that honor God's intentions for sexuality prior to marriage?

The ubiquity of the question highlights the importance of a sexual ethic that provides clarity. I'm not yet convinced that an abstinence commitment provides sufficient clarity. It falls short in two distinct ways. First, the idea of waiting until marriage to engage in sexual intercourse leaves open the question of whether any forms of physical affection aside from intercourse can reflect morally appropriate ways to express love. If we think of a range of sexual actions as being along a continuum, a pledge to "wait" seems more clear at the end of the continuum where we'd find sexual intercourse, but less clear at the end where we'd find an affectionate embrace. The moral boundary becomes very fuzzy! A pledge to abstain must clearly identify the actions from which one is abstaining.

An abstinence pledge must also provide, at least as a foundation, a clear rationale that explains *why* one is abstaining. As we've already seen, it is much easier to provide a biblical rationale for abstaining from sexual intercourse outside marriage than it is to provide a biblical rationale for waiting until marriage to kiss someone. The reasons that support the moral boundary become fuzzy, too, and increasingly so as we move further away from sexual intercourse. Abstinence programs presume that intercourse is wrong because the act itself is a violation of a biblically established boundary. In other words, it is seen as sinful. But there isn't such clear teaching about an intense make-out session. The argument implied here is that it is a temptation to do what is wrong, not that the act itself violates a biblical boundary. An ethic of caution advises us not to do what tempts us to sin. But different people are tempted in different ways. In the end, abstinence pledges leave many people feeling a vague sense of guilt about anything sexual, without knowing why or whether the guilt is actually justifiable.

One additional and unintended result of vague boundaries and vague reasons for those boundaries is an "everything but sex" approach. We are sometimes taught to say no to sexual intercourse but left with a huge void regarding other sexual practices. As I often hear students say, "Anything leading up to intercourse seemed acceptable, since my sex education was silent about all of that." An individual's misunderstandings can't always be blamed on an approach to sexual ethics, but I found it both troubling and interesting that a former student who proudly wore a "purity ring" saw nothing wrong with engaging in oral sex in casual relationships. She had pledged to abstain from sexual intercourse before marriage, had been obedient to that pledge over and over again, and had said no to many guys—a source of great pride! While this might be an extreme distortion of what advocates of an abstinence pledge intend, it's understandable. Her abstinence education had been very clear about one thing, and she had taken that prohibition seriously. It had been silent or vague about everything else, so if it wasn't forbidden, then apparently it was allowed. This misunderstanding has plagued many of my students over the years, leading them to engage in sexual practices they have sometimes come to regret (typically, only if the relationship didn't lead to marriage) or to feel vaguely guilty but uncertain whether the guilt was justified.

2. Saying No to Sex Needs to Be Balanced with Saying Yes to the Goodness of This God-created Gift

That doesn't mean giving sexual license to what ought to be prohibited, but it does mean that the reasons for saying no should not be grounded primarily in negative language. Abstinence pledges are undergirded by a strong sense of dualism, in which sexual desire is part of our sinful nature—rather than part of our God-created nature. When our thinking becomes dualistic, sexual desire is associated not with our God-created natures but with lust and the temptations of Satan. The moral line supporting the "no" to sex before marriage becomes, in subtle and perhaps even unintended ways, a no to desire and to physicality. Body and spirit start to appear at odds with each other, when in fact sin pervades all of life—not just bodily life, and not just sexuality.

It's easy to understand why this dualistic tendency arises. Abstinence pledges are mostly about saying no to a powerful human drive. That drive is connected to our yearning for intimacy, supported by genetically determined physiological factors, and encouraged by popular culture. This combination of factors creates a strongly undergirded urge! One way to encourage effective resistance is to attempt to create a negative counterbalance to all that affirms and drives sexual expression. If people can be encouraged to fear the negative consequences, for example, perhaps it will serve as an effective control mechanism. If sex before marriage is Satan's way to lure people away from God, if it is direct disobedience to a divine command that seeks your well-being, if it is likely to ruin marriage, destroy faith, and isolate you from those you love—well, you can see why abstinence makes sense! Negative reasons are reasons, and they are sometimes very powerful ones.

The power of negative reasons does not justify the dualism that associates sex only with sin. As we've seen in two previous versions of a boundary ethic, saying no to sex before marriage can be grounded in the goodness of sex, too. Striving for a biblically grounded balance between affirmations and prohibitions does not need to mean eliminating boundaries. But finding the right balance requires careful and even subtle language and analysis. From my analysis, it seems that too often, programs advocating abstinence lean too far toward dualism to reflect a theologically holistic approach to sexual ethics.

3. Actual Impact on Behavior

Research on the phenomenon of "promise rings" and virginity pledges and emerging evidence about how they affect sexual behavior supports the conclusion that pledging to obey sexual boundaries has had less influence on actual sexual behavior than defenders of pledging might hope for.

In a recent study of youth who took an abstinence pledge of some form, researchers found that the sexual behavior of virginity pledgers does not differ from that of non-pledgers.[7] The incidence of premarital sex, oral

---

7. Rosenbaum, "Comparison of Sexual Behavior," 110–20.

sex, frequency of sex, and age of first intercourse is statistically equivalent for those who took an abstinence pledge and those who didn't. This study was careful to compare youth who were similar (for example, those with similar levels of religious commitments) so that it controlled for other differences not accounted for in previous studies.

Commenting on the findings of her study, Janet Rosenbaum said, "It seems that pledgers aren't really internalizing the pledge."[8] Internalizing the convictions behind the boundary is clearly a key challenge for a boundary ethic. Is it possible to give reasons that are compelling enough to influence behavior? Can giving good reasons to observe the boundary make boundaries effective? If the behavior of virginity pledgers doesn't differ significantly from that of non-pledgers, it is reasonable to conclude that taking a pledge has insufficient impact on behavior to make a difference. Why might that be?

The lack of effective behavioral impact might result from at least three different factors. Each would need to be explored more carefully, but they suggest areas where abstinence commitment programs might fall short.

One reason a pledge might not change behavior is that the reasons aren't clearly understood—at least not enough to be compelling. Advocates of sexual boundaries like Smedes and Hollinger provide a good foundation for understanding the reasons behind the lines. However, in other contexts, those lines are often reiterated but too rarely explained. Boundaries gain effectiveness when reasons not to cross them make sense and are powerful enough to compete with biological and cultural pressures that vie for dominance.

A second reason pledging might not change behavior is that it functions as only one of many social mechanisms in our complex social environment that affect decisions about sexual practice. Pledging might affect the pledger, but it does not change the rest of the social environment. It is likely (a hypothesis to be tested) that when a pledger breaks the pledge, other factors have been strong enough to overcome the prior commitment. If so, pledging will only be effective when other environmental factors help support the pledge. Abstinence is an individual choice, but it seems to be a choice that is most easily lived out when it is part of a subculture that encourages, supports, and rewards it.

Even the research that indicates there is little difference in pledgers' behavior suggests that when pledging does impact behavior, it does so because the pledge movement is an identity movement. Taking a pledge has the potential to change one's self-identity and, even more powerfully,

8. Quoted in Stein, "Premarital Abstinence Pledges Ineffective."

to cause one to identify with a larger identity group. This identification might actually make the biggest difference. Adding *identity* to a *boundary* and even to good *reasons* to obey the boundary creates a more complete formative package. In the rest of life, many of the important boundaries we observe are supported by cultural systems that encourage conformity. Boundary violations are met with social disapproval, systems of punishment (laws, police, courts, jails), and other well-defined negative consequences. Boundary observance is rewarded by positive feedback, good reputations, and social rewards. The mere act of taking a pledge will have less impact than pledgers, pastors, and parents hope for unless there is a cultural system and concrete community in place to sustain the pledge. The community also sustains the identity of the abstinence pledger by providing a social space for shared discernment and dialogue. Pledging programs are rarely prepared to provide the context needed. In its absence, pledging programs are left with fear and guilt as their tools to encourage faithfulness to the commitment and are as likely to produce guilt and isolation among violators, of whom there are many.

4. REGRET—AND SAVING YOURSELF FOR YOUR FUTURE SPOUSE

A popular theme in several recent books on Christian sexual ethics is the importance of "saving yourself" for the person you will one day marry. This idea often overlaps with other themes in sexual morality examined in this chapter, but sometimes gets voiced by young Christians as the essence of their sexual ethic. This is also a boundary ethic, at least by implication, because "saving" implies that there is some boundary not to be crossed. Saving one's virginity is the most common explicit boundary. Virginity is seen as a "gift" one gives to a future spouse, and since it can only be given once, the clear boundary is to save sexual intercourse for marriage.

It's not only virginity that seems to be at stake. At another level some authors recommend that dating conduct should always be guided by what you would want your future spouse to share with someone other than you. Eric Ludy asks readers to consider how they would feel if their future spouse had been less careful and considerate than they had been.

> If my future spouse followed me around throughout my day, every day of my life, would she feel cherished and adored by me as she watches me interact with other girls? Would she come away each day saying, "He sure does love me!" or would she be deeply hurt by the way I give what is hers to other women?

> She [my current wife] would have wet eyes and a crushed
> heart because I was giving my love and affection to someone
> other than her.[9]

Leslie Ludy advises readers to be aware of how much of one's heart, emotions, affection, and time are being given to someone other than a future spouse. If now or later you would disapprove of a level of emotional or physical affection being shown to your future spouse, this creates a boundary for current dating relationships: "Until God brings my future husband along and I know it's him, I'm not available."[10]

In the contemporary culture of dating, some people end up in a series of serious romantic relationships that do not lead to marriage—although one may think it's "the one" at the time. The romance may be short and intense or long and stable—and, in both cases, seem to be leading to marriage. But relationships end, hearts are broken, or people just mutually decide they aren't meant to be together any longer. Each new relationship provides the opportunity for some level of sexual activity, and as experience shows, the level of sexual activity often increases from one relationship to the next. If it doesn't increase, then at the least it usually reaches the plateau determined by one's moral line more quickly from one relationship to the next.

The potential moral problem arises when one or both individuals find that they have engaged in a level of sexual activity that they had (at least mentally) reserved for the person they would marry. But now the relationship is over. It's no longer possible to share only with one's spouse the level of intimacy you've already shared with someone else. This can leave people with a deep sense of regret—wishing that some parts of the past hadn't happened. A morality of caution would advise: don't do anything with another person that you want to share only with your future spouse. It may not be *morally wrong* to do it, but it's dangerous if you are really intent on "saving" that kind of physical or emotional intimacy for one person in marriage. Depending on how much this matters to you, it may be that sexual activity is just not worth the risk.

One of the things being protected by this ethic of caution is *respect*. Every person you date will *potentially* be someone else's husband or wife, and someone else may be dating your future partner right now. When Leslie Ludy says, "I'm already taken," this implies that both she and the other person need to respect the future. An ethic of caution urges people to respect other people's future partners. At the same time, it encourages people to

---

9. Ludy and Ludy, *When God Writes Your Love Story*, 99–104.

10. Ludy and Ludy, *When God Writes Your Love Story*, 94, 118.

respect the person who will someday be their future partner by refraining from sexual activity today that they would regret in the future.

Positive Insights

It's wise to avoid behaviors one will likely regret in the future. This is especially the case when regret stems from a violation of deeply held values or enduring hopes. Saving oneself for a future spouse is often a combination of these. First, there is an implied boundary that sexual intercourse should be reserved only for the person you will one day marry. Perhaps going beyond this, there is an acceptance of a boundary ethic that reserves sexual intercourse for marriage. The enduring hope is that one will remain a virgin until meeting and falling in love with that one person you will marry. This allows the "gift of one's virginity" to be given only to that person and avoids the regret of having given it too soon to someone else.

If someone is likely to carry the baggage of regret into a marriage, it's best to make decisions that minimize or eliminate that regret. I've seen people struggle with this regret on both sides.

In one woman's story, she had a very hard time breaking up with a boyfriend with whom she had engaged in sexual intercourse. Prior to that romance, she would have told you that she intended to have sex only with the person she would marry. Now she's had sex with someone who she knew (cognitively) she didn't want to marry. But she almost felt that she needed to marry him eventually in order to maintain her moral aspiration. After a drawn-out breakup she had to give up the aspiration, which led to some serious regret. Nearly a decade later she is now in a happy, healthy marriage, having forgiven herself fully enough to let go of the regret.

In another woman's story, she had discovered that the person she was engaged to had been in a previous, very serious romance that included sexual intercourse. He sincerely expected that he would marry his previous girlfriend. But that romance had ended and now this couple was engaged. She had "saved herself" for him, and he wished with all his heart that he had done the same. But he couldn't undo the past. And she was now uncertain whether she could marry him since he had "cheated on her" prior to knowing her. She decided in the end that she needed to forgive him and allow the forgiveness to cleanse her way of seeing him.

A Critique of "Saving Oneself" for a Future Spouse

An ethic of caution that seeks to avoid future regret presumes a more precise moral standard that it doesn't directly state. It presumes that some level of sexual activity would be wrong and worth regretting. But an ethic of caution itself doesn't tell us how to go about determining that moral standard, and those who advocate an ethic of caution appear to have many different standards at work in the background.

There is a high level of subjectivity involved in popular versions of this approach to sexual ethics. An ethic of non-regret is grounded in a personal sense of what one would actually regret. From person to person, that line will differ. It's a matter of personal preference whether one will care that a husband or wife has said "I love you" to someone else whom they loved or thought they loved. Whether a prior kiss elicits jealousy isn't universal.

Subjectivity in an ethic of caution isn't a bad thing, as long as we recognize what is being claimed. One could say with a degree of a certainty that it's good to act in ways one won't regret in the future. What each person would regret will differ, so in that way one's line is relative to what each person will regret. It would be a mistake to do what you'd regret, but it isn't wrong for someone else to do it—unless it is wrong for reasons other than regret.

A moral line that's so subjective is likely to be troubling to many Christians. Behind the personal lines drawn because of what you'd regret is a deeper question: Is it really *wrong*? Would it truly be dishonoring to God and others? Does it violate a boundary that is based on more than my personal preferences?

I would propose that in actual experience, many people wish in retrospect they had felt and experienced emotional and physical intimacy only with the person they married. But this wish, which functions more like a romantic ideal, doesn't necessarily lead to a serious level of regret. Continuing my conjecture, I'd also suggest that when two people's sexual histories have been similar, they are less likely to regret their past than someone who "saved himself" but ended up with someone who didn't.

But we must also acknowledge that sometimes, rather than regretting their past, Christians believe they have been acting responsibly in sharing some level of emotional and physical intimacy in a series of dating relationships. They look back on their romantic journey with a sense that they did their best, they were forgiven for wrongs, and they grew into responsible and healthy partners as a result of their experiences and the lessons learned. They embrace the past as part of their personal narratives, knowing that they are loved by God and their romantic partner.

Finally, there is a practical difficulty associated with the ethics of non-regret. How do you develop a relationship that grows and matures in preparation for marriage, if the emphasis is on saving yourself for a future relationship? Some relationship will actually be the one that ends up in marriage, if marriage is in one's future. But there is never a sure way to know that in advance. It's easier to say after the fact—as is common in books written by married people. It's easy to say, "*I* didn't save as much of myself as I wish I had, but *you* should wait until you know you've found the person you'll marry." It's impossible to say how you can ever know you've found the "one"—at least until you both say "I do." While one can choose to save sexual intercourse for the honeymoon, it's much harder to imagine how a romantic relationship can mature prior to marriage without an increasing level of emotional investment, growing affection, words of endearment, and, most likely, some level of physical affection. Since this is a central critique of the idea that we should "guard our hearts," we can now consider this related idea.

5. GUARD YOUR HEART

Another thing an ethic of caution seeks to protect is your heart. I can't even begin to count how many times I've heard this notion, and it is clearly popular in the educational approach taken in Christian youth groups. To be honest, I'm not usually impressed by the vague, mushy image often used to explain this idea, so let me try to cast it in the best light possible. Our "hearts" seem to stand for that deep and sometimes mysterious place within us that is capable of giving and receiving love. It's our capacity to connect with another that seems to touch the very center of our selves. Perhaps it's also our uniqueness, what makes each person different and special and wonderful in his or her own way.

If that's what we mean by our hearts, they are certainly worth guarding. An ethic of caution would advise people to realize that we can be careless with our hearts, giving ourselves too quickly and too completely to someone not worthy of that much trust. You ought to be very careful when you place your heart (that deep center of yourself) in someone else's hands. And you ought to treat another's heart, when it is entrusted to you, with the utmost care. Such caution protects us from being hurt, used, disrespected, or betrayed.

Too many sad stories warn us that not everyone treats people with the respect and care they deserve. So giving your heart to anyone is dangerous. And sometimes giving our hearts is associated with giving ourselves physically to another person. In reality, we are not bodies *and* hearts, but we are whole selves. What touches our body touches our hearts, and what we feel in our hearts we sometimes express with our bodies. All of this heart language can clearly have a sexual component.

Positive Insight

In a culture where sexual activity is often separated from matters of the heart, guarding one's heart may mean being careful not to let the meaning of sexuality activity get distorted by what we might call "heartless sex." This would mean avoiding any sexual activity that isn't even intended to express the love that comes from that deep "heart space" within us but instead separates the physical sexual activity from the true nature of the relationship. It is possible to cheapen sex just like we devalue other things that matter. "Hooking up" is one way we do this, and the cultural practice of anonymous, casual sex teaches us to create and live out a narrative in which we learn to treat sex as if it "doesn't mean anything." Those who know that it has a deep meaning will want to guard their hearts from lived narratives that tell us lies about sex.

A Critique of "Guarding Your Heart"

There is a downside to this image of guarding one's heart. Consider this object lesson I have heard about many times. I've never witnessed it in person, but it goes something like this: a paper heart represents your heart. You have a romantic relationship in which you give a little of your heart away. To illustrate that, a piece of tape is placed on your heart, and then when the relationship ends, it is torn away. A little piece of your heart is torn away with it. Or a little piece of the paper heart is actually torn off. Each relationship results in the loss of more of your heart. In theory, too many romances and too much sexual activity could result in a badly torn and almost destroyed heart! Now, common sense and everyday experience tells us that this could really happen to someone. They might be so emotionally destroyed by their past relationships that they are incapable of healthy love. There are real hurts that need time to heal.

But romance and physical expressions of love do not always literally involve giving our heart away, nor are they always destructive. Sharing, expressing, and feeling love is not necessarily a loss of anything, and that's where the analogy falls short. You don't give a piece of yourself away when you share your love with someone. We are just as likely to remain whole and even find our hearts growing when we are in healthy relationships, even if they end. And we are just as likely to find our lives enhanced when others share their hearts with us, even if only for a time.

Building relationships is as much about *sharing* our hearts as about guarding them. Too much emotional and physical intimacy can clearly expose us to hurt, but too little emotional and physical intimacy threatens to keep any relationship at a very superficial level. Loving anyone is always a risk, even while it has the potential to bring the greatest joy. An ethic of caution reminds us that discernment is always in order. It is important to know how much to risk, with whom, and how soon. So an ethic of caution calls for the kind of wisdom that comes from the accumulated wisdom of a community, and partly from personal experience, sometimes even after experiencing deep hurt.

But hearts usually heal. Even when badly torn. That's why loving someone is worth the risk, and it is why I think the simplistic analogies about "giving parts of your heart away" can be misleading.

CONCLUSION

Even though I cannot wholeheartedly endorse approaches to Christian sexual ethics made popular in recent decades, they may convey wisdom and insight that readers would like to incorporate into their own sexual ethic. To do so might be consistent with moral commitments you valued before reading this book and that you continue to affirm as you near its end.

Since my summaries and reflections are part of what I called an in-house conversation, it wouldn't be surprising to find readers who still want to affirm some of what they've learned through their own tradition of Christian nurture. Perhaps that will mean holding on to some previous ideas, but with some necessary revisions brought about by careful consideration of the critiques offered above. Perhaps it will mean incorporating some insights from these contemporary approaches into one of the models of sexual ethics presented in previous chapters.

7

Can Men and Women Be Friends?

(Or Does Romantic Interest Always Get in the Way?)

CAN MEN AND WOMEN be friends, or does the sex part always get in the way? The question is posed by the famous and much-discussed claim in the 1989 film *When Harry Met Sally . . .* Harry says they can't be just friends, and the allegation that such friendships are threatened by sexual interests or romantic attraction plays a key role in the argument. But Harry can't be completely right. Non-romantic friendship between heterosexual males and females is a lived reality for some people, so they're clearly *possible*. Friendship is rooted in common interests, compatibility, personality, temperament, and character, and the chemistry that brings two people together as friends can be independent of gender. Still, this doesn't mean such friendships are without complications.

I'd like to pose an alternative claim: men and women *can* be friends, but normally such friendships will need to negotiate some real dangers and tensions that are not present in (heterosexual) same-gender friendships.[1] This cautiously affirmative response to the question steers a middle course

1. In this chapter I am obviously presuming friendship between heterosexual males and females, where romantic attraction could be expected. Perhaps the issues in same-sex friendships between people who are homosexual closely parallel those raised here. I expect so but would hesitate to make that claim without further study. I leave it to others to explore those matters more carefully.

between two alternatives. One gives an unqualified yes, naively denying that any difficulties exist; the other, all too aware of the difficulties, denies the possibility of anything beyond casual acquaintanceship.

Christians sometimes worry about opposite-gender friendships, fearing that they will lead to marital unfaithfulness. As one denomination's General Assembly warned, "Christians should be careful in how they approach friendships with the opposite sex. It is important that they build safe boundaries in order to protect themselves from temptation, sin, and accusation. This is especially important for married individuals." A common warning suggests that our fallen natures make opposite-gender friendships unwise and dangerous if the friends are close and spend one-on-one time together. Knowing this is important because danger sometimes lurks silently in the background: affairs almost always begin as innocent friendships. It would be naive to deny that the dangers are real. But how does that acknowledgment factor into developing a responsible ethic of male-female friendship? Should our conclusions be based primarily on the potential dangers posed by such friendships, or is that only one factor to consider in formulating responsible moral guidelines? The question is complicated even further by the difficulty of actually quantifying the dangers. Are the familiar warnings exaggerations? The majority of people seem to believe that men and women *can be* platonic friends. But in the same survey reporting that 83 percent of respondents believed this, the survey also revealed that 62 percent of respondents had been in a platonic relationship that crossed the line and became romantic or sexual![2] What weight should be given to anecdotal accounts of friendships ruined by romantic interests? Harry warns that "the sex part always gets in the way." Might we say, instead, that while potential romantic interests pose real challenges, they *need not* "get in the way"? This question is at the heart of what we'll explore in this chapter. To begin, let's think about what we mean by friendship, and then honestly name the challenges of male-female friendship and consider how they might be faced.

WHAT DO WE MEAN BY FRIENDSHIP?

Textbook definitions fall far short of capturing the depth and richness of friendship, which is probably better *described* by the stories we tell about our friends. But a working definition of friendship will provide helpful common ground for thinking about male-female friendship.

2. Chatterjee, "Can Men and Women Be Friends?"

C. S. Lewis' treatment of friendship in *The Four Loves* makes two important distinctions that I find helpful for clarifying the meaning and nature of friendship. First, Lewis identifies friendship as a form of love, but as a love that is distinct in character from other loves.

> Those who cannot conceive Friendship as a substantive love but only as a disguise or elaboration of Eros betray the fact that they have never had a Friend. The rest of us know that though we can have erotic love and friendship for the same person yet in some ways nothing is less like a Friendship than a love-affair. Lovers are always talking to one another about their love; Friends hardly ever about their Friendship. Lovers are normally face to face, absorbed in each other; Friends, side by side, absorbed in some common interest.[3]

The cultural dominance of a romantic paradigm for love keeps many of us from thinking about friendship as a form of love. In fact, if cross-sex friends said "I love you" to each other, it might introduce lots of confusion! But Lewis reminds us that the bond between friends *is* love—just love of a different kind. We don't have language that conveys it without ambiguity, though. If we followed Lewis' way of thinking, where the Greek term for friendship (*philia*) is another word for love, we could simply adopt the convention of saying "I friend you" as a way to express love.

Lewis makes a second distinction that helps us narrow the focus. He distinguishes *companionship* from *friendship*. While Lewis does not elaborate much, companions are people we associate with in everyday life. They are our classmates, teammates, coworkers, and neighbors, among others. We know them, talk with them, and share mutual activities because everyday life circumstances bring us together. Often, we even *call* them friends, because the word *friend* is sometimes a label for almost anyone we know. The fact that someone can have hundreds of friends on a social network exemplifies how the term has come to be used so broadly that it loses its classical meaning.

Lewis says that friendship arises out of companionship when we discover a shared interest, activity, insight, or even taste that leads us to proclaim something like "What? You too?"[4] Friendship is about seeing or caring about the same truth. Whether or not that sets the bar too high, Lewis meant to point to something richer and deeper in friendship than one finds in companionship. There's nothing wrong with companions, but they aren't friends.

3. Lewis, *Four Loves*, 61.
4. Lewis, *Four Loves*, 64–66.

If we accept Lewis' distinction, we can supplement his description of friendship with some additional characteristics that help capture the uniqueness of friendship. There are at least three additional characteristics that extend his definition, and other accounts of the nature of friendship could add several others.

First, we choose our friends through an intentional act of showing preference for them. There's an exclusive element to friendship, because we choose some people as friends from among all the possible options. Occasionally, the choice seems more like a mystery than a thoughtful decision, and we sometimes call that "chemistry." But it doesn't happen with everyone. While we don't usually go around saying it, most of the people we know are not actually *friends*.

In addition to the fact that friends usually share interests or care about the same truth, a second dimension of modern friendships is that friends "delight in" each other. We find a special quality in our friends that brings us joy. Perhaps they lighten our spirits with good humor or stimulate our minds with probing questions or insightful observations; they share and deepen our love for art, or sport, or nature—or whatever else we enjoy doing or talking about together.

A third characteristic of friendship is that friends intend each other's well-being. This characteristic draws on a very old idea. Aristotle saw the highest form of friendship as that based not on a friend's usefulness to us, nor on the pleasure we find in their company, but on virtue. Friends love each other because they love the good embodied in the other. Having such friends helps make us good, because in this kind of friendship, friends seek to enhance the good in each other. Good friends call out the best in us and hold us accountable to shared standards of excellence.

If this description of friendship sounds something like contemporary romance, that's not surprising. We usually expect a romantic partner also to be a friend. Sometimes friendship leads toward romance, while at other times "falling in love" starts a relationship that eventually becomes friendship. In either case it's common in an era of increased equality to find romantic love and friendship love coexisting in couples who are "in love." And once that blending of loves occurs, it's hard to disentangle which love is which.

This very brief overview of the nature of friendship and its distinctiveness as one form of human love provides a foundation for further considerations of the challenges and possibilities of male-female friendship. It is this kind of friendship we are asking about when we inquire into whether and how men and women can be friends. So, to reframe our basic question: can men and women be friends in the same way that same-gendered people can be friends with each other, minus the differences that individual personalities or gender might make?

GENDER AND CULTURE

The potential for sexual tension, temptation, or inappropriate sexual activity is not the only reason opposite-gender friendships can be challenging. Gender differences may account for another kind of challenge, and one that won't be discussed in detail here. Still, it is important to acknowledge. Some of these gender differences seem to be intrinsically part of our sexuality as men and women, in spite of the fact that there is considerable variation in the way individuals express their gendered selves. Other differences that make friendship challenging seem to clearly result from the ways men and women are socialized in particular cultures.

In the first case, the presumption is that men and women are "just different" in ways that make friendship difficult. The discussions sometimes move toward a "men are from Mars, women are from Venus" approach and suggest that, whatever the sources of these differences, establishing real friendships across genders will require overcoming the barriers they present. Ironically, the differences that threaten to make male-female friendship harder to sustain are often the same differences that are mentioned as key benefits of male-female friendship!

The way culture is structured creates another kind of challenge. Our socialization as males and females accounts for some of what we experience as gender difference, so depending on the kind of gender formation people experience, cross-sex friendship will be more or less difficult. Barriers to male-female friendship aren't just built into our genes but even into the way our culture shapes how we express our gendered sexuality. C. S. Lewis, speaking out of a social context in which men and women apparently had too little in common to become friends, concludes that when men and women have different educations, daily activities, and family responsibilities, it is improbable that they can become friends. Friendship requires equality, which in turn makes it possible for friendships to form around shared interests and shared activities. Gender inequality created by culture can make these opportunities rare. So historically, when social structures create gender inequality, men form friendships with each other and women do the same.

BENEFITS OF CROSS-SEX FRIENDSHIP

In spite of the challenges posed by gender and culture, both men and women report that being friends with members of the opposite sex has many benefits. Some of the benefits they describe arise from the fact of our gender differences. There's some reason to hesitate about these due to the stereotypes implied, but with that in mind, we can grant at least some validity to these frequently voiced testimonials. Males and females regularly say that being friends with each other gives them a better understanding of the way the other gender communicates, thinks, feels, and acts. Friendship provides a window into a perspective that might be gender-specific and helps us act and react with greater wisdom (assuming we recognize the uniqueness of individual males and females) in all of our opposite-gender social interactions.

Another list of advantages focuses more on the subtle spark of sexuality that might sometimes be present in the background of friendship. Being friends creates a zest, vitality, or zing. And both men and women report that their opposite-gender friendships affirm their femininity or manliness. It reminds them that people of the opposite gender find something about them attractive, even if there's no romance or sex involved.[5]

Both men and women identify benefits that reflect some of the common images of gender-specific friendship styles. Males report that having female friends provides an opportunity for more emotional intimacy and emotional depth. It helps them connect with a part of themselves that male-male friendships seem not to allow for. Females report that friendships with men have less "drama" and provide opportunities for male-style interactions and activity-oriented friendships that aren't as easily found in friendships with women. These oft-repeated comments clearly adopt the research findings and conventional wisdom that male friendships are more activity-oriented, while female friendships are more talk-oriented and attentive to the emotional dimension of life.

Both men and women find cross-sex friendships valuable because there is less of the same-sex competition they often experience—there is less jealousy and less game playing. And when compared to romantic relationships, being "just friends" sometimes seems more authentic. Having friends of both genders also brings more diversity into our lives. These comparisons suggest that many men and women find their cross-sex friendships to be refreshingly different because some negative things they've experienced in same-sex friendships aren't so apparent, and some of the gender differences

5. Rubin, *Just Friends*, 157–62.

that are one ingredient of the friendship add a valued and even exciting dimension.

As important as are the benefits that arise from differences, deep and mature friendships between men and women also transcend gender differences. They are grounded in the mutual admiration of someone's character, insight, competence, humor, and all those subtle traits of personality that make us unique and loveable. Gender differences and cultural systems might get in the way of noticing and appreciating these, but when we go beyond those limitations to see and know real people, anyone can become a friend. Men and women can express friendship to a person of the opposite gender in ways that make the benefits of friendship gender-neutral. This means that when we hear someone describe the advantages of their friendship with Jamie or Taylor, we have no idea of the friend's gender. At this level, a friend is a friend, and that friendship is valued for all of the reasons you value your deepest friendships.

DIFFERENT CIRCUMSTANCES, DIFFERENT CHALLENGES

The circumstances of particular male-female friendships are not all the same, and different circumstances produce unique challenges. In order to assess the challenges, it's important to first distinguish the *relational circumstances* in which they occur.

Circumstance #1: Single/Single

Sometimes a single male and a single female become friends. Anecdotal evidence suggests that sometime later, at least one of these friends is apt to develop a romantic interest in the other, even if that was entirely absent earlier. The "possibility of something more" enters people's minds. This shouldn't be surprising. The kinds of things we experience in friendship—support, encouragement, trust, honesty, emotional intimacy—are the same things that can easily contribute to romantic attraction. Whether or not we plan it or even want it, this fact makes it likely that romantic attraction will sometimes find its way into a friendship.

There isn't necessarily any problem here. If friends become romantically interested in each other, their friendship might simply serve as the foundation for romance. The "sex part" doesn't "get in the way" as long as we accept the possibility that friendship can turn into romance and that the two can then coexist and even be mutually enhancing.

Falling in love with a friend is risky, even if it's permissible. How would my friend respond to knowing how I feel? Would my profession of love be reciprocated, or would I hear those feared words "I'm sorry, but I don't feel that way . . . can't we just be friends?" Would things be awkward after that? Would the friendship even survive the experience of unrequited love? Is it worth the risk of damaging the friendship to profess love? And what if nothing is said? Will my emotions keep running wild, or can I make falling in love go away? Is it dishonest to say nothing? Or can it even be successfully hidden?

The confusing array of emotions and questions sets the stage for some game playing, and that's when the mix of friendship love (*philia*) and romantic love (*eros*) can make things uncomfortably messy. Since many of these challenges lead us primarily in the direction of situation-specific relationship advice, I won't deal with them in detail here but will simply identify some of the dilemmas and challenges single people often face when they develop a romantic attraction toward a friend.

- *Risk of losing the friendship.* Single people who fall in love with a friend often face a disclosure dilemma: should I tell the friend how I feel? The drive to do so is fueled by romantic interest and all that nature and culture contribute to that. The hesitancy is often fueled by the fear of rejection. "I'm sorry . . . I don't feel the same way about you . . . let's just be friends." Ouch. Unfortunately, things aren't always the same after that. Can the friendship survive the rejection and potential awkwardness that now exists? Uncertain about the response and it's potential to damage the friendship, friends sometimes hesitate to reveal romantic interest. If they take the risk and find out their romantic interest isn't reciprocated, what happens to the unrequited love? Does falling in love go away with intention and effort? Can you ever get back to "just friends"?

- *Risk of failed romance.* What if the romance does work . . . but only for a while? If it works, one of the barriers the friends will have surmounted is learning how to incorporate a new kind of love (*eros*) into a preexisting relationship characterized by *philia*—friendship love. But romances don't always last, and they are notoriously more short-lived than many friendships. Can you be friends after a breakup? I don't have any survey results but have heard students tell stories about this for many years. The cumulative answer seems to go like this: The friendship rarely lasts, especially when the breakup is one-sided. When it does work, the friends need to get through an awkward period first, and then they can sometimes reestablish the friendship. A mutual decision to end the romance makes this success far more likely. Everyone has their own stories to tell about what they have experienced and observed. But since this account seems to be common wisdom, at least among many, beginning a romance with a friend carries the very real risk that a failed romance could ultimately doom the friendship.

- *Hidden agendas and hesitant trust.* Single people know ahead of time that any friendship could eventually develop into romantic attraction, whether or not it's intended or welcomed. Unfortunately, friendship is sometimes used as an intentional strategy to start a romance, but without disclosing this fact. When one friend turns down the eventual invitation, he then discovers that the other "friend" wasn't really interested in friendship at all—and quickly disappears. To the friend without any agenda, this feels like abandonment or even betrayal. It doesn't take many instances of this for people to develop a hesitancy to trust people of the other gender who seem to want to be friends. Distrust becomes a way to protect oneself from manipulation and hurt.

Single people who can become friends but who could also become lovers face unique challenges that will have to be negotiated if cross-sex friendships are to survive and flourish.

Circumstance #2: Single/In a Committed Relationship or Both in a Committed Relationship

Sometimes a single person becomes friends with someone of the opposite gender who is already in a committed romantic relationship. Or perhaps both friends are in committed relationships; they may even be married. If one or both of their commitments exist at a serious level (which we will assume here, even in relationships falling short of marriage) romance with anyone else is "off limits." Unlike a friendship between two single people, which could appropriately move into romance, there is now a moral boundary supported by both faithfulness to one's commitments and respect for another person's commitments. This relational status produces a different set of challenges, and most of the challenges discussed below arise in this context. Even if this doesn't apply to you at this time, most people (statistically) will be in this category eventually, and since social conditions increasingly encourage opposite-gender friendships, the majority of us will face these challenges.

Circumstance #3: Opposite-Gender Friendships and Social Roles

Whatever the relationship status of the people involved, friendships with people of the opposite gender sometimes develop between people who are otherwise separated by the boundaries arising out of their social roles. Among the many examples, I'm thinking here of healthcare providers and their patients, teachers and students, supervisors and employees, clergy and their parishioners. Within these defined roles there are typically policies in place that are designed to identify and eliminate sexual misconduct. This provides an advantage that doesn't exist in more "normal" friendships where boundaries are often fuzzy. One might think of the principles, virtues, and safeguards below as an "opposite-gender friendship conduct policy" that tries to bring greater clarity to opposite-gender friendship in a way similar to how sexual misconduct policies bring greater clarity to professional and workplace settings. But sexual misconduct policies don't usually prohibit friendship, and rarely even address it. The presumption seems to be that friendship is allowed, as long as it doesn't become sexual and as long as there is no abuse of power.

CHALLENGES AND ISSUES IN MALE-FEMALE FRIENDSHIP

Since we're considering this issue in the context of broader reflections about sexual ethics, it's necessary to limit our consideration of the challenges of opposite-gender friendships to those that broadly raise concerns about sexual attraction. But this still leaves us with plenty to consider! You'll need to turn elsewhere to find wisdom about how to address the challenges faced because of gender or enculturation.

In its broadest strokes, the central challenge here has been described in similar ways by a variety of people. Opposite-gender friendships are obviously more complicated because sexual tensions or attractions may arise, even if by surprise. As a result, they "will always have to face certain difficulties that will not be present in same-sex friendships."[6] What are some of those specific challenges?

---

6. Meilaender, "Men and Women—Can We Be Friends?," 11.

1. Blurry Boundaries and Fuzzy Images

When I talk to adults from my parents' generation, it doesn't take long to discover that the opportunities for opposite-gender friendships and their frequency have undergone considerable change since then. Increased opportunities for women today, especially in education and the workplace, have created the kinds of conditions for men and women to become friends that didn't commonly exist a generation ago. It wouldn't be unusual for someone who married in the 1950s to say now that the only opposite-gender person they would consider a close friend is their spouse. While the phenomenon of opposite-gender friends isn't new, its prevalence is. However, we haven't yet developed clear norms—or at least shared norms—for how to conduct such friendships with integrity. The lack of clear norms means that we find ourselves operating with a generalized sense of uncertainty about boundaries and expectations. Things are a little fuzzy. As a result, we are sometimes a bit confused about our own opposite-gender friendships and suspicious of those we observe!

Social scientists tell us that when social practices become common, they become scripted.[7] This means they follow a loose set of rules or guidelines or expectations that we can learn by observation and practice. Subsequently, we internalize the script and are able to use it to conduct ourselves in those social contexts. If something is socially scripted you'd be able to ask people, "How does it work when . . . ?" and hear similar descriptions. But when there aren't abundant examples in our everyday lives or in the media, we don't have an opportunity to learn the script. We don't know how it works. Consequently, opposite-gender friends must improvise, managing their friendship without the advantage of readily available cultural wisdom.

The friendship script we've learned is that of same-sex friendship. As one researcher suggests, friendship between a male and female is a mysterious anomaly because it's so overshadowed by the paradigm of same-sex friendship. Consider what your own reaction would be to hearing that someone's best friend is of the opposite gender, or the reaction you'd get from others if you revealed the same. Male-female friendships just don't fit comfortably into our common images of friendship.

Another way to account for the fuzziness of the opposite-gender friendship script is to notice the prevalence of another potentially competing

---

7. I found Kathy Werking's *We're Just Good Friends* to be an excellent and helpful way of framing the issues of male-female friendship from the perspective of a social scientist. Her ideas especially helped sharpen my understanding of why we have fuzzy images of male-female friendship.

one. It can be argued that we've been trained to see male-female friendships primarily through the dominant paradigm of romantic love.

> In American culture, adult women and men are expected to form romantic bonds rather than platonic bonds with one another.
>
> The dominance of the romantic ideology is maintained by denying the legitimacy of alternatives to the romantic heterosexual ideal.
>
> "Is it possible for men and women to be close friends without engaging in sexual or romantic activity?" In asking this question the questioner assumes that sexual activity constitutes the core of man-woman relationships.[8]

If we are in the grip of a romantic paradigm that creates normative expectations for our male-female relationships, it's not surprising that cross-sex friendships are often ambiguous. It is not easy to see friendship as friendship when we've been taught to think about these relationships only within a paradigm of male-female romance. Opposite-gender friendship is considered abnormal at best, and many people just don't get it. This is because such friendships too easily get translated into the only framework we've learned: romance. If we try to claim an alternative ("we're just friends!") we are met with either disbelief or suspicion. If either is internalized as self-doubt it makes things seem even fuzzier.

The fuzziness of our male and female friendship images is compounded by the fact that friendship and romance have many similar characteristics, no matter what gender combinations are involved. If we wanted to use the characteristics of a friendship to decide whether it's friendship or romance, would that clear things up?

The following scenario, though fictional, may help clarify how easily this fuzziness occurs. Let's say that a friend who is in the initial stages of developing a romantic interest in another friend comes to you for advice. The friend asks, "Do you think she *likes* me? "Well, tell me about your relationship," you reply, seeking a little more information. The response goes something like this: "We can talk about everything! Conversations are so comfortable and I trust her completely. I've told her things I hardly ever tell anyone. And when we don't see things quite the same way, I feel completely accepted for who I am. I don't have to pretend or hide to know I'm accepted. She's always there for me when I need some emotional support and makes time for me even when I know it's not always convenient. I try to do the same. I'm sure we'd do anything for each other. We have so much fun together, too,

---

8. Werking, *We're Just Good Friends*, 3, 39, 87.

even just doing silly things. I just feel better when we're together; it just lifts my spirits! That's why I think we want to be together so often."

Friend or lover? I doubt that we could make that determination yet. It could certainly describe opposite-sex college-aged people who have been friends for months and who are now falling in love. But it could also be the testimony of your best friend for many years as easily as it could be the loving proclamation of a bride on the eve of her wedding, or a couple who have been married for fifty years. It doesn't tell us if romance is present, even though we might expect to find the same story in a healthy and stable romance. Sometimes friends have trouble figuring out what's really going on, because friendship looks so much like romance that it can easily be mistaken for it. Perhaps it's happened to you!

The confusion is also illustrated by the range of general advice we hear about opposite-gender friendships. On one hand they are affirmed, but with some guidelines that provide wise safeguards. Be honest with yourself and your friend, make the friendship public and transparent, and don't cross lines that move into the realm of romance. But other forms of advice seem much less affirmative and more cautionary: don't spend one-on-one time together, don't meet for lunch or coffee, base the friendship on a shared interest (not simply an appreciation for each other) and avoid the appearance of impropriety. The second list treats opposite-gender friendship as too dangerous to allow it to flourish in ways similar to same-gender friendship and doesn't permit it to be guided by the same set of norms.

We are left with fairly blurry boundaries for the conduct of friendships in which romance could become an issue. What are the boundaries of appropriate forms of touch? Can you hug an opposite-gender friend? Which kind of hug is appropriate? What about a back rub or a tender touch on the shoulder, leg, or arms? Since the social script isn't clear about these, they are prime candidates for misinterpreted intentions. Can you share emotional intimacy in the same way you would in other friendships? Or is there a different standard? What is it? Can you meet in private, or only in public? How often can you see each other? The list of boundary confusions abounds.

The challenge posed by fuzzy guidelines could be addressed by rejecting male-female friendships altogether. But that would be the easy way out. It can also be addressed by making the norms clearer. Along with this we'd need to be patient for a social script to emerge in society at large but also within the Christian community, presuming that Christians may have something distinctive to contribute. Kathy Werking concludes her book with a challenge I find inviting. She argues that opposite-sex friendships illustrate that they can be characterized by loving and caring deeply in non-romantic ways and that they are often based on mutual respect and on symmetrical rights and obligations. In order to sustain friendships that have real value in a social context where they are often confusing, it's essential that we find ways to "contest the prevailing assumptions that close, affectionate ties between men and women necessarily evolve into sexual or romantic relationships."[9]

2. Attraction

The primary challenge to male-female friendships that occupies our attention in this chapter is the possibility—some would even say *likelihood*—that friends will develop a romantic attraction for each other. There is a normative cultural expectation that relationships between heterosexual males and females will have a romantic component. Studies of male-female friendships and anecdotes from many of my college-aged students indicate that attraction does indeed occur. Somewhere between 30 and 60 percent of survey respondents report the development of sexual or romantic attraction to opposite-gender friends. There are reasons for this that won't be surprising. Sexual attraction is in our nature. It can happen whether we want it to or not. Emotional vulnerability and deeply shared intimacy seem to promote attraction, so friendship is a natural place to see it spring up. When a single person has a close friend there is often also social pressure to think about that friend as a potential lover or spouse. Non-romantic male-female friendships are a lived reality, but the potential for romantic attraction is just as real.

In what ways can attraction be a challenge or threat to friendship? Several challenges have been identified in studies of cross-sex friendships, and I think they reflect the familiar responses that come to mind when we think about familiar experiences. For people already in committed relationships, the central challenge is that romantic or sexual attraction to a friend threatens the violation of another already established relationship boundary. Studies of opposite-sex friendship tend to draw on research participants who are single, however, and many of the challenges that exist for single people are expectedly distinct. Let's start there and then revisit the implications of attraction for people in committed relationships.

Attraction itself is a complex phenomenon, and making some distinctions may help us understand a further complication for friendship. Heidi Reeder distinguishes four kinds of attraction that can occur: subjective physical attraction (I find him/her physically attractive), objective physical attraction (I can see why people would find him/her physically attractive),

9. Werking, *We're Just Good Friends*, 164.

romantic attraction (I'm attracted to him/her as a romantic partner or potential spouse), and friendship attraction (I'm attracted to him/her as a friend—but wouldn't want to be in a romantic relationship for various reasons).[10] Using these distinctions, it's easy to imagine that someone might be attracted to a person physically but not romantically. This might create some sexual temptation but not a desire to establish a romance. Sometimes when that attraction is mutual, friends decide to include a sexual component in a relationship defined as friendship, not romance. Reeder says that individuals with a conventional value system tend to avoid this and consider sex a threat to friendship. People with less conventional values sometimes believe that being "friends with benefits" might have positive outcomes.

The primary concern among people along the conventionality spectrum is that romantic attraction and sexual activity threaten to harm friendship. This is one of the main reasons friends hesitate to disclose romantic feelings, even when as single people it would be appropriate to do so. Friends fear that introducing romance or a sexual component into the friendship will destroy what makes friendship valuable and a distinctively good kind of relationship. In one study after another, interviewees mention increased complications and conflicts in romantic relationships. They say that along with a sexual relationship comes a level of commitment, exclusivity, and possessiveness that are refreshingly absent from friendship. They worry that romance is more self-serving, jealous, and less authentic than friendship. These fears suggest that on balance, it makes more sense to protect a good friendship by not undermining it with the additional layer of romance. If this conventional wisdom makes sense, "friends with benefits" threatens friendship. Adding sex to friendship is just too messy.

Some of the fears expressed in explaining the risk reflect a depressingly negative view of romance! Perhaps that's because too many of the college-aged research subjects have had mostly negative experiences with romance and mostly positive experiences with friendship. A healthy, mature romance can be characterized by high degrees of authenticity, selflessness, and trust. Nevertheless, it is probably accurate to assume that adding romance to friendship makes the relationship both more complex and challenging. It's legitimate to wonder whether one should risk changing the nature of a fulfilling friendship by adding this new level of complexity. While two people may have learned to successfully negotiate the challenges of friendship, there's no guarantee that a romantic couple will be able to meet the new challenges with the same success. So, sometimes friends who experience

10. Reeder, "I Like You . . . as a Friend," 329.

attraction decide that divulging this information isn't worth the risk of harming the friendship.

Revealing romantic attraction also creates the possibility of rejection. "Let's just be friends" might sound like an invitation to a deep and meaningful relationship, but to someone who's developed a crush on a friend, those words can be painful. Can friendship survive such rejection in cases where the attraction is only one-sided?

Researchers and their subjects reflect an emerging consensus that friendship is a unique kind of love, and outside of an exclusive dating relationship that might include both, friendship thrives best when it is the single goal (or good) being sought. When attraction emerges, then, one clear option is to choose friendship alone. This means the attraction must be resisted. Research suggests that this is not only possible but often a normal part of the development of a cross-sex friendship. Reeder relates that "while a few participants reported that their romantic attraction had grown at some point during the friendship, the most common change was dissipating romantic attraction."[11] The stories told by opposite-gender friends suggest that attraction is often a fleeting experience that need not complicate friendship when friendship and not romance is the goal. The internal mechanisms that account for dissipating attraction are probably as mysterious as those that account for its presence in the first place, but the intention to resist attraction and focus on friendship, along with a little patience, seems to be sufficient to avoid the complications that attraction creates.

3. Jealousy

When at least one of the friends is in an already existing romance that includes some degree of commitment, jealousy is likely to be among the most common challenges to opposite-gender friendship. At its lowest level of intensity, the person who isn't directly involved in the friendship may have an uneasy feeling of discomfort, simply based on a fear that the friendship might be a threat. Perhaps a little distrust is part of the mix. Add some insecurity and the jealousy is heightened even more.

The sense that an existing romance is threatened by a friendship might not focus on the possibility of sexual interest but simply on the potential that the friend will become the primary source of emotional intimacy. Does that fear arise in the same way in same-sex friendships? Perhaps—and when it does, the fear is a reminder that our culture sees romance in such a way

11. Reeder, "I Like You . . . as a Friend," 161.

that there's a common expectation that one's lover fills a variety of exclusive roles. We often expect our romantic partners to be exclusive best friends as well as sexual partners. Any threat to that exclusivity can generate jealousy. Harry explains this problem in our classic movie example:

> If the two people are in relationships, the pressure of possible involvement is lifted . . . That doesn't work either, because what happens then is, the person you're involved with can't understand why you need to be friends with the person you are just friends with. Like it means something is missing from the relationship and why do you have to go outside to get it? And when you say "no, no, no it's not true, nothing is missing from the relationship," the person you're involved with then accuses you of being secretly attracted to the person you are just friends with, which you probably are. I mean, come on, who the hell are we kidding, let's face it. Which brings us back to the earlier rule before the amendment, which is men and women can't be friends.[12]

His theory puts us in a no-win situation where jealousy is presumed to be inevitable, even in legitimate friendship, and where attraction is assumed to be inherent in any cross-sex friendship. If the latter were true, it would only support the inevitability of jealousy!

People consistently tell me that they like the idea that their romantic partner will feel a little jealous. It seems to confirm love. We apparently like the idea of being possessed at least a little—as long as it's just a tender emotion. A lack of jealousy seems to some people like not caring.

Unless jealousy is paired with trust, people in committed relationships will find it difficult to have opposite-gender friendships. While I haven't yet found studies to support my hypothesis, I would suggest that the less trust we find in a relationship, the more jealousy we find. That would explain why jealousy is such a common threat to either romance or friendship in very early stages of dating or perhaps even in early stages of marriage. That's when we're most apt to find a fearful partner expressing the expectation that the friendship will end for the sake of the romance. This might be a frustrating request for someone who is worthy of trust, even if a partner hasn't become confident enough to extend that much trust. The prospect of having to end a longtime friendship with a person of the opposite gender because one's partner is jealous creates tensions that can be hard to negotiate.

---

12. Harry Burns' monologue in *When Harry Met Sally . . .* (1989), written by Nora Ephron, directed by Rob Reiner.

As trust increases, jealousy typically decreases. If this is true, stable and secure romantic relationships that have produced high levels of trust can make room for either person to have friends of the opposite gender. While there is still always a theoretical risk of unfaithfulness, trust can replace fear as the lens through which we see our partner's friendships.

4. Temptation and "Moral Weakness"

The possibility that a friendship might turn into romantic attraction creates a temptation for persons who are already in an exclusive romantic relationship. We might wish it wasn't so, because when we are truly intending friendship and nothing more, romantic attraction is an intruder that only makes things more difficult. We don't want our friendships to tempt us to be unfaithful. Good friendships are supposed to nurture our character, not threaten it.

The possibility of temptation becomes an even more serious issue when we think about the part of our fallen nature that I'd call "moral weakness." The phrase is borrowed from Aristotle but seems to capture the universal experience Paul describes in Romans 7: "I can will what is right, but I cannot do it. For I do not do the good I want, but the evil I do not want is what I do" (7:18b–19). To call this "moral weakness" is meant to include the possibility that we often do very good things, borne out of love and reflecting God's intentions for human well-being. But if we are honest with ourselves, we know that we sometimes don't follow through on our best intentions, and more often than we'd like, we don't have the strength to resist the temptation to do what that little voice inside us says we shouldn't do. Sometimes, it seems, we just don't have the strength to be as good as we want to be. That's what I mean by moral weakness. It creeps into every part of our life.

Since the possibility of temptation is real, the important question is how it should be addressed. To answer that we need a little more clarity about what counts as temptation and how it differs from sin. Temptation is the "incitement" to sin. It's something inside or outside of us that takes the form of a suggestion, encouragement, or enticement to do what we shouldn't do. But no matter how strong the temptation, if we don't willingly give in, it's still just a temptation. A temptation is dangerous, but it isn't wrong.

The blanket approach found in much of the advice given by moralists is to *avoid* temptation whenever possible. That makes sense, since temptation is dangerous and there is wisdom in avoiding danger: Don't keep your favorite cookies in the house if you're are on a diet (avoiding the temptation to gluttony); don't turn on the TV if you'll end up watching it for hours when you have more important things to do (avoiding the temptation to sloth); and don't expose yourself to sexually arousing images (avoiding the temptation to lust). Advice like this seems reasonable. If having an opposite-gender friendship seems to pose a degree of danger that you think wisdom requires you to avoid, then avoiding such a friendship may be your best choice. However, there might be a second responsible option.

What if we consider friendship a high-level value? Sometimes we decide that certain risks are worth taking. What conditions make that a responsible risk and not a careless one? First, we'd need to know that the goal mattered enough for the risks to be considered "acceptable risks." This isn't always easy, but we'd need to know that when honestly weighing the risks and the benefits, they were at least roughly even.

Next, we'd expect the risk-taker to be aware of the danger. Quickly dismissing it leads to false confidence. If the dangerous outcome were almost certainly to become a reality, we'd consider the risk a foolish one.

We'd also want to know that the risk-taker has good reasons to be confident that the danger can be avoided. In the context of opposite-gender friendship, this raises the important issue of willpower or self-control. When faced with a powerful temptation, being confident in one's ability to exercise self-control is one of the most reliable reasons to be confident. Most of us know which kinds of temptations we find hardest to resist, and also where our self-control is an effective guard against falling to temptation. Richard Foster provides a perspective I find helpful, since it takes both the risks and our ability to act responsibly with equal seriousness:

> Most intimate heterosexual friendships have erotic dimensions to them. And it does us no good to deny that fact of life. Rather, we should accept these feelings. But to accept them does not mean to act upon them. Sexual feelings are not to control us; we are to control them. It is an illusion to think that sexual feelings are uncontrollable.[13]

Foster's perspective suggests the possibility of making a shift from *avoiding* temptation to *resisting* temptation. The idea that we can resist temptation creates a middle way for Christians to deal with temptation, at least in some settings. Resisting temptation falls between ignoring it (a form of naive optimism leading to moral carelessness) and allowing the possibility of temptation to so control our lives that we are paralyzed by it (a form of naive caution). This is another version of a morality of caution, described in an earlier chapter using this analogy: the view from the edge of a precipice can be breathtaking, but one ought to avoid the danger of standing too close

13. Foster, *Money, Sex, and Power*, 116.

to the edge. However, the fact that one *could* fall isn't a good reason not to venture out to a safe vantage point. A fence would make things easy. But in the moral life, there aren't usually fences and guardrails in place to protect us. In friendship there isn't a clear line that marks the danger zone, and we're left figuring out what limits, principles, or safeguards are necessary to protect what matters; in my mind what matters is both the friendship and the integrity of our other moral commitments. Can we protect both?

5. Public (Mis)Perception and Arousing Suspicion ("People Will Talk")

Let's assume that friends who are highly principled people of high integrity conduct their opposite-gender friendship in ways that honor the friendship, their other commitments, and the boundaries that separate friendship from romance. Now a new challenge emerges: it's possible—or even likely—that their male-female friendships will be suspect. Outside observers will wonder and whisper. After all, how many times have you seen the response "We're just friends" met by skepticism? People will wonder if there is "something else going on," and the mere questioning can be the spark that ignites rumors or voiced suspicion. Aware of this, there's a common wisdom that's expressed in familiar form: "You can't be too careful."

In this scenario, we have to question where the problem really lies. Is it the friendship? Is it the human proclivity to gossip? I'm strongly inclined to say that the "talk" or suspicion is the problem, but even so, it does create a real challenge that must be faced. We might not like the idea that people who gossip can ruin meaningful relationships of all kinds, but it's true.

There are two directions one might choose to take in response to this challenge. The first is the path suggested by caution. Play it safe. This option is described by the cluster of advice that says we should keep opposite-gender friendships at a casual level, avoiding intimacy. Deep friendships should be sought only with those for whom romantic attraction wouldn't be an issue. Associations with casual friends of the opposite gender should always be public and should only occur in groups, in order to minimize any one-to-one connections. In other words, the friendship should be conducted according to guidelines that assure that others will have nothing to talk about. The need to avoid suspicion becomes the standard used to create friendship guidelines.

There are substantive values at stake here, and protecting those values is important. Even though appearances aren't reality, they can become reality to others, and that reality can create real tensions in either of the friend's other relationships or social networks. Suspicion (even when unjustified) can create jealousy as easily as reality. False rumors can effectively destroy one's reputation as long as they are believed. Appearances of impropriety can undercut trust even when the underlying reality, if known, would increase it. Stability in our relationships, maintaining a good reputation, and being seen as worthy of trust are all worth protecting. Sometimes we might decide that an opposite-gender friendship, even if morally appropriate, is worth sacrificing for the sake of other values we deem paramount.

Another option that also values morally appropriate opposite-gender friendships is one that refuses to allow false perceptions to disqualify anyone from friendship. Instead of "playing it safe" by creating limits designed to avoid misperception by outsiders, friends choose to conduct their friendships with such integrity that they are beyond reproach. This doesn't mean throwing common sense to the wind. But it does open the door to real friendships, where both the standards and the possibilities of friendship with people of the *same* gender also apply to people of the *opposite* gender. The perception of outsiders does not become the basis for a double standard. No artificial barriers need to be erected to protect the friendship from suspicion, since there's nothing about the friendship that justifies suspicion or judgment.

This option refuses to give suspicious people the power to decide who our friends will be. Doing what is right and living with integrity becomes the primary standard. This is obviously more risky, since we have no control about how others see, think, or talk about us. We only can *influence* perceptions by our behavior.

There is another risk associated this approach. Rather than using the social setting to insure propriety, it puts the onus on the friends to insure that even with the artificial barriers down, they will still stay within the boundaries of appropriate friendship. For example, if one's romantic partner, other friends or coworkers aren't always present, friends need to regulate their own behavior. If meeting for coffee, they must insure that their conversations are always appropriate. Without an external source of control, the locus of control is now internal to the friendship and to each individual. Without external accountability, self-discipline becomes more important.

We aren't left without guidance here, however, and we'll end this chapter with some suggestions about the kinds of guidelines friends could use to hold themselves accountable to standards of integrity that will help insure the propriety of their friendship.

NURTURING AND PROTECTING MALE-FEMALE FRIENDSHIP

The challenges people face when they seek to maintain cross-sex friendships are real, even though they are experienced differently depending on specific circumstances and unique personalities. These challenges need to be faced honestly. To ignore them is careless, since ignoring dangers is one of the easiest ways to succumb to them. The common alternative to avoid them is probably the safest, but one can ask whether opting for the safest approach is always the best route. If living cautiously also asks us to sacrifice what is of real value, we're left needing to weigh the relative merits of what we're avoiding and what we're giving up.

In response to my comments about the dangers of male-female friendship, one of my students responded like this: "People assume the worst. Maybe if we stopped lowering the bar, we would be surprised how many people rise to the occasion. We should expect more from people and give more room for human integrity to prevail."

I liked the guarded optimism expressed in this response. It suggests that instead of allowing fear and caution to rule, we use our realistic assessment of male-female friendship to guide us down an appropriate path, steering clear of the dangers as much as possible and seeking to maximize the blessings and benefits of friendship. I'd suggest that the best way to both nurture and protect friendship that comes with the kinds of challenges we have explored above is to

1. conduct our friendships on the basis of fundamental commitments that arise from Christian faith, supported by

2. the integrity of the persons involved, and by

3. friendship practices and practical wisdom that seek to embody our commitments and character.

1. Christian Commitments

In addition to the orienting convictions discussed in chapter 2, which provide a theological account of how we see ourselves, others, and human sexuality, there are a few specific affirmations that are especially relevant to this discussion of male-female friendship.

Friendship is a gift. God clearly created us with the capacity for *philia*—the kind of love shared between friends—and the wisdom of the ages testifies to its power to enrich our lives. In his account of friendship, Christian theologian Paul Wadell describes this well:

> Friendship is one of the greatest gifts of life; without friendship our lives would be impossibly impoverished. We can appreciate the great significance of friendship when we think how different our lives would be if certain people had never entered into them. Not only would our history be different, but we would be different as well. Our friends shape our character. They influence our attitudes, values, and perceptions. They challenge us, they teach us not to take ourselves too seriously, and they give us hope. Most important, friends want what is best for us and help us achieve it . . . It is in company with these good friends that we come to understand better what life means for us, the kind of person we ought to become, and what will really make us happy and free. Good friends not only change us, they make us better persons.[14]

Friendship is a positive good that can be considered an end in itself. It is of such value to life that it is worthy of pursuit. I assume there is little argument over this fact, but it is important to affirm. The question being posed in this chapter is whether *all* friendship is of equal value, and whether even valuable friendships sometimes come with a risk or cost that is too high.

I want to affirm that when the social conditions exist for true opposite-gender friendship, Wadell's description of the gift of friendship applies to all friendships, without regard for the gender combinations involved. Sometimes we experience the gift of friendship with people who are of the opposite gender—and could be potential romantic partners too, under the right circumstances. Individual experience with opposite-gender friendships varies greatly, so not everyone's story includes close friends who are the opposite gender. Not everyone would even want to be close friends with the opposite gender! But when those friendships emerge, they have the same value for our lives as any other and deserve to be seen as a gift that ought to be celebrated, nurtured, and protected.

Honoring covenant commitments. God is a covenant-making God. Time after time, from Noah to Abraham to Moses and beyond, God makes promises and keeps them. In the keeping of covenant promises, God is revealed as faithful—even in the face of obstinate disobedience that requires divine patience and grace. God's faithfulness engenders confidence and trust. Many dimensions of human life mirror this activity of covenant

14. Wadell, *Becoming Friends*, 40.

making. Keeping promises is central to daily life, and especially to the cooperative behavior necessary for social interactions. Marriage vows traditionally include a promise to love exclusively and unconditionally until life's end. Contracts of various sorts enable us to count on agreements when we are engaged in economic activity. Making and keeping covenants seems central to so many human endeavors!

In a rare biblical story about devoted friendship, a covenant also comes into play. We're told that Jonathan made a covenant with David, symbolized by giving David his clothing and armor. The details of the covenant aren't explained. It seems to express the friendship commitment evident in the story: "The soul of Jonathan was bound to the soul of David, and Jonathan loved him as his own soul" (1 Sam 18:1–4).

Since Christians worship a God who is faithful to covenants, one of the fundamental convictions one brings into a cross-sex friendship is the *inviolable primacy of covenant commitments.* The word *inviolable* invites a particular way of seeing. Covenants demand a level of committed obedience that puts everything else into perspective and sets priorities when we see all of our activities through the lens of the covenants we've made.

Our covenants also form our identity. In baptism, Christians recognize themselves as being "baptized into Christ" (Gal 3:27). In my own tradition's liturgy, we acknowledge God's covenant making ("I will establish my covenant between me and you, and your offspring after you throughout their generations, for an everlasting covenant, to be God to you and to your offspring after you" [Gen 17:7]) and remind the community of faith that "baptism is a sign and seal of God's promises to this covenant people."

A marriage covenant similarly establishes a new identity as well. A wedding liturgy proclaims, "Christian marriage is a joyful covenanting . . . that proclaims before God and human witnesses a commitment to live together in spiritual, physical and material unity . . . acknowledging that the love God has shown to us enables us to love each other." Having established this new identity, we often find that even in daily social settings, married people sometimes introduce themselves as their spouse's husband or wife. The covenant tells us who we are, defines our mutual belonging, and makes our promises and obligations part of our identity. When people in covenants enter friendships with others, they bring this identity into the friendship. I am your friend and I am my wife's husband. And while unmarried couples haven't usually entered into formal covenants, they have often made promises and established mutual understandings that function in similar ways.

Covenantal relationships provide a basis for trust both within the covenant and beyond it. When we live out of our covenantal identities, we find greater clarity about friendship boundaries that arise from our status as partners in a covenant. Expectations are clearer. And the covenant creates a clear context for assessing the quality of the friendship, since conversations and activities and all of our choices are made in light of covenant commitments.

Truth. The Christian commitment to truthfulness is grounded in the commandment that forbids bearing false witness (Exod 20:16). The ninth commandment addresses the importance of truthful testimony in judicial proceedings in its most focused application. But the tradition has extended this to include the veracity of our testimony in all of our verbal communication as well as the testimony our lives bear. So truth is a matter of both what we say (and don't say) and what we live. Words can correspond to the facts and lives can correspond to one's identity as the people of God and a follower of Christ.

In opposite-gender friendships it is especially important to think of this commitment to truth holistically, as is expressed in a quotation I picked up somewhere: "Live the truth first, then speak it." It's possible to hide untruth behind a veil of silence ("What he doesn't know won't hurt him"). Living a lie that's invisible to the public doesn't reflect a commitment to the truth. It betrays the hope that one won't get caught! Using the guise of friendship only to foster romance doesn't necessarily require telling any verbal lies, but it does involve hiding real motives, creating false impressions. Saying things in a way that avoids telling the real truth creates a facade designed to fool others. Living the truth demands more than appearances and momentary words. Truth is a way of life as well as honest speech.

There's a familiar intuition that communication is at the heart of the success or failure of human relationships at almost every level. Treating good communication as a panacea certainly oversimplifies things, but the intuition also taps into an important insight. Telling the truth is more than wise advice or a rule we're supposed to obey. It is at the heart of what makes human community possible. Truth creates bonds that connect us to those we love and trust and lays a foundation for the kind of cooperation that is central to the flourishing of human shalom.

2. Character and the Integrity of Persons

One of the things Christian ethicists have come to realize over recent years (or remember from earlier periods in the Christian tradition) is that the moral life is far more than obedience to a set of rules and figuring out how to apply them in complex dilemmas. Becoming a follower of Jesus also involves learning to be disciplined by a set of dispositions (or virtues) that comprise the character of a disciple of Jesus. In chapter 5 ("An Ethic of Sexual Integrity") I've already provided a model of how we might think about Christian sexual ethics in terms of dispositions that ground our sexual lives in the sort of person we are, not only in boundaries we observe or consequences we seek to avoid or achieve.

Trusting people of good character to conduct themselves with integrity in male-female friendships is an alternative to retreating from such friendships. The character of people involved in friendship is of paramount importance because we depend on the integrity of friends to keep friendships healthy in ways that honor God, our friends, and our covenants. Without integrity of character, the dangers of opposite-gender friendships would be much harder to avoid! Consider just a few examples of the kinds of gifts, virtues, or dispositions that matter to male-female friendship.

Self-Awareness

The literature on friendships between men and women suggests that constant monitoring is necessary in order to negotiate mutual understanding and socially acceptable practices. In order to monitor accurately the quality and character of our friendships we need to have a high level of honest self-awareness. Is romantic attraction creeping into the friendship? Is real friendship the motive for pursuing this relationship? Am I sacrificing important values to pursue this friendship? In order to answer these questions honestly, individuals need a clear self-awareness. Otherwise, our judgments are too easily clouded by hidden motives (motives we hide from our conscious awareness because we don't want to face them). Knowing the answer to the question, What's really going on here? is a central starting point for moral conduct.

Self-Control

One of the primary concerns in cross-sex friendships is the intrusion of romantic or sexual interest. If it's appropriate for friendship to become romance, open communication is more important than saying no to romantic feelings. If there's mutual interest in romance, the nature of the relationship changes into a romance between friends. If romance is off limits, however, one must find a way to suppress the romantic feelings so they have little or no impact on the friendship. Can that be done?

As Richard Foster has already reminded us, to accept the presence of romantic feelings is not to act on them: "Sexual feelings are not to control us; we are to control them. It is an illusion to think that sexual feelings are uncontrollable."[15] Foster isn't claiming that it's easy to stop "falling in love" with a friend, but he is holding out the possibility that we can choose to set romance aside for the sake of friendship. In the movie *When Harry Met Sally . . .*, Harry's claim is that men and women can't be friends because "the sex part always gets in the way." The alternative to that claim is that with self-control, the "sex part" might be present, but we can choose not to let it get in the way. Friends who report having had a romantic interest in the past typically also report that an intentional decision to pursue "only friendship" allowed them to move beyond their romantic interest so that it was no longer a factor in the success of a healthy friendship.

Respect

Respect is one of my favorite words when talking about Christian morality. It isn't a prominent biblical term, but it does capture important biblical themes. Biblical translators sometimes use the word *respect* to translate what in other versions is rendered as "honor." We are exhorted to respect parents and elders (Lev 19:3, 32). Their roles and importance to the community gives them divinely recognized status throughout the Hebrew Scriptures. Respect is also something we should strive to be worthy of. And in contrast, being the kind of person who does not earn the respect of others is a sad fact and a status to be avoided. Jesus criticizes religious leaders who think they ought to be respected but aren't actually worthy of it (see Matt 23, for example). In the New Testament epistles, respect is something one seeks to be worthy of by living in ways that earn it.

In sexual ethics, respect is something we can be expected to give and something we deserve to receive. In either case it is grounded in the conviction that we are creatures made in God's image. At this basic level, respect as I'm using it here isn't the same as the honor we earn through our achievements or social status. You deserve respect even if your life is a mess. You deserve respect from others even if you don't respect yourself. You deserve respect even if you're in no condition to show it to others at the time. In other words, basic respect is an attitude and act grounded in grace. Because it isn't earned, it's unconditional. That idea makes us grateful when we receive it, but it also makes it very hard to show respect toward people who don't seem to deserve it. When showing respect is an expression

15. Foster, *Money, Sex, and Power*, 116.

of Christian character, it recognizes in others a God-given worth that isn't extinguished by any disrespect we show. Respect is both an attitude and action that can become part of our character.

MORAL PRACTICES AND PRACTICAL WISDOM: GUIDELINES AND SAFEGUARDS FOR CROSS-SEX FRIENDSHIP

One of the best ways to resist feelings and actions that, after careful reflection, we decide are morally inappropriate or unacceptable is to take up practices that embody the alternative we seek. I use the word *practice* here in a semi-technical sense. Our personal and social practices shape our attitudes and habits in subtle ways we're not always aware of. We can reshape them when we intentionally choose to take up a set of practices that embody the convictions we want to live out. Practices are powerful. Christians can use them to define identity (worship and liturgy), nurture faith (education, mentoring), and model Christian discipleship (healing, caring, forgiving). Our practices bring our ideas and convictions into reality. Practices also have the power to contest or resist alternative practices. They are a way of saying no to one way of thinking or acting by engaging in an alternative (saying yes).

In the context of male-female friendship, this means that we say no to inappropriate expressions of friendship by taking up practices that provide models of healthy and morally appropriate ways for men and women to be friends. This is an alternative to saying no to the practice of male-female friendship altogether. It is a way to resist what's negative without abandoning the entire endeavor.

Over several years I have accumulated a personal list of some practices that resist the dangers of cross-sex friendships and embody an alternative that embraces the possibility of establishing friendship without regard to gender, yet sensitive to the unique challenges described above. Some of these have been learned from experience, others from reflection, and still others from the accumulated wisdom of reading and listening to others. The list is brief and in flux and is reproduced below without much elaboration. The adequacy of this set of practices will be determined by whether they address the full range of challenges, fully embody relevant and important Christian commitments, and effectively reduce or eliminate the dangers implied in the challenges people face in cross-sex friendships.

1. The Practice of Covenant Faithfulness

When people in covenant relationships (like marriage) are in cross-sex friendships, their faithfulness to the covenant is an absolute responsibility. This means that friendships should be structured and carried out only in ways that are fully in accord with covenant obligations. In other words, practicing faithfulness is a prerequisite when either person in a cross-sex friendship is married. While this may seem obvious, and while covenants are sometimes broken, the intentional and conscious practice of faithfulness is a practice of resistance. If our everyday decisions and actions are an accumulation of faithfulness, both marriage and friendship will be honored.

2. Practicing Honesty and Forthrightness

Because Christians are committed to truthfulness in all human interactions (this includes being honest with oneself) it's important to embody the truth not only narrowly (by not telling lies, for example) but in exhibiting a level of honesty and forthrightness that "tells the whole story" without hiding behind ambiguity or technicalities. Practicing honesty and forthrightness contests the kinds of things we say and do to conceal what we're ashamed to admit to ourselves or others. Honesty is one of the first casualties of a guilty conscience. For single people this practice will mean avoiding the manipulative strategy of using friendship as a pretense for initiating a romance, and for those in a committed relationship it means at a minimum conducting the friendship openly in order to minimize suspicion and build trust.

3. Practicing Expansive and Inclusive Friendship

Friendships based on shared interests flourish when others join the circle. You have probably had the experience of being with a small group of friends when someone is missing. It just isn't the same. What they add to the friendship makes it qualitatively better. There is something about friendship, so claim the ancient and contemporary theorists, which is naturally expansive and inclusive. Sharing our friends and our interests with others is a practice that celebrates friendship while also protecting it from exclusivity and isolation. If you are in a committed relationship, it would be normal to include your romantic partner in the friendship at some level. Sometimes this will include casual references ("I had a great conversation with _____ when we met for coffee today!") and other times might include doing things together.

4. The Practice of Mutual Respect and Support

Within the Christian community we honor and respect not only the covenants we make ourselves but also the covenants others make. This would mean, for example, that friends make intentional decisions to act with sensitivity and respect toward the other person's spouse and the other person's covenant obligations. A deep respect for both each other and each other's romantic partners will help maintain appropriate boundaries.

5. The Practice of Respecting Boundaries

The lack of social scripts for male-female friendship in society and within the Christian community means that friends are often left to improvise boundaries because there aren't clear communally shared and publicly modeled guidelines. Some proposed boundaries are so strict that they essentially limit men and women to casual acquaintances, and some friendships fall apart because there weren't adequate boundaries to protect them. It's difficult to propose boundaries that carry authority. Still, the practice of respecting them protects friendships and other relationships. Perhaps being left with the task of improvising isn't all that problematic. Many boundaries we'd choose to observe are matters of common sense, given the convictions that undergird friendship. For example, there will be boundaries for the physical expression of affection. If it would not be appropriate for the relationship to develop into romance, physical expressions of affection in friendship that create sexual arousal should be avoided. The activities friends engage in should be appropriate to friendship rather than dating. Boundaries for opposite-gender friendships will be generally consistent with those in same-gender friendships.

6. Practicing Self-Awareness

While at some level, a high degree of self-awareness might be a gift that some have and others don't, it seems essential to many areas of the moral life that we nurture within ourselves an awareness of our thoughts, emotions, and motives. This may mean creating time and space for conscious self-reflection. The spiritual discipline of meditation is a long-standing practice. Self-awareness provides an opportunity to monitor the moral quality of a cross-sex friendship. Is it having any negative impact on your committed romantic relationship? Is it becoming an obsession? Are you feeling infatuation within the friendship? Are you jealous of your friend's romantic interests in others? Is the relationship becoming a romance cloaked in friendship? Asking oneself questions that challenge friendships in constructive ways and looking inside ourselves for honest responses will help us embody integrity in those relationships.

7. The Practice of Self-Regulation

Whenever inappropriate feelings or actions arise in opposite-gender friendships, we are responsible to regulate our emotions and our behavior. For example, romantic fantasies are not appropriate in friendships unless it would be appropriate to begin a romantic relationship. Such fantasies should be resisted rather than dwelt on. One should intend and expect that they will go away. When any friendship is conducted in ways that begin to threaten other important relationships, we are responsible to adjust our choices and our actions in ways that honor and respect those other relationships. Friendships of any kind can be powerful, but that can also make them dangerous. Many powerful goods in life also have the capacity to do great harm. It's easy to get "carried away" by things that are good and to rationalize our behavior by its association with a positive good. We avoid the potential harms by taking responsibility for our behavior and choosing to regulate what we do in accordance with our deepest moral convictions.

CONCLUSION

In the face of threats and dangers, I continue to affirm the value and practice of male-female friendships. One of my students put things well when she said, "When we are capable of developing a friendship with a person of the opposite sex, we give ourselves the opportunity to be the best that we can be." I have characterized male-female friendship in a way that makes it some-times difficult but almost always possible—but only if we act with integrity. So it's not really so different than most of the worthwhile relationships we pursue in life. Every relationship of love, no matter which kind of love it is, has the capacity to bless our lives beyond measure, or to hurt us deeply. We nurture the former when we live as people of virtue and conviction.

8

Healing Our Hurts and Recovering a Healthy Sexual Self-Image

INTRODUCTION

SEXUAL HURT TAKES MANY forms. Rape may involve physical violence and deep, complex emotional pain.[1] Poor choices (judged after the fact on more careful reflection) have consequences, and they leave wounds and scars that can last a long time. Behaviors that violate our moral values damage our self-identity. When we hear people call others names ("She's sure a slut!") we might realize they'd say the same about us if they knew our story. There's a continuum of sexual hurts too, though one must be careful about assigning levels of seriousness. To make things even more complicated, people experience the same hurts in many ways and heal in as many ways, and on a variety of personal schedules.

---

1. One important omission from this chapter is the topic of sexual assault. Skipping this important topic isn't meant to assign it lesser importance. On the contrary, the physical, spiritual, and emotional pain is so deep and so unique that it would be better addressed (and at greater length) by those who are more expert. Many personal and print resources are already available, and I advise readers struggling to heal from the hurt of sexual assault, and those seeking to support others, to consult specialized literature on the topic and, when necessary, professionals who can provide more focused personal assistance.

This chapter cannot substitute for the formal and informal therapeutic methods we use to aid our own healing. Professional counseling, informal conversations, self-talk, a journey of forgiving, and the healing balm of time will contribute to personal healing. At best, reading about sexual hurt and healing can help name the kinds of hurt we've experienced and can give us some clues about how to take positive steps toward healing, health, and wholeness. Those are the modest goals of this chapter.

BECOMING AWARE OF THIS TOPIC AS AN ISSUE

I gradually became aware of the importance of this topic through hearing the honest and deeply personal stories my students told as they struggled to articulate their own sexual ethic. They found this task especially difficult after having engaged in past sexual activities that reflected a morality very different from the one they now wanted to claim. I remember one young woman proclaiming, "Well, it's too late for me! I'm already damaged goods."

The self-perception was real. She had a history of casual sex that she now looked back on as meaningless. She allowed males she didn't care about to use her for their own sexual pleasure and was also honest enough to say she had done the same to them. She had violated the sexual ethic she had adopted somewhat automatically from her family and church and now carried a vague sense of guilt and shame. She didn't like her sexual self but had also been taught that past violations of sexual boundaries left her in a permanently broken, damaged, or impure state. "Damaged goods" now seemed like a fixed part of her sexual identity. If she was honest about her history in future relationships, she expected that everyone else would see her that way too. Changing her behavior, she assumed, would do nothing to change that status. Having already crossed a sexual threshold, she felt condemned to repeat and relive the past, as much as she disliked it.

I refuse to accept those conclusions, even though I have learned to recognize that they feel very real to people. The reality must be respected. But I also believe that the power of redemptive healing can overcome the depth of our pain, guilt, and regret and can re-create our sexual self-image, even though it usually involves a gradual journey of healing and restoration.

SEXUAL HURT: LIFE HAPPENS . . . AND SOMETIMES IT HURTS

"How did I ever get into this mess?" If you've ever found yourself in a moral place you didn't like, you have probably asked a similar question. As I think back over the stories I have heard, there are some repeated patterns that help answer that question in at least some very general ways.

1. Sometimes sexual hurt happens in a way that seems somewhat random. A lover pressures us with caring words and a little guilt. A manipulative or forceful partner, perhaps someone who is almost a stranger, pushes us way past our sexual limits. Was it rape? Sexual assault? A consensual mistake? Was intoxication a factor, so that decision-making became fuzzy? When we are victims of sexual pressure or actual sexual assault, what happened doesn't feel like our choice—but still, it happened. Sooner or later you wish that it hadn't.

2. At other times we find ourselves in a moral place that seems unlikely—it isn't morally familiar territory, and we wouldn't have expected to be here if you'd asked a few years ago. No momentous decisions were made and no one forced us to do anything. But here we are, engaging in a level of sexual activity that creates lots of moral or personal discomfort, wondering how we got to this place. Sometimes the answer is "gradually, one small step at a time." Gradualism is an easy way to pass moral limits with a minimum of cognitive and emotional dis-ease. We find that circumstances have simply led over time to increased levels of sexual activity. People get "caught up in the moment" or, if it's a slower process, caught up in the relationship. One thing leads to another, and the circumstances of these sexual encounters overwhelm internalized sexual boundaries—especially when they haven't been consciously owned.

   The thing about gradualism is that it can feel so automatic. You hardly have to make any decisions. Each small step is incremental, so that it feels morally similar to the step just before it. No major crisis emerges over the course of ten small steps—though it might have been a big decision to move from step one to step ten all at once. Gradualism cheats moral decision-making by fooling us into thinking it isn't necessary. But sometimes we wake up and find ourselves at a place we don't want to be. And then we wish that we'd made more conscious decisions along the way. But now it feels too late!

3. A third reason that accounts for some of our regrets about the past is related to the fact that cultural trends show that levels of sexual activity are beginning at earlier ages. As a result, sexual activity often begins well before people are mature enough to make thoughtful, informed decisions. In other words, immaturity gets us into situations we wouldn't choose from a more mature vantage point. But by the time we're mature enough to realize that, it's too late to undo the events—although not too late to heal or change! Regret often enters the picture here: "I wish I had thought about these things before this, because I wouldn't have made the same choices." That's probably true. We learn new things, develop new convictions, and grow wiser with experience. Maturity brings us to a new place and creates new opportunities for the future. But it doesn't give us a way to change the past; it only provides a way to re-vision the past and to move beyond it.

4. Peer pressure is an obvious reason we sometimes do things that our moral convictions tell us not to do. "Everyone's doing it" almost becomes its own moral maxim in the sexual arena, especially in the absence of moral convictions that give us another way to look at what everyone else seems to be doing.

   A male student tells this story: "My church taught me that sex was for marriage and I should wait. My health class taught me that sex was dangerous and scared me away. But my teammates were all about having as many sexual encounters as possible, and they made me feel like there was something wrong with me if I didn't keep up. Eventually the group norms made multiple sexual encounters seem acceptable. We even became proud of being so experienced."

   Morality is taught and lived in community, and peer influence is naturally powerful. We'd expect the most powerful community we're a part of to have the most impact on our lived morality. So when that formative group is comprised of school friends, it's not surprising that we conform to the popular morality around us. It doesn't happen to everyone. There are nonconformists and strong-willed people who resist the pressure to follow the crowd. But many people who find themselves at a more mature place in life look back on their sexual histories as enactments of peer-group behavior.

5. Since sexual activity is often justified by an ethic of "love and commitment," it's common to find people looking back with the realization that they have had an inflated sense of love and commitment. *Love* is a vague term. Being "in love" shares in indistinct notions we associate with the general concept of love. It's fair to ask, "What kind of love

were you in?" But at the time, we didn't necessarily stop to think about that. Was it infatuation? Was it fairy-tale love? Was it wishful thinking? Looking back, it's often easier to see that it wasn't really love. And what about commitment? If commitment is a prerequisite for sexual activity, what kind of commitment counts? Exclusive dating for as long as it lasts? Thinking it will be "forever" and hoping the other person sees it that way too? Planning a future together? Exchanging vows of faithfulness? Looking back, it's often easier to see that there wasn't really much of a commitment.

Conscientious individuals in early stages of sexual morality might think they have reached a fairly advanced stage of moral thinking when they realize that sex doesn't belong in casual relationships that are more recreational than relational. A more advanced realizition might be that it is only appropriate within a relationship characterized by love and commitment. But it's typical for a single twentysomething to have been in many such relationships since he started dating ten years ago. Yet, when looking back, it's easier now to see that what counted as love and commitment was something quite different than what we mean by those words today. The inflated sense of these important-sounding concepts can make it easy to engage in sexual practices that one would have liked to reserve for a relationship characterized by a deeper and more developed understanding of love and commitment.

NAMING SEXUAL HURT AND MOVING TOWARD HEALING

Naming and understanding the kinds of sexual hurts we've experienced is the first step in moving toward healing. Naming hurt helps bring a vague sense of painful memories and feelings into focus. That's not always a comfortable process. Seeing our past hurts clearly, however, gives us more power over them than when they lurk in the shadows. Furthermore, what we mean by healing begins first with the nature of the injury, hurt, or condition that needs to be healed.

And as soon as we try to name it, we will find that *hurt* is not always the best overall term. Victims of sexual violence, for example, have clearly been harmed, but "hurt" seems to diminish the seriousness of the harm. In other cases, the term *hurt* implies to some people a sense of moral judgment. That's not intended here. The hurts I identify reflect the self-perceptions of people who have interpreted the results of their experiences as a form of hurt or pain. Perhaps it's best to think of the term *hurt* simply as a starting point for describing some of the past experiences described below.

Consider some of the ways people experience sexual hurt and, in conjunction with them, some ways we might move toward healing.

Hurting: Living with Unresolved Guilt

Guilt is a form of pain. We usually want to get rid of it if we can. In the Christian tradition, guilt can play a positive role in the moral life. It often serves as a warning that our actions don't correspond to God's will and that there's something wrong. In fact, it means that *we've* done something wrong. Guilt is like a warning light that signals us that something needs attention. We might wish the warning light hadn't gone off, and it might call for a response that we'd rather ignore. But warning lights, like guilt, serve long term well-being, and we need to pay attention to them.

Engaging in sexual practices that violate our moral convictions (our beliefs about what God requires of us) can create a deep sense of guilt. It signals a disconnect between our moral convictions and our lived actions, much like the reality Paul reflects on in Romans 7:19: "For I do not do the good I want, but the evil I do not want is what I do." It also creates a disconnect between a desire to live a life that honors God's will and intentions for us, on the one hand, and the kind of life that's engendering the guilt, on the other. In combination, we might feel like we're caught up in a vicious cycle of sinful behavior that dishonors the God we've decided to love and serve.

When we're caught in a pattern of behavior that fits the cycle Paul describes in Romans 7, guilt becomes more than a momentary warning. If we keep on doing what our conscience tells us is wrong, guilt becomes a permanent discomfort that creates spiritual barriers and threatens to damage our person. When Adam and Eve realized their guilt, they wanted to hide from God. Guilt creates distance, isolation, separation.

Our psychological well-being is also threatened by living in a perpetual state of guilt. Being and feeling guilty isn't meant to be permanent. When the warning light is always on, the machine is under continual stress and runs the risk of serious damage. People sometimes describe this as a "nagging sense of guilt," which implies that they know they are guilty but aren't addressing it directly. Yet if while driving we say, "That bothersome oil light is on again . . . I wish it would just stop nagging me!" we see that dismissing the warning isn't the way to insure health and wholeness. If the oil light is on, you'd better stop and check the oil level and add oil! If our sexual warning light is on, some serious self-examination is called for—and, most likely, a change of behavior.

Sometimes there's such a thing as false guilt. We might have been taught to feel guilty about things we shouldn't feel guilty about. We get rid of that kind of guilt by learning to consciously assess our actions in light of moral convictions that we have embraced. When we do that it's possible to discover that what we once thought was wrong (or were taught to see as wrong) isn't really wrong after all. Discerning whether it's real guilt or false guilt requires careful reflection. It also requires having a clear sexual ethic that can provide a standard for determining which kinds of behaviors nourish us and which we should repent for.

Healing: Repentance, Accepting Forgiveness, and Forgiving Ourselves

Sometimes guilt is legitimate. When it is, guilt indicates a need for repentance, receiving God's forgiveness, and forgiving ourselves. True repentance also includes finding a restored sense of sexual identity by working to bring actions into conformity with moral convictions. This is part of the redemptive process that turns our lives around and sets us back on a journey of striving to live in a way that honors God. It doesn't imply perfection but does imply serious intent and conscious effort.

For some people, knowing that God has granted forgiveness is much easier than forgiving oneself. Why we find it so easy to hold our sins against us when God's grace has already ceased to do that is somewhat of a mystery. God's forgiveness is a transformational experience. St. Paul writes, "So if anyone is in Christ, there is new creation: everything old has passed away; see, everything has become new!" (2 Cor 5:17). But until we accept and affirm God's forgiveness, we don't experience the newness. Someone once said that forgiving yourself means giving up hope for a better past. It seems that we must give up that hope in order to create a better future.

Poet Maya Angelou shares this reflection about forgiving ourselves: "I don't know if I continue, even today, always liking myself. But what I learned to do many years ago was to forgive myself. It is very important for every human being to forgive herself or himself because if you live, you will make mistakes—it is inevitable. But once you do and you see the mistake, then you forgive yourself and say, 'well, if I'd known better I'd have done better,' that's all . . . If we all hold on to the mistake, we can't see our own glory in the mirror because we have the mistake between our faces and the mirror; we can't see what we're capable of being."

Maya Angelou's insights are consistent with a Christian theological understanding of forgiveness. God's forgiveness releases us from the past and frees us to move on toward a more faithful life. But how do we do that? Sometimes with great difficulty! If we draw on the wisdom of others who have described forgiveness, it's possible to summarize some widely recognized steps or stages. In real life the process isn't always so neat and linear. Nevertheless, thinking about steps to forgiving ourselves as a way of nurturing our healing can be helpful. When we can't forgive ourselves, it's sometimes the case that we are wallowing in guilt and just need something to grasp onto in order to start making some progress. Consider this advice, gleaned from many sources:

1. Categorize the offense by naming the wrong you have done. What is it, exactly, that needs forgiving? To name the offense is to face it honestly—something that's already implied in repentance. Naming the offense is also a way of containing it, narrowing it, bringing it out of the cloudiness of our consciousness and into clear focus. Now we know what needs to be forgiven.

2. Identify the hurt that you have done to yourself or others. Doing something wrong usually has negative consequences, and naming the hurt names those consequences. We often feel as bad about the consequences as we do about having committed the offense. This may be true, in part, because we've been taught to be consequentialists and to identify actions as wrong *because of* the negative consequences they produce. But however one resolves that argument in ethics, common sense tells us that actions and consequences are hard to separate, and consequences matter.

3. Repent and apologize. Confession is a rich part of the Christian liturgical tradition and an important spiritual discipline. The practice of confession affirms that it matters when we violate God's will and, at the same time, affirms that a gracious God is already waiting to forgive us. Neither truth should be sacrificed to the other. God's grace doesn't mean that sin doesn't matter. At the same time, intimate knowledge of our sin and the pain that it has caused us and others doesn't cancel out the depth of God's grace. The act of confession, in which we repent and receive God's forgiveness, is at the heart of the Christian tradition: "If we confess our sins, he who is faithful and just will forgive us our sins and cleanse us from all unrighteousness" (1 John 1:9).

A second dimension of forgiveness can be experienced when we have hurt someone to whom we can offer an apology. People aren't always as full of grace, or as ready to forgive quickly, so there's no guarantee that an apology will yield immediate words of forgiveness. But often one of the best and easiest ways to receive forgiveness and then to forgive ourselves is to offer a sincere apology.

4. Stop replaying the past. When we get caught in a loop of reliving the past, the things we did "back then" gain the power to control the present and future. We can't change the past. We can only move forward. But memories heal slowly, so it's also unlikely that healing will be as easy as pressing a stop button. It is possible to shift our focus, however, slowly but intentionally. One place to refocus our attention is on change.

5. Resolve to change things. When Jesus forgives the woman who was brought to him after being caught in the act of adultery (John 8:1–11), he includes in his words of forgiveness and affirmation an important admonition: "Go your way, and from now on, do not sin again." If we need to be forgiven, it's because we've committed a wrong. And if it was wrong, sincere repentance means that we intend not to do it again. We don't always succeed, but our honest intention should be to change, as hard as we think that may be.

A focus on change replaces a cycle of guilt with a positive, constructive goal. The prospect of acting in ways that honor God and that contribute to our physical and emotional well-being is now something to celebrate.

Hurting: Shame and a Damaged Sense of Self

A female student recently told me,

> Sometimes my friends will use words like "trashy," "slut" or "easy" to describe someone we know. I find myself joining in and doing the same thing. But then, when I am honest with myself, I realize the same words could be used to describe me, because I'm doing the same things that earned other girls this reputation. Then I find that I start to think of myself as a slut.

Another explained it like this:

> I've become little more than a sex toy, because I have let other people use me for their own sexual pleasure when I knew that they didn't really care about me as a person. Part of me knows I'm not a sex toy, but when I keep letting people use me and dispose of me, it's hard to think of myself any other way. How can I heal my broken self-image?

When our lived reality contradicts our more ideal image of ourselves, that lived reality can easily erode the ideal. We start to see ourselves as people we don't even like. Seeing ourselves in negative terms as a result of sexual behavior, and internalizing social judgments associated with that behavior, redefines our sense of self in ways that may tell the truth, but it is not the truth we want to claim. If we get to this place, we are living with a sense of *shame*. Sexual shame is a complex topic about which entire books have been written. But it is a common form of hurt we experience, and this summary of the concept can help name an experience some readers will want to learn more about.[2]

We experience shame when we realize that our behaviors don't match up with the ideal self that we'd prefer. The distance between the actual and ideal self is measured by a standard that we absorb from the communities that matter to us—perhaps from family, the church, and the culture that surrounds us. Shame enforces the moral agenda of those communities. That agenda is communicated by explicit rules, unspoken subtle messages, punishments, and the stigmas that get attached to violators. An especially dangerous situation arises when shame is created by unrealistic standards or by people who expect us to be moral heroes when most of us are simply moral commoners struggling to be good as we can be.

The most natural reaction to shame is to hide, due to a sense of unworthiness. The more shame we feel, the more we wish we could just disappear so that no one would notice us. When shame is internalized, it reshapes our sense of self by defining us as defective, contemptible, unwanted. Sometimes we simply wallow in our shame, keeping it hidden. But shame can have more serious impacts on our lives. Studies show that in more extreme cases it can lead to anger, jealousy, control, and the exercise of inappropriate power over others. So whether shame hurts our own self-image or motivates us to hurt others, it clearly needs healing.

Shame isn't always negative. It can also create a powerful motive to make changes toward a more healthy way of expressing ourselves sexually. Shame is an effective motive, experts tell us, when we experience it in a context that is generally loving and supportive. In those settings, shame becomes a temporary state that moves us to address whatever is causing it. It's only when shame becomes a pervasive feature of our lives that it can put down deeper roots and overtake us.

Shame and guilt are obviously closely related. While guilt is a response to a behavior identified as sinful and is resolved by forgiveness, shame affects a more generalized sense of self. Shame may result from the same behavior

2. My summary depends largely on McClintock, *Sexual Shame*.

that creates guilt. But shame occurs when the self-portrait created by our behavior doesn't match up with the idealized self we'd like to be. Shame initially tells us "that sort of behavior is not 'me' . . . it shows me myself in a new way that is utterly shocking. I am not the person I thought I was after all."[3] Shame has the potential to infuse our whole self-image with a sense of unworthiness.

Healing from Shame and Learning to See Myself as a Person of Worth

Christians often willingly accept the designation "sinners" as part of their self-identity. That's a good thing, since to deny it is a form of self-deception and easily leads to charges of hypocrisy. Being able to honestly identify our sins is an essential step in moving toward forgiveness, healing, and renewal. At the same time, however, "sinners" does not define any of us *fully*. We are also God's amazing creations, full of the potential to love God and our neighbors and blessed with a variety of gifts that make each of us wonderful in our own way. Affirming this truth as well helps us know that even sinners are people of worth who are lovable and worthy of being loved by others.

As we've seen above, forgiving ourselves in response to God's forgiveness is inseparable from restoring a positive self-image. But rehabilitating our self-image can involve additional positive steps.

Self-image is a reflection of what we think, say, and do. There's an exception to this, however. The image we have might be skewed, too, when we internalize what others think of us or when we compare ourselves to the implied standard or to the explicit behavior of another person or group. Then it's not what we do but how we fail to measure up to the standard of comparison that creates the picture of the self we dislike. In the sexual arena, this happens frequently. When we compare ourselves to others who are deemed more attractive, more popular, more experienced, or more (fill in your own example), it's easy to judge ourselves as inferior. Or when we compare our own lack of self-control, lack of chastity, or undiscriminating sexual practices to people who seem more "pure," it's easy to see ourselves as morally degenerate (or choose your own negative attribution).

So where do we begin? It's easy to see how a renewed sense of self could help change the behaviors that led to a negative self-image in the first place. If I think I'm dirt, it's more likely I'll let others treat me like I am. Their treatment confirms my negative self-image, and a vicious downward spiral continues. But it's also easy to see how a change in behavior could renew

3. Keyes, "Meaning of Shame and Guilt," 2.

our self-image, creating a new story of our lives, giving us a new sense of confidence, and creating a new self to see in the mirror. So what comes first: A change in self-image or a change in behavior?

Let's begin with a foundational affirmation or two. You are loveable, plain and simple. Henri Nouwen reminds us that a Christian self-image begins with the central truth that God created each one of us and claims us as "beloved." It's an unconditional claim. It precedes our accomplishments and our shortcomings. It's just the way it is: as God's creatures we are loved, period. It doesn't matter what anyone else thinks. It doesn't matter if anyone is *in love* with us or not.

But Nouwen knows that it isn't always easy to hear God's voice reminding us that we are God's "beloved."

> The negative voices are so loud and persistent that it is easy to believe them. That's the great trap. It is the trap of self-rejection . . . When we have come to believe in the voices that call us worthless and unlovable, then success, popularity, and power are easily perceived as attractive solutions . . . As soon as someone accuses me or criticizes me, as soon as I am rejected, left alone, abandoned, I find myself thinking, "Well, that proves once again that I am a nobody."[4]

These other voices, Nouwen says, contradict "the sacred voice that calls us the 'Beloved.' Being the Beloved constitutes the core truth of our existence."[5] This fundamental truth about us challenges the image that shame has created and invites us to see ourselves through the eyes of grace.

Now we can add another layer, a conditional element. Try this exercise: Make a list of twenty things you love about yourself—qualities, characteristics, gifts, and traits. Then expand the list by adding twenty things others could or should love about you. Finally, add a few things *aside from* your personal characteristics that make you worthy of love and respect.

Hopefully, you have a long list of reasons to see yourself as lovable. Of equal importance is your own recognition that others owe you the care and respect these lists imply. While many of us run the danger of thinking too highly of ourselves, I often find that in the arena of sexuality, we have learned to think of ourselves as lowlier than we ought to. The downward spiral we see in the above testimonies reminds us of the danger. I would prefer that people adopt the attitude that says "Hey, watch it! I'm too good to be treated that way!" Or in more a more positive tone: I am a person of worth. God created me with a body, heart, and mind; I am a physical,

4. Nouwen, *Life of the Beloved*, 31–32.
5. Nouwen, *Life of the Beloved*, 33.

emotional, and intellectual person, loved by God in all the fullness of my being and worthy of being loved by others in the same way. Whatever my sins and shortcomings, there are many things about me that are lovable and worthy of being noticed and respected by others. This is true not only of me, but of all God's creatures. Find ways to remind yourself of this.

Finally, there is a third layer necessary for an honest rehabilitation of our sexual self-image. Trying to think differently about ourselves without trying at the same time to embody the differences would be to create a sham. A changed self-image helps support lifestyle changes, but lifestyle changes also help restore a positive self-image. What kinds of changes will support your self-affirmations? What do you need to *do* to bring your actions in line with your emerging or ideal positive self-image as a beloved creature of God?

Hurt: People Sometimes Get Caught Up in a Whirlwind of Sexual Activity That May at First Seem Exciting and Adventurous

Perhaps it's a game of pursuit and conquest. Or it may be a mission to find someone who sees us as attractive, desirable, and sexy. But over time we can also find this to be a whirlwind that threatens to swallow us up in a perpetually dissatisfying series of sexual escapades. What was once exciting now seems both mundane and meaningless. Rather than feeling like sexual freedom, it begins to feel like we're in servitude to a lifestyle that is hard to escape from. It's like a prison without walls.

Getting caught up in a subculture within one's school environment is one way we may find ourselves in this situation. The term *hookup culture* is one way to describe the powerful cultural forces that seem to hold us in their grip. A college sorority member described it like this:

> All of my friends in the sorority always go out [partying] on the weekends. We drink too much, hookup with guys we hardly know, and do things sexually that often make us feel disgusting the next day. But that's what everyone does, and if I don't want to sit home alone on the weekends, I don't have much choice. I'd like to say no to hooking up like that, but when I look around me, I don't really see an alternative.

Stories like this one are sad because they portray people who seem to be living in a self-imposed slavery to a cultural practice (hooking up) they don't like. But our subcultures are powerful, and they create constraints that make the word *self-imposed* a bit too simplistic. Part of what makes a culture is a set of practices that become routine. When we engage in those practices, they get inside of us in the form of habits, dispositions, attitudes, and expectations. This process of enculturation is almost invisible most of the time. But once culture has been internalized, we feel at home in it, and it creates a "world" within us that generates a kind of comfortable conformity. When this happens, it doesn't *feel* like we are imprisoned, but if we want to resist cultural pressures, or even escape from a segment of culture altogether, the bonds of culture will be hard to break.

Escaping from this source of sexual hurt will require finding the personal and social resources that can empower us to take charge of our own lives rather than letting culture or peers subtly manipulate us into acting in ways that are contrary to what we really want. That task will likely involve creating cultural alternatives within the realm of our local communities, since resisting powerful cultural influences is best accomplished when people with shared convictions band together to embody an alternative.

We can get caught up in our own habitual behavior as well. While this normally happens in conjunction with larger cultural pressures, it can often feel more personal, and perhaps without an awareness of larger social forces. After all, our choices are both free expressions of our will and at the same time complicated expressions of formative factors that impinge on us from outside. When we focus on our individual choices, we highlight the dimension of life that can be understood with terms like *habitual*.

Another student's testimony: "I keep making the same bad choices over and over again. I've become a habitual consumer of casual sex. How can I escape from this pattern and learn to trust myself? How can I heal my old habits and replace them with a new quality of romantic relationships?"

Social scientists tell us that habits are complex patterns of behavior that are formed in association with social cues and an associated response in our memory.[6] In studies of habit formation and attempts to change bad habits, students have identified several examples of habitual patterns they want to change: staying up too late, eating junk food, partying too much, getting caught in cycles of negative thinking, and engaging in risky sexual practices, to name a few. These are obviously complex behaviors when compared to biting one's fingernails. But researchers claim that they are often habitual behaviors. They have become automated responses prompted by particular environments and social cues and learned through a process of repetition.[7]

6. Neal, Wood, and Quinn, "Habits," 198–202.

7. Neal, Wood, and Quinn, "Habits," 198.

Habitual behaviors are hard to change. While habit formation isn't fully understood, studies confirm what we experience in everyday life: once formed, habits are hard to break. One reason for this is that habits don't require conscious thought, and they are therefore less affected by our good intentions. We can't easily change bad habits simply because we want to. "The mechanisms of habitual control pose a particular challenge for changing behavior . . . Changing minds does not necessarily mean changing behavior."[8]

When our intentional goals and commitments conflict with behavioral patterns that have become habitual, it's easy to feel like we're unable to get off the treadmill. Perhaps this is just the other side of the coin: sometimes we feel like slaves to the cultural pressures bearing down on us and at other times we feel like slaves to the habitual behaviors we struggle to change. When the habits that grip us are also dissatisfying and meet with our own moral disapproval, they create a serious negative dissonance in our lives.

Healing Repetitive Life Patterns and Lifestyle Habits

Habits get deep inside us due to repetitive action. They make being good (virtuous) seem like second nature sometimes, but that also means that our vices sometimes become second nature as well. We unlearn bad habits by taking up new actions that break the old connections. We heal old habits by replacing them with new ones. But this is a case where the truism applies: *easier said than done.* There aren't any formulas to make it easy.

Healing habitual patterns of behavior begins with developing a clear sense of what the alternative will look like. You can't start re-habituating yourself if you don't have something specific in mind. In our sexual lives, this means having a clearly understood and well-defined sexual ethic. In this sense a sexual ethic serves something like a moral mission statement for our sexual lives. It directs us toward sexual activity that is life-enhancing and creates health, wholeness, and happiness. In other words, a morality grounded in an understanding of what God wants for our sexual lives provides theological grounding for the development of new habitual patterns.

A psychological understanding of how habits are formed provides some practical assistance in bringing about change. Research has shown that behavioral cues that come from *situations* and *contexts* are often more powerful than our intentions or our "willpower" when it comes to changing habitual patterns of behavior. That's why we often find ourselves doing

8. Neal, Wood, and Quinn, "Habits," 200.

what we just said we wouldn't do! "Habits form when people gradually learn associations between a response and cues in the performance context."[9] If this theory is accepted, the best way to break bad habits is to break the connection between situational cues and the unwanted response. If situational contexts elicit habitual behavior, one strategy is to change the context. Context change can disrupt the normal patterns of negative behavior, making it more likely that our intentions will be free to create new patterns of behavior that correspond with our values and goals. But contexts can't always be changed, so researchers also suggest that we can use "vigilant monitoring." This involves a "don't do it" response in the context that elicits the habit, creating a disruption that gradually erodes the more automatic, habitual response.

Find a community of partners. It's easier to act with others, especially when changes in behavior and social context are involved. That's probably part of the reason Jesus called his followers to form communities that could resist dominant culture and reshape character within the moral community we've come to call the church. Calling people into the community of the church means calling them out of other communities. In similar fashion, sometimes changing our sexual activity requires changing the structure and activity of social life. If friends are creating a social context that encourages negative habitual behavior, it would be easier to change if our friends decided to change too—or more radically, if we found new friends whose social life supported the goals we're striving to embody.

The concept of accountability is closely associated with the idea that change happens more effectively in community. Accountability has become a popular word in recent years, but there is wisdom behind its popularity. If changing bad habits means disrupting the connection between the social cues and the response they elicit, then voluntarily having someone hold us accountable can strengthen the disruption, whether it takes the form of changing contexts or monitoring habitual responses more closely. When people whose company we value add their support to our good intentions, we often find added strength to say yes to what's good (but hard to do) and no to what's destructive and unhealthy (even though it's sometimes the easy path).

After making a serious attempt to eliminate habits we deem bad and to replace them with those we consider good, it makes sense to step back and do some honest self-evaluation. Do I feel healthier, happier, more fulfilled? If so, this will serve as an intrinsic reward.

9. Quinn et al., "Can't Control Yourself?," 499.

Hurt: Destruction of Trust

Another form of sexual hurt involves the destruction of trust. As a student recently told me, "I've been hurt by so many men, so many times, that I find myself unable to trust any of them anymore. You talk about finding a guy who will respect and care about me, but where do you find guys like that? I'm sorry, but I just don't trust them." While repeated experiences like this solidify the damage, sometimes it only takes one experience of broken trust to create hesitancy and pessimism. The harm can happen in any gender combination, too. Once trust is broken, it's hard to regain.

When people or experiences destroy our trust, they harm a central part of us, and a part of us that is necessary to make relationships healthy. When we try to enter a new relationship unable to trust, it soon becomes obvious that an important foundation is missing.

Trust is always a risk. People take advantage of us, manipulate our emotions, tell us lies. When we recognize this, it becomes harder to trust. Even the people who claim to love us sometimes let us down. Fragile hearts can be broken and mistreated in so many ways and can take a long time to heal. Trusting again, it seems, will only open us to new possibilities of pain. Why lay our hearts open in such unprotected ways—especially if it seems so likely they will be hurt? Of course the only way to completely protect ourselves from broken trust would be to create an island of human isolation. Since, I assume, most readers find that unacceptable, we seem to be stuck with needing to take the risk. That doesn't make it an easy one.

Healing Our Willingness to Trust

Anyone who has already taken the risk and been hurt knows that learning to trust again feels like a much bigger risk the next time. Innocence is lost, the costs of broken trust have already hurt, our fears have been fed, and it's not easy to trust again. Recovering broken trust is sometimes a journey of small steps over a great distance. This can be true whether we're learning to trust again the specific person who violated our trust or whether we're learning to give someone else a chance. Some steps toward relearning how to trust might include the following.

Learning from the Past

Trust is compatible with wisdom and caution, and it certainly includes taking reasonable steps to protect ourselves from future harm. While serious hurt is best avoided, one advantage of having faced difficult situations in the past is that we can learn from them and assess new choices on the basis of newly acquired wisdom. When we have learned some things from the past, we have new resources for moving forward. Perhaps the term *cautious optimism* describes the next stage. *Caution* about new relationships (as opposed to avoidance) is a realistic recognition of potential dangers. *Optimism* indicates a shift from not trusting to being willing to give trust a chance, replacing pessimism with hopefulness.

Guarding Our Hearts

I'm critical of this phrase in another section of this book. When it's taken too far it suggests rejecting closeness and intimacy in ways that hinder healthy growth. But the phrase is so commonly used in some Christian circles that is seems worthy of rehabilitation. And that suggests a helpful analogy. If you've ever been injured, perhaps even to the point of needing physical therapy, you know that there's a transitional phase as you move from "keeping off" the injured limb to regaining full use of it. Rehabilitating our trust, like rehabilitating our bodies, is not an all-or-nothing approach. It involves a gradual movement from serious protection (guarding) to stages of progressive rehabilitation and on to full, healthy use.

Following a situation of broken trust, injured hearts need time to heal. Guarding hearts in a very protective manner makes lots of sense here. But hearts (as a metaphor for the emotional and passionate dimension of a person) are also meant to be used, like arms and legs. People with open hearts and welcoming hearts express the fruits of God's Spirit. Learning to trust again, like learning to run again, requires a process of rehabilitation, during which we make careful, wise, and healthy choices and do our best to insure that we're building strength and endurance and won't be injured again.

Trusting Wisely

Trusting wisely includes assessing benefits and burdens. This implies that trust is both an overall view of the world and, at the same time, a conscious choice based on careful discernment. Sometimes we say, "He's sure a trusting soul" when someone's overall disposition of trust seems to omit the necessary discernment in specific situations. Becoming *trusting* as an enduring feature of our character is a trait that's built up over time. Deciding whether to trust an individual in a specific time and place is also a situation-specific decision. Since trust is unavoidably a risk-taking venture, it makes sense to think of it as a process of weighing benefits and burdens—a decision process sometimes used in medical decision-making. Careful discernment doesn't guarantee the outcome, but it does bring our best thinking to the forefront and makes future hurt less likely.

There are many possible benefits to trust that we might find applicable in whatever circumstances we're thinking about. Trusting someone else often invites them to trust us too, and mutual trust is a foundation for strong relationships like friendship and romance. Trust eases our fears and anxiety, and does so increasingly as we learn that the other is worthy of the trust we've given them. Trust makes space for sharing our faith, ideas, viewpoints, personal stories, hopes, and dreams. These are the things that build and deepen relationships and make them increasingly valuable and meaningful. Trust gives us a sense of security; we can rest in it, be assured by it, and depend on it.

The risks of trust are real too. People can use the trust we place in them to take advantage of us. Trusting someone presumes that they are decent, caring, respectful people. If they fall short of these qualities in ways we don't recognize, it's like walking out onto a bridge that can't really carry the weight. Trust risks that someone else will put our well-being before their own. But people don't always keep our secrets when they see some benefit in breaking confidence, and they sometimes put themselves first when deciding how to use information we have shared. When it comes down to it, people sometimes just aren't trust-*worthy*. We assume trust functions like a safety net that will never let us fall. But due to our humanness, our imperfection, sometimes the net breaks.

Is it ever worth trusting someone, especially after we've been badly hurt by broken trust? That's a question each of us must answer by carefully and honestly weighing the benefits and burdens involved in deciding to trust a person or situation . . . and then hoping for the best.

The Hurt of Unresolved Regret

Among many of my students I've found a recurring theme of sexual hurt that takes the form of regret. It gets expressed in several ways; here are three examples:

> I've been naive. But now that I stop to think about it, I don't like the way I've lived. I guess I just never really thought much about sex, and ended up going further than I wanted to with more

people than I wanted to. I wish I had thought about my limits and values before I started dating.

I never really intended to have sex before I was married. But when I did it, I thought I was in love and wasn't really old enough to know what that meant. Now I wish I had waited.

I wasn't against sex before marriage, so when my relationship with my former girlfriend reached the stage where we were talking about marriage, we decided it was OK to have sex. But now I'm engaged to someone else who waited for marriage (and for me) and she's having a very hard time with the fact that I'm not a virgin. I regret the decision I made a few years ago and I wish I could undo the past.

Whether or not we think each of these people *should* regret the past, the fact that they do creates a very real form of sexual hurt they carry with them. When regret is present, it can be a source of real pain.

I must add that there is a minority report on this matter. Some students reflect back on their sexual histories from their present vantage point and disapprove of what they've done—but they are quick to add that they "have no regrets" because "it was a learning experience" and it helped make them who they are today. I use quotation marks here because this testimony is stated so similarly from one person to the next that I wonder if they're quoting someone! If we take these reports at face value, it seems that not all of our self-acknowledged mistakes are worthy of regret.

Regret is different from guilt, and it's important to distinguish them. Guilt is a response to doing what we believe is wrong. Guilt results from violating God's will, whether we find it revealed in laws, commands, principles that can be drawn from biblical teachings, or examples set by Jesus. Repentance and accepting God's forgiveness, and the forgiveness of those we've wronged, is the Christian response to guilt. In contrast, regret is usually the result of looking back from our present vantage point and knowing we could have done better. It's the result of wishing we had made choices in the past based on what we now know, believe, and care about. A sense of regret arises when we disapprove of past choices and the consequences of past actions.

It's easy to get caught in a recurring loop of regret. When we look back and assess the past on the basis of who we are today, we find ourselves applying a new standard that we didn't have then. Notice the way people state their testimonies of regret: "Now that I stop to think about it, I don't like the way I've lived." We realize that if we could return to the past as the people we are today, we would make different decisions that would likely have better consequences, possibly preventing the outcome we now regret. But we weren't the same person back then, so we made choices based on what we had to work with at the time. Even if many things haven't changed, our perspectives have, so we see things differently. We didn't have the advantage *then* of seeing the way we do *now*. But the differences can go deeper than hindsight, and we might have been even more different than we realize. We acted as the people we were, based on the way that our time, culture, personality, and social location shaped our person and our choices *at that time*. No one has yet discovered a way of undoing the past based on the insights and wisdom of the present.

Healing Our Regrets

Moving beyond regret will obviously require something other than changing the past according to our present values. If we shift our way of thinking about it, regret is actually self-affirming and focused on the present. It is self-affirming because it embraces our current way of looking at our sexual practices and wishes that these values could have existed before. It is present-oriented because it implies a new way of thinking and acting today, even if that can't change yesterday. Unfortunately, regrets are hard to shake and there are no magical formulas. But here are some steps to consider:

- Moving beyond regret first means deciding to give up on changing the past. You can't "take it back" or ask for a "do-over." It's already out there. What's done is done. No amount of hand-wringing or instant-replaying will change anything about what has already happened, so neither of those are very productive ways of handling regret.

- We can embrace the growth that has produced a new perspective and let it (rather than the past) define our lives. Even though the past is unchangeable, the present and future are not. This change in thinking allows us to make positive use of our regret by identifying the lessons we've learned and asking how we can apply them. Regret can become motivation to reshape our future in ways that correspond more closely to the values we've used to disapprove of certain aspects of the past. "I wish I had never . . ." can become a resolution: "I'm going to try my best to . . ."

- Progress in the journey to leave regret behind will be hindered by an expectation of perfection. Regretting our imperfection serves no useful purpose. Still, many of us tend to be perfectionists. Perhaps as long as we are realistic perfectionists, this can work. If perfection (or perhaps we should call it *moral excellence*) serves as an ideal to strive for in the future, it serves us well if we see our lives as a journey toward sanctification. But if it serves as a standard to measure the past, we will always be burdened by regret. We can only do our best with what we have and who we are today, and we can't know for sure until tomorrow, or in God's distant future, whether we're making the right choices today.

Hurt: Sexual Activities Can Ruin Our Reputations

Since reputations are valuable, and because they also become part of our identity, this can be a serious form of sexual hurt. Of course, it can also be a sexual hurt for which we say, "The only person to blame is yourself." There have been a lot of public cases in which prominent individuals have hurt their reputations by making sexual choices that violate popular morality. (After all, reputation is based on popular morality, whether we agree with existing moral norms or not.) A former governor recently revealed that he had a child with another woman. A member of the U.S. House of Representatives just admitted sending "lewd" photographs to women he'd met online. Not long ago a famous married golfer had several simultaneous affairs. Famous people may fall further and with more publicity, but a damaged reputation can hurt anyone.

A student wrote, "I've ruined my reputation. Everyone knows I'm easy. No good guys want to date me. The only ones who are interested only want me for sex." Another wrote, "People who know me know that I party and hook up a lot. They also know I regularly attend chapel on campus. I know they all see me as a hypocrite."

Bad reputations hurt because they serve as reminders of our dark side. It makes it harder to ignore or hide from. But reputations aren't like internal guilt. We can't always hide from our guilt, but we can often hide it from others. Reputations have gone public. Bad ones advertise what we wish no one knew. They define our identity to others in ways that can affect what people think of us and how they act toward us.

Healing Bad Reputations

Bad reputations are easy to acquire but hard to rehabilitate. The people who are aware of them aren't necessarily aware of the whole story, the depth of one's personal struggle, or a more recent history of reform. Even when we work hard to overcome a bad reputation, it's hard to erase. Reputations are always partial representations at best. Even good reputations could be stained if everyone knew the whole story! Bad reputations would often be softened if people had more information. Often, knowing more about the whole person would lead to more nuanced and more generous assessments. That's why it's easy to excuse our friends for the same behaviors that can lead us to condemn others. In the end, we don't have much control over what others know and think. If we know we have a reputation we don't want, we are also likely to feel a sense of helplessness to change it—even if we change ourselves. That sometimes means living with the consequences for a while.

There is no simple way to repair a bad reputation because nothing we do can be guaranteed to have quick results. Like most forms of healing, healing from a bad reputation takes time and patient effort. Here are some steps toward healing to consider:

- Reputations are usually reflections of our behavior, even if they are not wholly accurate reflections. The first step in changing our reputation is adopting behaviors that will eventually create the kind of reputation we desire. This presumes the value of integrity, where reputation isn't a sham but a truthful reflection of the way we live. The ideal is to adopt a sexual ethic that makes sense and then strive to live by it. Obviously, repairing one's reputation requires repairing one's lived morality, so it's a very demanding and difficult kind of work!

- Since changing our behavior is difficult, especially if it requires undoing established patterns or standing against cultural norms, it is important to set realistic goals for personal change and take one step at a time. Cinderella was changed in an instant by a magical fairy. Change doesn't happen that way in real life, at least not for most of us. Setting specific and attainable goals and moving one step at a time helps break a task that looks overwhelming into manageable steps. Patterns of sexual behavior and the reputations that arise from these weren't formed in a day, and for most of us, restoring a good reputation will be a gradual process requiring persistence and patience.

- Don't expect perfection. If others seem to expect you to be perfect, they are probably living with a double standard that you can't do anything about. Reputations are by definition connected to what other people think, so when we are concerned about reputation, what people think does matter. But at another level, what you know counts most. When people observe an isolated action, they don't know which direction you're moving. If a slip-up is taken by others as evidence that your bad reputation is deserved, only you will know that you are headed in a new direction. Instead of focusing on perfection, focus on the efforts you are making to change.

9

Responding to Questions from My Students

INTRODUCTION

During a course that I have taught many times, students are invited to submit one or more of their own questions about sexual ethics. In case there's something we didn't cover that they think must still be addressed, this gives us a chance to ponder and respond to real questions from people who are grappling with them in everyday life.

From among the many pages of questions I've collected over the years, I have chosen eight to reflect on here. They are the questions that have been asked most often and most persistently. Many important questions aren't included here—and when it comes right down to it, every question, if it was posed seriously, was important to the person who asked it.

My responses unavoidably draw on what has already been said in previous chapters, and if someone skips ahead to read only the answers, they can't be fully understood without thinking about the foundational convictions and approaches to Christian sexual ethics already explained. The "answers" are intended to give real guidance to those who are asking them. But in getting to a conclusion, there's some "thinking out loud" that goes on along the way. That's mostly because this book has been an invitation to the reader to *think about* sexual ethics and not simply to learn the answers.

THE QUESTIONS

1. *Is it morally appropriate for an unmarried Christian couple to receive or give any form of oral sex? Is oral sex the same as sexual intercourse as far as its permissibility or non-permissibility in a nonmarital relationship? Can you still consider yourself a* virgin *and a* God-honoring *person if you participate in oral sex?*

2. *What exactly is lust? Is there a distinction between lust and sexual desire? Do you have to feel guilty about lust if there is no action associated with it? Or are thoughts just as sinful because they will eventually lead there?*

3. *Does it make any sense to claim a "second virginity"? Is there such a thing as a "born-again virgin"? What would it mean to say that you've gained back your virginity?*

4. *What should you do if your partner's sexual ethic is different from yours? Can a relationship survive and be healthy if this is the case? If a couple has sex and only one of them decides it was a mistake, is it possible for them to stay together and be abstinent?*

5. *Are there any absolutes in Christian sexual ethics, or is it just up to each individual or couple to decide for themselves? Can a universal line be drawn about what kinds of sexual practices are allowed before marriage, or is it up to each person to draw this moral line for herself? If there are universal Christian standards, how should we respond to Christian friends who violate those standards? As a Christian, is it fair to judge another person for having sex?*

6. *When you are engaged and know you are getting married, is it morally wrong to have sex before the actual wedding? If marriage is necessary, when are you actually married? Why isn't it enough to know that you are in love and intend to live together forever?*

7. *Am I a bad Christian if I engage in sex outside of marriage? How do you deal with past actions that you are ashamed of? Can you ask forgiveness for something you're pretty sure will happen again?*

8. *What does God say about masturbation? Is it right in light of Christian morality? Does masturbation count as sex? Is masturbation considered unethical?*

1. Oral Sex

Is it morally appropriate for an unmarried Christian couple to receive or give any form of oral sex? Is oral sex the same as sexual intercourse as far as its permissibility or non-permissibility in a nonmarital relationship? Can you still consider yourself a virgin *and a* God-honoring person *if you participate in oral sex?*

Whether or not it's morally appropriate, oral sex is a common form of sexual activity in both casual and serious relationships. According to data from the Centers for Disease Control and Prevention, about 80 percent of males and females between ages 25 and 44 have engaged in oral sex with persons of the opposite gender. When the statistics focus on teens aged 15 to 19 (both male and female), 48 percent report having already engaged in oral sex.[1] From a health perspective, oral sex itself carries no risk of pregnancy and is *perceived* to have a lower risk of sexually transmitted disease than sexual intercourse—even though the risk actually remains high.

People engage in oral sex in a variety of circumstances. For some, oral sex is simply a casual recreational activity, one means among many of giving and receiving sexual pleasure with no strings attached. It is not regarded with a high degree of moral importance or meaning. Oral sex might also be a form of youthful sexual experimentation. In more serious relationships it might be an alternative to sexual intercourse for those who aren't yet ready for sex or who believe that oral sex is allowed, while sexual intercourse is prohibited. And for others, oral sex is a form of foreplay leading to sexual intercourse.

Prior to considering a Christian assessment, we could evaluate oral sex using what we might call common standards of human decency. At least three basic principles come to mind. The first is *consent*. Our bodies are considered private space, and the right to touch, caress, or sexually stimulate them is based on the freely given consent of each person involved. A second widely recognized principle is the requirement to *do no harm* to others. While people might vary in their assessment of what counts as harm and whether they are likely to experience harmful consequences, this standard obligates participants to do their best to evaluate their actions and to conduct themselves in ways that seek to avoid harmful consequences. In addition, the requirement to treat others with *mutual respect* is a norm that applies to our social interactions. At a minimum this means that we treat each other as people of worth who have feelings, ideas, values, and goals that matter.

1. Centers for Disease Control and Prevention, "Key Statistics."

Judging the morality of oral sex by these standards might raise concerns about oral sex under certain circumstances, but they provide no universal basis for disapproval. Christian sexual ethics typically accepts these standards as minimal requirements but goes beyond them to provide a richer, theologically informed moral stance.

In serious and committed relationships, including those of Christian couples, oral sex often serves as an alternative to sexual intercourse, especially when having sex isn't yet considered appropriate. I have encountered many college students over the years who have engaged in oral sex but have not engaged in sexual intercourse. Most were taught that "sex outside marriage is sinful"—but little or nothing was said about oral sex. So they reason, "But it's not intercourse, right? So (perhaps) it's permissible." Still, some doubt often lingers, as it does in the question we're considering here.

From a number of surveys done a decade ago it's clear that many teens and even health educators don't think oral sex "counts" as sex. Instead, it functions as a substitute when a couple is not yet ready for coitus or when there are health or pregnancy risks. Even in educational programs designed to promote abstinence, the line dividing abstinence from non-abstinence is often vague.[2] Confusion about what counts as sex obviously complicates how to apply moral boundaries.

Is oral sex simply going *too* far? To ask about oral sex this way is to ask a version of the familiar question, How far is too far? In my experience, unmarried Christians ask this question when they are in a serious and exclusive romantic relationship that is moving from less intimate to more intimate forms of physical activity but wonder whether there is some line that shouldn't be crossed. However, their willingness to entertain the possibility of oral sex grows out of a desire to find appropriate physical expressions of love that are intended as part of a meaningful relationship of love growing between the couple.

When this context and these intentions accompany oral sex, its *meaning* as a sexual act is different from the meaning of the same physical actions when they take place in a casual, recreational context. If, after a casual hookup, a partner asked, "What did that mean to you?" it wouldn't be surprising to hear a response like "What do you mean, what did it *mean*? It didn't *mean* anything! I thought we were just doing it because it felt good." But the fact that oral sex is more meaningful in some contexts than others doesn't yet answer the question!

The only way to give a definitive answer is to adopt a moral framework that provides reasons to say yes or no. In other words, it all depends. The

2. Remez, "Oral Sex among Adolescents."

answer depends on your sexual ethic. While that may sound like an easy way out, I see no way of avoiding it. As I have argued in prior chapters that explore approaches to Christian sexual ethics, the moral conclusions one draws are inescapably connected to the presuppositions one starts with when deciding how to approach moral choices and the kind of people we want to be. Here are some ways we might approach the issue:

Nonmoral Aversion

Some people simply have an aversion to oral sex, for whatever reason. Perhaps this takes the form of a nonreflective moral judgment they have absorbed from family, friends, or society. We often come to express moral disapproval this way. "It's just wrong!" But when pressed to say why, we aren't sure. Maybe it is, maybe it isn't. An aversion of this type is prerational. Someone who feels this aversion might find their reasons in one of the options below.

"I don't like it."

Or perhaps oral sex just seems disgusting. That's a matter of personal judgment. I sometimes refer to this kind of moral assessment as the "yuck factor." Much of our moral training identifies some things as "dirty" in order to ingrain an aversion to those things. Oral sex might have been one of those. Or it might just be something that people don't like, don't enjoy, or don't want to do. That's not a moral judgment yet, it's simply a fact about how someone thinks or feels. Whenever someone has an aversion to any form of sexual activity, the first responsibility of others is to respect that fact. While oral sex might not be morally wrong to one partner, it would be morally wrong not to respect another's choice not to engage in it.

A Boundary Violation

If one approaches this question with a boundary ethic in mind, one might claim that oral sex is *never* appropriate outside marriage (or, for some, even within marriage) because it crosses a moral boundary. Oral sex might be seen as an example of what could be included in the biblical phrase "sexual immorality" (see 1 Cor 7:2). This might be especially so in connection with either kind of aversion described above, since there's a commonsense connection between immorality and things we find dirty, disgusting, or immoral—even if there may not be a solid foundation for thinking they are. But the Bible never specifically identifies oral sex as immoral, so those who include it are making a pre-biblical choice about what actions to include in the phrase "sexual immorality."

But perhaps oral sex isn't simply one among many forms of sexual immorality and is actually "the same as intercourse." If it is, then it could be evaluated using the same considerations that Christians apply to sexual intercourse outside marriage. But is oral sex the same as intercourse? That all depends on what one means by "the same." Physiologically it isn't. Different body parts are involved. Another reason to argue that it isn't the same is to note that oral sex isn't a procreative act. But sexual actions need not be procreative to be considered good. The capacity of sexual activity to express love and create unity can make non-procreative forms of sex significant and meaningful. If oral sex isn't the same as intercourse but is nevertheless an action that can participate in its own kind of goodness, it's clear why someone might claim to be a virgin even if they have engaged in oral sex.

But if by "the same" we mean that it has a similar emotional intensity requiring similar levels of trust, and demanding a similar level of personal vulnerability, then oral sex and sexual intercourse start to look very much alike. Oral sex and sexual intercourse can also be very much alike when we consider the motive and intent. Either might be used to express a deep and intimate love, to create or nurture a close personal bond, or to give and experience physical pleasure through orgasm. It is this similarity that easily leads someone with a boundary ethic to consider oral sex to be the kind of sexual act that belongs on the marital side of the boundary.

Relational Ethics and Conditional Approval

What Christian approach to sexual ethics might see oral sex as a healthy and appropriate way to express love in a serious committed relationship between people who aren't yet married? A relational ethic provides a way to answer the question with qualified permission. A relational ethic says that the morality of sexual activity is based on the quality and characteristics of the love present in a relationship. What makes a sexual act good is that it reflects the deeper goodness of the relationship in which it occurs and the depth and character of the love that it communicates. (In order to fully understand how a relational approach would apply, the reader needs to understand the overall approach described in chapter 4.)

If one assesses the morality of oral sex within the framework of a relational ethic, it could be seen as morally appropriate when it is a *meaningful* expression of love at an appropriate stage in the development of the relationship. Without repeating the detailed explanation of a relational ethic, this would mean that oral sex communicates a deep and holistic love that is present in a variety of ways in the nonsexual components of the relationship. In this approach to sexual ethics, oral sex is appropriate when it means the same thing each person means by all of their other expressions of love and by the way they care for each other in every aspect of their relationship.

One of the most important components of a relational ethic is the expectation that sexual activity is a meaningful expression of love in the holistic context of a relationship. Consider this set of questions as one measure of the meaning of a relationship: Do you trust each other with those parts of your life that matter the most? Do you feel safe sharing issues and concerns and fears that are private and personal? Do you know each other intimately and expect to be treated with care, compassion, and respect as you reveal the deepest parts of yourself to the other? When sexual expressions of love take place in the context of honest responses to questions like these, a relational ethic judges it as a good thing. But notice that one doesn't draw this conclusion lightly. It's the product of careful consideration of the variety of factors that are part of a relational ethic.

An ethic of character also does not automatically rule out oral sex as a way to express love through acts of physical intimacy, even prior to marriage. Once again, a more complete understanding of this approach is necessary to give us a thorough answer (see chapter 5). In brief, oral sex can be an expression of love by people who embody the concerns and character that are dimensions of an ethic of sexual integrity. The character of their sexual expressions of love is given positive moral value by the kind of people they are, and the characteristics of integrity minimize the possibility of distorting the meaningfulness of sexual expressions of love.

In Summary

If this "it all depends on your basic approach to ethics" response leaves you uncertain about oral sex, it's most likely that the uncertainty stems from a more fundamental one: the uncertainty about how to approach sexual ethics in general. I'm convinced that many people have mixed feelings about oral sex because they have mixed feelings about how to approach sexual ethics. A vague sense of boundaries makes one feel that oral sex is probably going too far. But at the same time, one realizes that the relational context and the qualities people bring to a relationship really do make a moral difference and that perhaps oral sex can be morally appropriate when the right relational factors are present. Mixing our approaches to sexual ethics, especially in an unconscious way, can generate lots of confusion.

Making a decision about the morality of oral sex is clearly connected to how one approaches sexual ethics. A boundary ethic provides a clear way to say that oral sex is wrong (especially outside marriage) because it is an action that is included in the biblical prohibition of sexual immorality. And even if one can't produce an explicit biblical condemnation of oral sex, one can claim that it is sufficiently similar to sexual intercourse that it ought to be reserved for marriage.

Both a relational ethic and an ethic of sexual integrity provide a way to understand how oral sex, under the right conditions, could be a meaningful and appropriate way for people to express their love for each other prior to marriage. In both of these approaches, the quality of an action is grounded in the intentions, meaning, and character of the act rather than on predetermined boundaries.

2. Lust

What exactly is lust? Is there a distinction between lust and sexual desire? Do you have to feel guilty about lust if there is no action associated with it? Or are thoughts just as sinful because they will eventually lead there?

Jesus clearly warns against lust in the Sermon on the Mount: "But I say to you that everyone who looks at a woman with lust has already committed adultery with her in his heart" (Matt 5:28). Since the moral seriousness of lust is equated with adultery, it is clearly a weighty matter. So for starters, it's important to know what the warning against lust actually prohibits.

Whatever it is, the word itself conjures up lots of negative images. Lust isn't something you'd want others to see you doing. It sounds darkly secret. Lust is associated with unbridled sexual passion and is the presumed driving force behind pornography and prostitution—sex for sale. But those familiar images of lust aren't very helpful when it comes to deciding more carefully how to control and conduct ourselves sexually—and especially how to keep our sexual thoughts under control in ways that honor God.

There seems to be a lot of confusion about exactly what's being prohibited when the Bible identifies lust with sin. One can easily find hints in the Christian tradition that say virtually anything associated with sexual pleasure is lust. But if we cast the net too broadly, too much gets caught up in the category of the sordid and sinful, and that creates a lot of false guilt. So first let's distinguish what lust isn't, and then what it is.

Lust is not the same thing as sexual desire. To simply equate the two quickly leads to a sense of false guilt. God created us so that sexual desires are part of our humanness. These desires emerge naturally and are part of the "normal" that God intended for us. This doesn't mean that they shouldn't be channeled and controlled. What is good and natural can be distorted by sin. But it can also be nurtured to honor God and God's intentions for human sexuality. When used rightly, sexual desire can glorify God and celebrate our life and our sexuality as God intended it. Sexual desire is part of our God-given humanity and is not something to feel guilty about.

Sexual desire leads us to seek the unity and love Christians celebrate in marriage. It leads us to the bodily unity (one-flesh union) experienced in sexual intercourse, and it encourages us to bring new life into the world. Sexual desire encourages the bonding of two lives into one, and in that oneness creates new ones whom we love and nurture. We could have been created to reproduce through mere physical, instinctual behavior. But God didn't make us that way. Human sexual activity is enveloped in thoughts and feelings. It involves deep emotional intimacy and intense physical pleasure. As a result, it produces not just offspring but also creates, communicates, and celebrates—sometimes even in ways that seem mystical—the bonds of love we experience in communion with another. Desire prepares us to merge our bodies with those with whom we are also merging our hearts and minds in a life union.

There are some things that get associated with lust that we need to keep separate, since they are more aptly associated with sexual desire. Physical attraction is one of these. There's nothing wrong with finding someone attractive or physically appealing. Like all good things, we can take this too far, but the appreciation of someone's physical characteristics isn't sinful. Neither is sexual arousal, which can occur whether you want it to or not, with no conscious decision. It's just the way we are made. And perhaps most important, sexual temptations aren't in themselves sinful either, even though temptation is a danger zone. But temptation can be resisted. It need not turn into the actions it suggests.[3]

3. This list was suggested by Joshua Harris' own list in *Sex Is Not the Problem (Lust Is)*, 35.

So What Exactly Is Lust?

One of my favorite lakes in Michigan is formed by a dam. At the other end, miles away, a river flows into the lake. Several times, I've taken a canoe from the lake into the river. But when, exactly, did I enter the river? Well, that's hard to say. There's no distinct line. First, the lake narrows considerably. Then, there's a winding path of clear water through a marsh. It looks a little like a river now, but you could still paddle through the marsh grass, and the shore is off in the distance. But eventually you know you are in the river. The current is clearly discernible and the shoreline distinct and close. I don't mean to suggest that there's a long path toward lust but instead that it's easier to describe it by a *cluster* of characteristics than by a distinct line one crosses. But if straightforward definitions are helpful, here are a few examples:

- Lust is craving sexually what God has forbidden (Joshua Harris). For this definition to be helpful, you also have to know what God has forbidden.

- Lust is sexual desire minus honor and holiness (John Piper). Piper's definition doesn't identify sexual desire itself as lust but acknowledges that even something good, like sexual desire, can be distorted by having the desires in the wrong way—that is, by having them in ways that dishonor both God and the person who is the object of the desire. All of our conduct as Christians, including our sexual desires, should be characterized by holiness—which means they ought to be done in accord with God's intentions, rules, and goals.

- Lust is "the inordinate craving for, or indulgence of, the carnal pleasure which is experienced in the human organs of generation. The wrongfulness of lust is reducible to this: that venereal satisfaction is sought for either outside wedlock or, at any rate, in a manner which is contrary to the laws that govern marital intercourse." This definition, from the *Catholic Encyclopedia*, merges thoughts and actions and defines lust in a way that looks pretty much like sexual sin in general.

In the Christian tradition, the word *lust* names something sinful—something that misses the mark that God intends for human sexuality. As the term has come to be used, it identifies several different ways this might happen. But it is not quite the same thing as engaging in sexual *activities* that are wrong. The term *craving* is often used to identify what kind of "action" lust is. It's an action of our passions, thoughts, imaginations. Lust happens before we act with our bodies—or even apart from such actions. Lust can mean any one or any combination of the following things:

1. From "captivating" to captive: Let's say you're functioning like a normal post-puberty human male or female. You notice people with attractive physical characteristics, you're keenly aware of your sexual urges, you have fleeting feelings or fantasies. It's not something we necessarily set out to do but just something that happens to us and to everyone. None of this has turned into lust yet. These feelings and attractions are normal.

But here I want to draw on a helpful distinction made by Lewis Smedes (*Sex for Christians*). Smedes explains how the normal morphs into something that looks more like lust: "There is a difference between being aware of someone's sexual attractions and being dominated by a desire for that person's body . . . Attraction can become captivity; and when we have become captives of the thought, we have begun to lust. When the sense of excitement conceives a plan to use a person, when attraction turns into scheme, we have crossed beyond erotic excitement into spiritual adultery [i.e., lust]."[4]

If we think about lust this way, there's a line being crossed between appropriate natural desires and longings and those that are inappropriate. What makes them inappropriate? The next three characteristics of lust all seem to be implied by Smedes' distinction.

2. Popular Christian writer Joshua Harris defines lust as "craving sexually what God has forbidden." Understood this way, lust involves crossing into forbidden territory, at least in our minds. Most definitions of lust depend on some supporting notion of sexual sin, as this one clearly does. You can really only know what counts as lust if you know what God has forbidden. Some moralists would use the term *impurity*, while others speak of sexual behavior that isn't holy or God-honoring. Whatever the language, the idea is that there are certain behaviors that are wrong because they violate a standard of morality. And here's the point: to desire them is wrong as well. To desire sexual activity that God forbids is lust.

Some biblical interpreters argue that Jesus' admonition against lust in the Sermon on Mount actually refers to having sexual desires for women (or men) who are in some way "out of bounds." Women who are already married would clearly fall into that category, as well as those who were still virgins (by which the Bible would mean women not yet married). In this sense, lust is sexual desire that specifically targets anyone with whom sexual activity would not express the true nature of the love that is present, or that would not do so in ways that abide by biblical boundaries. This way of defining lust makes it a case of *desiring the wrong thing*. If we find ourselves dwelling on desiring the wrong thing, those desires should be resisted.

4. Smedes, *Sex for Christians*, 188.

3. Another common attribute of lust is that it involves (using the classical language) an "inordinate craving" of sexual pleasure. Simply put, lust means wanting *too much* of a good thing. More precisely, it means that sexual desire becomes problematic when it becomes excessive, and especially when it becomes a preoccupation, obsession, or addiction.

While it isn't an everyday word, the term *inordinate* can be a very useful moral measure. It implies that there is a mean between extremes. We think this way in many arenas of life and could find several illustrations in Christian morality. In the sexual sphere, someone with a prudish aversion to anything sexual would be at the opposite extreme from a lustful person, whose intense sexual cravings are inordinate or excessive. The mean or the middle, seen as the moral ideal between these inappropriate extremes, was defined by classical moralists as chastity. To be chaste means to desire sex in the right way, at the right time, with the right person. Contemporary Christian writers sometimes use the word *purity* where *chastity* would have been used in earlier days. The point is that lust misses the appropriate middle. It lacks the kind of self-discipline, balance, and limits that help keep sexual desire healthy and holy.

4. Another way to assess feelings of attraction is to test whether they are associated with other improper attitudes. For example, lust is sometimes described as a sexual attraction that is *self-indulgent*. Since sexual activity is an expression of love, and sexual pleasure is meant to be mutually given and received, it is not a selfish activity, even though we receive individual pleasure from it. In contrast, sexual fantasies about strangers are self-indulgent. When we nurture thoughts and fantasies merely to satisfy ourselves, we place sex outside the context God intended.

Lust is also sometimes associated with sexual desire that gets linked with thoughts or actions that are *degrading or dehumanizing*. This might be the case, for example, when sexual thoughts effectively reduce people to body parts or sex toys. Whether in action or in thought, Christians are expected to treat and think about people in ways that respect the fact that we are created in God's image, loved as God's children, and redeemed by Christ's death and resurrection.

When sexual desire is associated with these or other improper attitudes, something good gets tainted. It's not the sexual desire that's wrong but the company it sometimes keeps. Sexual desire is meant instead to be nourished by the kinds of virtues and values that are part of sexual integrity (see chapter 5).

Should We Feel Guilty If It's Just Thoughts?

Yes, given what's been said in answer to the questions leading up to this final query, we should feel guilty about lust. While I've described it in a way that intends to steer us away from false guilt, there's a core that is still inappropriate, given the kind of Christian convictions that inform my approach to sexual ethics in earlier chapters. Guilt is an appropriate response to lust as long as we understand guilt as an appropriate response to sinful, inappropriate thoughts and actions.

In spite of its bad name, I see guilt as having a few important functions in Christian morality:

- Sometimes it serves as a red flag that makes us stop and take notice that what we're doing probably needs some attention, assessment, and revision. I say "sometimes" because we can be taught to feel guilty about things we shouldn't feel guilty about, just as we can be taught not to feel guilty when we should!

- It serves as a stop sign. It reminds us that we've come to a line we shouldn't cross, an action we shouldn't take. It's our conscience reminding us of what we care about, what we stand for, and who we are.

- It serves as a motive for confession, forgiveness, and reconciliation.

What about this distinction between thoughts and actions? Does it make a real difference? Yes—and no! My analysis of lust explains why lust is wrong, even though it resides primarily in our minds. It's a wrong way of thinking about sex and about people as sexual objects. Wrong thinking is wrong.

But wrong thinking doesn't always have negative consequences equivalent to the consequences of wrong actions. You can have lustful thoughts without hurting someone else. But if you act on those thoughts, you are likely to do someone harm. The difference between thoughts and actions is real, but it's not the kind of difference that gets lust off the hook. And because a Christian sexual ethic seeks a holistic orientation to what is God-honoring, it makes sense to resist lust so that our attitudes as well as our behaviors coincide as much as possible with a sexual ethic that honors God, the creator of sexual beings like us.

3. Born-Again Virginity?

Does it make any sense to claim a "second virginity"? Is there such a thing as a "born-again virgin"? What would it mean to say that you've gained back your virginity?

A born-again virgin? "Wait a minute," you might say. "Can it be so easy? Either you are a virgin or you aren't!" Claiming to be a born-again virgin sounds like cheating. As one of my students asked, "I have a friend who lost her virginity, and then after regretting this, she just decided she was going to be a reborn virgin. Once you lose your virginity, can you get it back?"

On the other hand, it makes a lot of sense to claim a second virginity. But in order to understand why, we need to know why someone would make such a claim and what one would mean by saying it.

Is virginity something people go around announcing? Probably not with any regularity, but if it is announced, the setting would be an important part of ascertaining the meaning of the claim. In popular culture, virginity might be an embarrassment: I'm a virgin (sad face); help me do something about it! In a church youth group, the same fact might function as a badge of honor, indicating moral strength in a world of alluring temptations. But I'm not sure there is much value in public pronouncements of virginity or born-again virginity, unless they take place in the context of serious conversation with trusted companions.

Hearing someone claim to be a born-again virgin makes some people cringe. We are full of suspicion about what's really intended by this pronouncement. Are they bragging? Do they naively believe that once you've engaged in sexual intercourse you can somehow also never have done it? Do they think they are better than the non-virgins among us and are trying to make us feel guilty?

Being a born-again virgin (or claiming a "second virginity") clearly doesn't mean that you have never engaged in sexual intercourse. Of course technically, being a virgin means that you haven't had sex. But claiming to be a born-again virgin usually means that you *have* had sex and aren't technically a virgin. It isn't a claim about something magical happening, like traveling back in time and undoing an event in the past. It's not a statement about what you've done with your genitals or a denial of past practices.

So what's the point in saying it?

Above all else, I think the statement is usually meant as a way to reflect a new *moral* status. It means that someone has decided to adopt a sexual ethic that places value on abstaining from sexual intercourse, even though this might not have been so in the past. It's a change of heart and mind, not an erasing of past behavior. It means that while virginity is not a fact about one's past, it is a commitment that one intends to make part of one's future—at least until there are good moral reasons to change.

If you don't place a high value on virginity or sexual abstinence, perhaps because your own sexual ethic doesn't call for it, the idea of being a born-again virgin might still make you uncomfortable. But if it does, it might simply be uncomfortable in the same way we are uncomfortable when someone else's moral commitments conflict with our own. If a friend has decided to stop doing something (having sex) because they now believe it's wrong, and we are still engaging in sexual intercourse, the implied conflict is likely to be a little disquieting. We might wish they would just keep their commitments to themselves and stop making us feel ill at ease.

Repentance and forgiveness are the ways Christians have been taught to deal with guilt from past sins. A claim of "second virginity" can be a joyous announcement of the experience of forgiveness and having been made new. If one's past sexual practices are seen as sinful, repentance and forgiveness lift a sense of guilt and shame. How will this newfound sense of freedom be named? In general terms, Christians have called this kind of repentance and turning away from sin and toward a life of Christian discipleship "being born again." In the arena of sex, some have called it "born-again virginity."

Being forgiven of any wrong doesn't mean that the wrong never occurred. In fact, the act of confession involves honestly coming face to face with the wrong and acknowledging it. Likewise, if one's past sexual behavior is now seen as an example of having done something wrong, being forgiven means having been honest about the past—not hiding from it.

But it also means letting go of the past. And it means committing oneself to taking up a new way of life. Living as one who has been forgiven means that in some real sense our status has changed. The fact of being forgiven now means more than the wrong we have done. Forgiveness puts us in a restored relationship to God, it invites us to restore our relationships with those we have wronged, and it puts us in a new relationship to our moral convictions and intentions for the future. Calling oneself a "born-again virgin" *in this sense* makes a claim about a radical reorientation of one's sexual life.

Regaining a sense of one's virginity may also be related to one's sense of moral purity. If you have read chapter 6 you already know that I am somewhat troubled by a notion of purity as it is used in contemporary sexual ethics. But if we relate purity to forgiveness, it helps shed light on another valuable dimension of a second virginity. To reclaim one's purity can mean to claim that one has been "washed clean"—an image often used when the Bible describes forgiveness. The result of forgiveness is not technical or physical purity, but purity of the heart. To claim that one is a "born-again virgin" is to say that purity of the heart is what really matters.

Finally, claiming to be a born-again virgin is often meant to be an important affirmation of a renewed self-identity. It is something to hold oneself accountable to, an ideal to live up to. And if it is the product of a prayerful, careful, thoughtful process of moral discernment, it is an identity to treat with care.

In our sexual lives, our self-identity plays a powerful role in the way we live. We treat ourselves in ways that are consistent with our self-identity. If we believe we are God's creatures, worthy of love and respect, we are more likely to treat ourselves with love and respect. The same is true of our expectations for how others treat us. If we think we have little value and worth, we won't be likely to insist that others treat us as people with value and worth. Letting a romantic partner know that you are a born-again virgin announces not only an important dimension of your own self-identity but also an expectation. It invites someone to see you that way too, and it asks them to support you as you strive to uphold the moral commitment that goes along with this identity.

4. What Should You Do If Your Partner's Sexual Ethic Is Different from Yours?

Can a relationship survive and be healthy if this is the case? If a couple has sex and only one of them decides it was a mistake, is it possible for them to stay together and be abstinent?

It's already a complicated undertaking to figure out how you want to express yourself sexually. So what happens when your partner has figured it out too—but with different results? Or perhaps he hasn't thought about it as much as you have and is driven by somewhat unrestrained passion. Or maybe he just has a different sexual history, for a variety of reasons. In any case, differing sexual ethics can cause lots of tension, disagreement, or hurt feelings in a relationship.

Unwanted sexual advances, even when motivated by love, can feel disrespectful, leaving you wondering why someone who cares about you would make you feel that way. Unwanted touch may make you feel dirty or simply uncomfortable, even if it is intended as a gentle expression of love. Saying no engenders feelings of guilt, and this can be especially confusing when your no is rooted in deeply held convictions about what is right. Why should *you* feel guilty?

On the other side of things, being turned down can feel like a form of rejection, which is confusing in a relationship that is otherwise healthy and happy. If physical touch is your dominant language for expressing love, you might feel at a loss about how to express what you think and feel. Knowing that your sexual advances have felt hurtful to someone you love is likely to make you feel guilty—which is confusing if all you intended to do was to express your love.

People whose morality differs from our own are sometimes a mystery to us. Even though we know that it happens all the time, it's sometimes hard to imagine how someone could draw a different moral conclusion than the one we've arrived at. Our views seem so logical. They feel so right. When someone's morality differs from our own, whether it's a matter of their viewpoints or actions, it's easy to *see* them as wrong—or sometimes even as bad. Morality is about what's good, after all, and if someone believes in or does what you've decided is not good, what conclusion are you supposed to draw, you might ask?

The fact that someone has drawn different moral conclusions or perhaps given less thought to a moral issue doesn't make him or her a bad person. We don't have to agree with people about everything to be in a relationship with them as colleagues, friends, or lovers. But we do have to cooperate, and in some cases this means finding common ground that can serve as the foundation for unity.

So which ethic prevails? If you have drawn your moral lines in different places (to take the perspective of a boundary ethic), someone's line has to be the one that's obeyed. One person in the relationship will have to respect a line that isn't the one she's drawn. As far as I can see, there is only one choice: the more conservative line prevails.

Several virtues associated with the character of Christian love demand this and legal obligations require it as well. We *respect* the moral choices made by a romantic partner even when they are not the choices we would make. We set aside our desires and our decisions for the sake of another, embodying the *selflessness* that characterizes Christian love. We proceed with *patience*, both toward our own desires and toward the person who sees things differently than we do. Love sometimes means that we set aside what we want, being willing to wait for the right time and place. And even when it's difficult, Christians seek to embody *self-control*, since it is often the case that doing the right thing is not the same as doing what comes easy.

In practice, this means that the partner who seeks more sexual expression demonstrates a form of loving care for the other partner by showing restraint. The traditional word for this is chastity, and in a setting where one partner's sexual ethic calls for less sexual activity, chastity can be an even deeper expression of love than a bodily caress.

The danger of manipulation lurks in the background when this kind of tension arises in a relationship. The familiar and well-worn words "If you loved me, you would . . ." are often a red flag. In the best sense, saying this might mean "If you loved me the way I love you, and if your sexual ethic matched mine, it's likely that you would be willing to engage in the same level of sexual activity that I desire." But in practice, the words "If you loved me . . ." easily become a form of manipulation that uses guilt to get someone to act in ways they don't want to, in order to prove their love. No one you claim to love should ever be put in that position.

Can the Relationship Survive?
If So, What Does This Situation Call For?

Discovering that your sexual ethic differs from that of your romantic partner shouldn't have to be a revelation that ends things. It seems more like a challenge—not unlike others a couple will encounter. It's a test not only of morality but also of the maturity and depth of your love for each other.

First, *it calls for a willingness to do the hard work of learning to understand each other*. Respecting someone's moral commitments is easier when we understand them, so making the effort to explain your moral standards in a way that makes sense to others is good practice for the rest of one's life and relationships. I think it's worth striving for an ideal that I'd put this way: If a romantic partner understands *why* you say no when you do, he or she is likely to help you live by your own standards. You'll notice that this falls short of suggesting you will change someone's mind, converting her to your own way of thinking. That might make things easier, but it doesn't seem necessary. Instead you agree (through understanding) to disagree (I can see why you think that, but I still disagree with you). As a result, one partner says, "I believe I understand you, but I'm not going to change my limits." The other says, "I believe I understand you, and that makes it easier to respect and abide by your limits."

Second, *it calls for a willingness to sacrifice for the sake of the other's moral commitments*. If the ideal expressed above becomes part of a relationship of love, someone will have to make what is likely to feel like a sacrifice in order to make things work. That person will have to practice patient and loving respect for a moral viewpoint they don't share and will have to resist the urge to have everything their way. Exercising this kind of respect and self-control isn't easy. It might feel like a difficult sacrifice. But if it is genuine, it won't be a grudging sacrifice—the kind that pouts and complains and makes the other person feel guilty. Instead, it will be the kind of sacrifice that says "I love you so much that what you value is important to me. I want to help you live the way you want to, even if it's not what I would choose."

A Happy Ending?

As long as the more conservative partner's physical limits are respected, this seems to be a case where disagreement does not need to result in disunity. When a couple reaches a mutual understanding and agrees to an appropriate level of sexual activity, they've created a basis for increased trust, understanding, and respect. If things go well, they will look back and realize that their efforts to negotiate these differences helped create an even deeper bond of love.

5. Are There Moral Absolutes? Or Is It Just up to Me?

Are there any absolutes in Christian sexual ethics, or is it just up to each individual or couple to decide for themselves?

Christians don't all agree on an answer to this question, so an easy response is, "It depends on who you ask!" The controversy isn't limited to sexual ethics, either. One of the quandaries I have pondered for about as long as I can remember is how Christians can disagree with each other on virtually every controversial moral issue! Such disagreements have divided the church in the past (slavery) and threaten to create serious rifts in the present (homosexuality). If you've read the preceding pages, you already know that the approach to sexual ethics presented here isn't grounded in any simple-to-state absolutes but in several central moral convictions that are meant to shape Christian ways of living. Those convictions, grounded in the Bible and carried by the tradition, point us toward what is right and good. It's not just up to us.

I think we ask this question because we feel like we *ought to* recognize a moral absolute but at the same time feel like we *also* ought to assert our individual freedom over-against that absolute. The absolute, if there is one, has been generated and sustained by the Christian tradition. The moral line that says sexual intercourse belongs only in marriage is the best example of such an absolute, and I think it's the one people are usually wondering about. Most Christians have been taught about that line, even if it is the only thing they have been taught about sexual ethics. The fact that it *is* sometimes the only thing we're taught makes it seem even more absolute!

Why Do We Question Absolutes?

Believing in a moral absolute means believing that a particular moral truth is not affected by history, culture, consequences, or intentions. There are no conditions that can change the moral truth. If something is morally wrong, it's always wrong, no matter what. It always was and it always will be.

Many of us have grown up to be suspicious of absolutes, and perhaps also of anyone who claims to *know* what the absolute actually is. Where does that suspicion come from?

AUTHORITY

Somewhere I acquired a protest button that displays the simple words "Question Authority." It's now a virtue in our culture to question authority, and since any absolute is proclaimed or mediated by some authority (the pope, the church, the pastor, mom and dad), those who question authority are just as likely to question the absolutes they proclaim. Absolutes are virtually inseparable from someone who claims the authority to tell us what they are, and in a culture that questions authority, absolutes stand on shaky ground. Even if the Bible is the source of one's moral absolute, someone still has to interpret the text and decide that it has the status of an absolute. If human authority is always a mediator of what's absolute, it would seem that absolutes are based on imperfect, limited, and sinful humanity. If we can't trust the human mediator, absolutes become hard to establish.

TOO EASY?

Absolutes often sound too easy. When they take the form of principles or rules, the reasons behind them are often invisible until we dig deeper. When we start digging, the absolute frequently starts to look less certain. While careful investigation into what's behind an accepted absolute doesn't always undermine it, we do start to notice that historical context, human interpretations, power struggles, and other relativizing influences are part of the picture.

Context Matters

Absolutes, understood as moral truths that are true without qualification, contain the clear implication that context doesn't matter. That's the point! It doesn't matter who, when, where, why. But in our common daily experience, context often matters—we're leery of any claims (like a moral absolute) that ask us to set it aside.

History

Things people took as absolutes before aren't absolutes any longer. If new knowledge or changing moral sensitivities can undo the absoluteness of a belief about morality, theology, or the world, then it obviously wasn't an absolute. Maybe there are some absolutes, but the fact that we never know ahead of time which ones will be undone makes us hesitant to grant absolute status to the absolutes currently in vogue.[5]

We Disagree

You might simply disagree with an absolute someone else espouses. If it's really an absolute, then you're probably wrong. But if thoughtful, prayerful, careful investigation has led you to a conclusion in opposition to the absolute, your head, heart, conscience, and faith may lead you to oppose the absolute, even in the face of considerable opposition.

The Tension between Absolutes and Individualism ("It's my body, I can do with it what I want!")

A popular alternative to believing in absolutes is individualism. Libertarian sensibilities have shaped attitudes about morality, both within Western culture and also within the church. In this way of thinking people tend to practice a form of individualism that calls for noninterference in private matters. This means that instead of recognizing the morality of the authority or of the majority, we get to choose sexual values from a smorgasbord of options available.

Individualism is an attractive alternative at a time when obedience to authority is no longer a popular virtue. It has been replaced by the obligation

---

5. For example, Newton's physics and Euclid's geometry once had the status of absolutes until they were replaced by new ways of knowing in their respective fields.

to question authority, to think for oneself, to make up one's own mind. We've learned to feel a sense of accomplishment and self-satisfaction when we do that and are made to feel guilty when it seems that we're simply adopting traditions uncritically. Moral choices are commonly seen as decisions people need to make on the basis of whatever values they have internalized, in the context of whatever personal experiences they have lived. And when this yields wide differences in our morality, we are encouraged to respect or at least tolerate the diversity of viewpoints and lifestyles these differences produce. Predisposed to devalue conformity to any absolute standards, Christians are often as likely as anyone to reject absolutes in sexual ethics.

Evaluating the Options: Absolutism and Individualism

There are good reasons to be *cautious* about absolutes, and for those reasons it makes some sense to answer our question with serious reservations about there being an "absolute sexual morality" for Christians. But there are good reasons to be cautious about individualism as well, and for those reasons it makes sense to stop short of saying that sexual morality is something everyone should simply "decide for themselves."

One reason to be suspicious of absolutes is the hesitation about whether anyone really has access to absolute truth. That's a complex philosophical and theological question that the reader will have to pursue elsewhere. For our purposes, let it suffice to say that if it's not clear how we could *know* what moral "truths" are absolute, we must be at least very cautious and careful about assigning that status to our moral convictions.

A second reason is that caution about moral absolutes also stems, in part, from the way people have sometimes used them. Certain of their absolutes, crusaders for their cause sometimes seek to impose their absolutes on everyone else—even through violence. A belief in absolutes can also easily fuel judgmentalism. If I'm right, those who hold opposite views are wrong. But what comes next? Judgmentalism involves advertising your own sense of moral superiority and making it clear to those who don't see things your way that they are morally inferior. Things sometimes even go further. In the name of absolutes, individuals and groups have been ostracized, dehumanized, disenfranchised, or severely punished. One could readily find illustrations of these extremes, for example, in the history of absolute prohibitions of same-gender sex.

A third reason is that absolutes have even more destructive power when they are held by people with power. Majorities, governments, and people in control of social institutions have the ability to implement their absolutes in ways the less powerful might only hope for. This legitimately makes us suspicious, too, since the absolutes that get enforced are those held by the people with the power to enforce them. This is no guarantee that they are actually the ones that are right and true.

There are reasons to be suspicious of individualism, too, especially from a Christian perspective.

First, Christian life is shaped by a tradition—one that includes the biblical narrative and its interpretation, the history of the church, and the moral tradition carried by God's people over time. That tradition has authority. It's meant to shape our ways of thinking and living. Becoming Christian means being introduced into that tradition (a process historically referred to as catechesis) and taking up the way of life the tradition teaches (a process historically referred to as discipleship). Being Christian has always been about being part of something bigger than ourselves. In fact, it means learning to see ourselves differently, through a new lens. An important dimension of Christian conversion is learning to see that we are not our own (see 1 Cor 6:19–20). When we understand Christianity as a tradition that invites people to follow Jesus and take up a life of discipleship, this doesn't sound anything like individualism. Christian discipleship doesn't mean "do whatever you want."

Second, you've probably heard the idea of individualism presented like this: "I have the right to do whatever I want behind closed doors. Your values don't have the right to come into my bedroom." In other words, individualists identify a private space (or sphere) where outside interference is inappropriate. In the private sphere what we do is up to us, and us alone. "I can do whatever I wish in the privacy of my own home (or other private space)." But we recognize that there are limits to this. There are legal limits. While the notion of private moral space might grant us considerable sexual freedom, we can't abuse our spouse or child behind closed doors, even if we're able to provide some explanation to legitimize this as a morally permissible activity. And in the Christian tradition, the idea of walling off certain private spaces from Christian morality implies an incomplete commitment. Christians are called to honor God in all of the spaces of life.

A third reason is that at another level, individualism might simply be a myth. If we see individualism as a state of not being influenced by any factors outside ourselves, does this ever really happen in the real world? Are we ever really free from the culture around us, so that we can make up our mind? Mary Midgely says,

> A child growing up with no background culture at all would
> have a very thin and shaky life, not an enriched one. Giving

children a normal cultural heritage is not an interference, but an act of normal provision for human life.[6]

We never simply make up our own minds because our culture has already shaped our minds. We have absorbed or adopted cultural values along with cultural ways of thinking about and evaluating morality. This often happens so naturally that the process and product are invisible to us. This makes it easy to think we are influenced only by our own ideas, when in fact our own ideas reflect a complex matrix of the larger social life that shapes us. And this is true for matters like sex that might seem so private. We can ignore the influences that shape our minds or pretend that they don't exist. But we never truly make moral decisions in an individualistic vacuum.

Conclusion

Let's now revisit the original question: Are there any absolutes in Christian sexual ethics, or is it just up to each of us? Based on the considerations above, I think it now makes the most sense to affirm that Christian sexual morality is *tradition-formed* (an external moral authority stands behind the core convictions Christians affirm) and at the same time *individually owned*. So it is not "just up to us" to make up a Christian sexual ethic, but it is up to us to affirm the tradition and even certain voices (sub-traditions) within it. I would suggest that it makes more sense to refer to an authoritative tradition than to absolutes. The phrase "authoritative tradition" maintains the idea that Christian morality has truth value beyond the choices individuals make, while at the same time affirming an important individual responsibility—to think carefully, to give assent, and to make a commitment to embody the tradition.

First, faith is *giving assent* (the individual pole) to a *tradition* (the authoritative pole). Living according to a Christian sexual ethic is one dimension of what it means to have faith in God. Whether it's the Christian life in general or a sexual ethic in particular, a person decides to say yes to Jesus, or to the particular Christian convictions that inform one's sexual practices. This assent often involves the whole person: We recognize there are good reasons to affirm these convictions. We experience the veracity of living faithfully. We are motivated and affirmed by emotions of gratitude, forgiveness, and love. We are nurtured and sustained by a community of believers.

6. Midgley, *Can't We Make Moral Judgements?*, 64.

Whether or not we believe that it is God's Spirit ultimately making our assent possible, we experience this assent as an individual phenomenon, usually brought on by an identifiable set of experiences and motives. We might say that because God's Spirit uses the particularities of our individual lives, we experience the work of the Spirit in and through our individual selves. We experience faith and commitment as something we each do.

But faith is about more than what we do. Christian faith is faith in God, as known through the story of Israel and especially in the life, death, and resurrection of Jesus. His story and its meaning is carried by the church through time and culture, under the guidance of the Holy Spirit, as the church seeks to carry and live the story (although imperfectly) of what it means to exhibit signs of God's reign today, in the world we inhabit. Faith is faith in God, as understood through an authoritative tradition that continues to live in the real world. So while giving assent is the individual pole, the authoritative tradition is the "absolute pole" that stands outside of us.

Second, honoring the tradition and recognizing its authority doesn't mean giving up our critical capacity to think carefully about the moral life. Jesus' call to love God with our whole selves, including our minds (see Luke 10:27), affirms the importance of moral discernment. This means that figuring out how to honor God in our sexual lives is part of the responsibility of honoring God. Christians, in deciding to follow Jesus, are not called to stop using their minds and simply conform with blind obedience to whatever their parents or church have taught them about sex. But it might mean (voluntarily) sacrificing our freedom for the sake of something more important. For example, it might mean sacrificing the satisfaction of physical desires in order to build the kind of relationship that sanctifies sexual expressions of love.

Core Christian commitments, like those I have proposed as "orienting convictions," are not established merely by our own opinions or preferences. But that does not mean that they can never change or come to be understood a bit differently than before. A husband's right to sex on demand (once justified on the basis of a wife's duty to be submissive) is now considered marital rape, not only by law but by many (or perhaps even most) Christians in Western cultures. Whether or not people of the same gender may marry and express their love in sexual ways is now debated within the church and no longer presumed by all to always be sinful.

The fact that sexual ethics can be debated and changed over time through a process of careful discernment does mean that sexual ethics are private and up to no one other than me. But because Christian moral understandings have sometimes changed over time, and because the process of change requires tolerating new questions, ideas, and insights, Christians must always approach their moral convictions with a sense of convicted humility.

6. Is Being Engaged Enough?

When you are engaged and know you will be getting married, is it morally wrong to have sex before the actual wedding? If marriage is necessary, when are you actually married? Why isn't it enough to know that you are in love and plan to be together forever?

Deciding to become engaged often feels like the big decision we make in romantic relationships. The decision is often the result of a process of careful assessment, honest discernment, and long preparation. People think about it for months or even years. After that, the wedding might feel like just a matter of waiting and planning. Perhaps it's even seen as a celebration of what has already taken place. The engagement decision seems to be about the relationship; wedding decisions are about details. Where is the marriage in all of this?

Some people think that marriage is the event that takes place at the wedding. That's how the tradition sees it, and many Christian wedding liturgies expresses this as well: marriage takes place in and through the words and actions that happen in the wedding. Others seem to increasingly have the intuition that it happens well before the wedding, perhaps when someone says, "Will you marry me?" and the other responds, "Yes, I will." It sounds a bit like a wedding vow, doesn't it? Getting engaged might be experienced as a more profound change in status than "getting married."

What are people wondering about when they ask whether it's appropriate to engage in sexual intercourse once they're engaged? At the most basic level I hear the question as a plea for "early permission" from those who have been taught that sex only belongs in marriage. They are asking, Do we really have to wait that long? Isn't there a way around this rule, since our love is so mature and our lives are already bonded in so many important and meaningful ways? Doesn't that already qualify us for sex? While the question implies a lack of patience (an important Christian virtue), there are also responsible questions here that take sex and the relationship of love seriously.

The question might also arise from a cynical view of marriage. The thinking goes like this: Does marriage really matter or mean anything more than the statement of intent expressed in engagement? Is the wedding simply a formality? And marriage no longer guarantees permanence. Look at how many people get divorced or dishonor marriage! Some engagements are healthier relationships than some marriages. Amidst such cynicism one might easily believe that their "engaged love" has far more meaning and substance than a "typical marriage."

The question about whether it's necessary to wait until marriage clearly presumes the normative view that sex belongs only in marriage, most likely based on some version of a boundary ethic. So we'll proceed here using a Christian boundary ethic as our starting point.

A first step in responding to this question requires figuring out whether there is any meaningful difference between engagement and marriage. If there isn't, whatever makes sex morally permissible in marriage is likely to make it permissible during engagement as well. Are engagement and marriage essentially the same? Is engagement the beginning of a marriage? If not, what is it that makes marriage alone the morally appropriate setting for sexual intercourse?

People often talk about marriage as an "institution." In secular terms, this means that it is a social practice that has emerged over time. In this broad sense, marriage is defined and regulated by laws enacted by governments. Christians usually accept the legal definition of marriage, and possibly go no further in defining it.

I would suggest that beyond the legal definition, Christian marriage is a covenant relationship defined by the vows that establish the covenant. There are three central promises made in marriage covenants across a broad range of Christian churches. Marriage vows almost always promise *exclusivity* (I take you, and only you), *unconditional love* (for better or for worse), and *lifelong commitment* (until death parts us).

Marriage as a social institution is a public event—even if this only means that it is licensed and witnessed and meets the legal requirements. The basic elements of a marriage are (1) the parties' legal ability to marry each other, (2) mutual consent of the parties, and (3) a marriage contract as required by law.[7] As an act of Christian covenanting (making solemn vows), Christian marriage is also a community event where vows are exchanged in the presence of a community of believers who both celebrate the marriage and promise to provide the support necessary to sustain it. Christians typically combine the legal and covenantal aspects of marriage in a single event. In modern American culture, we typically call the ceremony in which this covenanting takes place a "wedding."

Is a wedding ceremony necessary in order to establish a marriage? As described above, it is—only because the wedding is the ceremony in

---

7. Cornell Legal Marriage Institute, "Marriage."

which the covenanting takes place. This covenanting might occur in a less traditional setting, but no matter how formal or informal, the event in which this covenant is exchanged could be called a wedding. At the heart of what constitutes a Christian marriage is the exchange of vows that promise exclusive, unconditional, lifelong love.

How is a "wedding-in-which-marriage-takes-place" different from an engagement? Keep in mind that we are considering here the kinds of differences that would be relevant for those holding a boundary ethic, since that's the approach that claims marriage is a necessary line that makes sexual intercourse morally appropriate.

1. The *decision to get engaged* is a decision to get married. It's a mutual promise to enter into a covenant at some point in the future. It's a public announcement that essentially says "We plan to get married." Apart from the desire to use engagement as a license for sex, people do seem to recognize the difference and know whether they are engaged or married.

It's possible to grant this distinction but still wonder why engagement isn't the boundary beyond which sexual intercourse is morally permissible. But from the perspective of the boundary ethics we've examined previously, sexual intercourse belongs only in a covenantal relationship of love, that is, marriage. Since engagement is not yet marriage, the essential conditions (the public covenantal promising of exclusive, unconditional, lifelong love) haven't become part of the couple's relationship. If they have already done this in what was called engagement, marriage and engagement have been merged into a single event, and they are already married (though not yet legally).

Engaged couples do not typically enter into a marital covenant when they get engaged. Rather, they exchange their intentions to do that in the future. So from the perspective of a boundary ethic, engagement is still on the premarital side of the line.

2. The *period of engagement* is a time to prepare for marriage, although this opportunity often gets lost when it is overcome by the complexities associated with planning the wedding and reception. Amidst the busyness of planning a wedding, the actual marriage might get ignored. In the context of a boundary ethic, the distinction between the time to prepare to be married and the time one is actually married makes all the difference. While advocates of a boundary ethic might explain that difference in their own unique ways, the common theme is that there is something about actually being married that makes so much of a difference that only in marriage should one engage in sexual intercourse.

3. There is a long tradition in the church of seeing the act of *sexual intercourse as the "consummation" of a marriage*. This means that the marital

covenant, followed by the act of sexual intercourse, brings to completion the process of getting married.

When we add the richness of a well-defined boundary ethic to this idea of consummation, it becomes easy to see sexual intercourse as a new level of sexual activity that corresponds to the new level of commitment expressed in Christian marriage. Sexual intercourse means what marriage means: I take you, for better or for worse, for life. One says that with one's words in the public covenanting, and one says it with one's body in the act of sexual intercourse.

In summary, a boundary ethic intends to say clearly why a particular boundary matters. In the Christian tradition, this boundary has been marriage, and we have already seen in the explanations of Smedes and Hollinger why marriage is the boundary that makes sexual intercourse permissible. And because engagement is distinct in a few important ways, and is *not* marriage, engagement is not the line that makes sex morally permissible.

Would a Relational Approach Offer a Different Answer?

Asking whether a boundary (marriage) is the right boundary invites reflection about the meaning of the boundaries. But I'm not sure that the question about whether marriage or engagement is the right boundary is really motivated by boundary-ethic considerations. Here's what I think is really going on:

Those who wonder whether people who are engaged are in a relationship that makes sexual intercourse morally appropriate have an intuition that sounds more like a relational ethic. They sense that people who are engaged (or maybe they are thinking especially of themselves) are in the kind of relationship that has the qualities and characteristics that make sexual intercourse a morally good way of expressing their love. So their question is really something like this: Isn't it possible that the quality of love we see in a couple who have publicly proclaimed their intent to get married is the kind of love that makes sexual intercourse morally appropriate?

This isn't really a question about boundaries at all. It's a question about the relational characteristics that make sexual intercourse a meaningful and healthy expression of love. A questioner might assume that some engaged people are already in such a relationship, while some married people might not be. But it's not the boundary that matters in this approach; it's the *quality of the relationship*. (The chapter on a relational approach to ethics examines the dimensions of what it means to talk about the quality of a relationship.)

A relational ethic leaves more room for making engagement equivalent to marriage, when the focus is placed on relational characteristics and the character of the people involved. From the perspective of a relational approach, one could easily agree with the distinctions made above between marriage and engagement. But from a relational perspective, those differences aren't the things that matter most. The relational characteristics matter most, and those, one might argue, can be present before the event of the marriage. In fact, many would probably argue that it is the presence and even flourishing of those relational characteristics that lead a couple to decide to marry.

Boundary Ethics or Relational Ethics?

Previous chapters have not recommended one approach to ethics but have explored the meaning of three streams of Christian thinking about sexual ethics: a boundary ethic, a relational ethic, and an ethic of sexual integrity. Perhaps readers are still struggling with which one to make primary, or how to combine the best elements of all three. But it is also probably obvious that one might reach different moral conclusions using different arguments, depending on which approach one takes.

When I apply a boundary ethic to the question about engagement or marriage as the proper context for sexual intercourse, it seems clear that the difference between engagement and marriage is significant enough to say no to sexual intercourse outside marriage.

But when I apply a relational ethic to the same question, it becomes easy to see why, especially in a culture that includes long dating relationships, a couple might develop a relationship that has the same relational qualities we'd hope for in a healthy marriage. *If those qualities alone are the determining factor*, then it's not the line of marriage or of engagement that necessarily matters. But if we accept the terms in the question, it does seem that everything that is necessary for sexual intercourse to be a morally appropriate expression of love (a certain set of relational characteristics, honest self-assessment, maturity, etc.) might be present in engagement . . . and get carried on into marriage.

7. Guilt about the Past

Am I a bad Christian if I engage in sex outside of marriage? How do you deal with past actions that you are ashamed of? Can you ask forgiveness for something you're pretty sure will happen again?

If you engage in sexual intercourse or sexual activity in circumstances where it would be wrong to do so, it doesn't mean you are a "bad Christian." What it does mean is that you have violated your own sense of what is right. And assuming that your moral convictions match what God actually expects of us, you have violated God's expectations or God's will too. There are a variety of common ways to describe this: you have sinned, acted immorally, and/or been unfaithful to God.

Let's just use the standard (and sometimes unpopular) word *sin*. In the Christian tradition, acting in a way that is sinful means acting in a way that is disobedient to God.[8] Romans 3 says that it is a universal human condition. Sin is part of the brokenness that exists in our relationship to God and to each other. A *sin* is an action that exemplifies this brokenness. So our questioner is really asking, "Am I a bad Christian if I sin?" If sex outside marriage isn't a sin, the answer to the question is easy. But the questioner clearly presumes that it is wrong to engage in sex outside marriage. So again, she is inquiring about one's status as a Christian when one engages in behaviors that are believed to be wrong.

It's certainly easy to *feel* like a bad Christian when we do the very things we know we shouldn't do! It's a very old tension in the moral life. As Paul writes in his letter to the Romans, "I can will what is right, but I cannot do it. For I do not do the good I want, but the evil I do not want is what I do" (7:18b–19). When we are honest enough to recognize that there is a conflict between our convictions and our actions, guilt is a natural consequence.

Given what's been said so far, let's assume that the label "bad Christian" simply designates a Christian who is aware of his or her sinfulness in a specific arena of life. Calling oneself a "bad" Christian seems helpful only if it points to the distance between actual behavior and a higher standard God calls us to. One might instead ask, "Am I a Christian who falls short of God's standards for sexual intercourse when I violate those standards?" Of course the answer is yes! So what do we do when we find ourselves struggling with this dilemma?

Doing things we believe are wrong is serious business, but thinking that one is a bad Christian because of it seems to put the emphasis in the wrong place. Putting oneself down ("I'm a bad Christian") doesn't accomplish anything good. The most appropriate Christian response to sin, guilt, or shame is confession: acknowledging the wrong and purposing with one's heart, soul, and mind to live in ways that are right and good. Confession is

---

8. The biblical understanding of sin includes both the idea of sin as *transgressing* (crossing a line that shouldn't be crossed, as in disobeying a commandment) and *missing the mark*. To miss the mark is to fail to abide by the standard (whatever this might be) that serves as the "target" for the kind of behavior God intends.

a restorative process that raises us up. In fact, facing sin honestly and caring about living more faithfully looks much more like being a "good Christian."

How do we deal with past actions we're ashamed of? First, we should do so with the same kind of grace and gentleness toward ourselves that we would hopefully show toward others! But it is often even harder to forgive ourselves than it is to forgive others, and knowing that God forgives us does not always dissolve our sense of guilt. Seeing ourselves through the eyes of grace is most important.

Lewis Smedes, whose work served as an important basis for explaining a boundary ethic, explains the experience of grace in the Christian tradition in simple but powerful terms:

> Grace is the beginning of our healing because it offers the one thing we need most: to be accepted without regard to whether we are acceptable. Grace . . . is the gift of being accepted before we become acceptable.[9]

A Christian's response to grace comes as both gratitude and as the determination to strive toward living in a way that corresponds to what God wants from us and for us. Grateful for unmerited acceptance, a forgiven Christian seeks now to honor God as a sign of gratitude and faith. This continuing journey describes Christian life in general, and how Christians live out their sex lives is just one among many areas of life where sin and recommitment are part of the rhythm of life.

But what if you're sure it will happen again? Or even: "What if I want to keep doing what is wrong? What if I don't want to change?" Sometimes sinful behaviors become part of our pattern of life. We don't break those patterns instantly, simply by deciding to change. It isn't surprising, then, that we might honestly guess that the confessed and forgiven sin will be repeated. It's all the more difficult to break the pattern when the behavior in question is a form of pleasure. How do you break an established pattern of pleasurable behavior when you identify it as wrong?

Asking forgiveness for actions you fear you may repeat is more like a form of ongoing dialogue than a one-time transaction. The point is to avoid pretending. That's what gives this kind of prayer integrity. You need forgiveness, but you need more than that. You need the strength to do what's right. Isn't this really part of living out one's faith every day in every arena of life?

I've never discovered any easy answer to the question, How can I change sinful behaviors that are difficult to change? The easy (but also

---

9. Smedes, *Shame and Grace*, 107–8.

truthful) answer is with patience, with persistence, and with prayer for the strength God provides that enables us to do what we cannot do on our own. But where this seems only to be a pious platitude, one might also need to call on other practical means to change. Accountability partners, the encouragement of a wider community of supportive friends, and counseling can be additional means that God provides to nurture Christian life. This answer doesn't pretend to be a self-help guide to change, though, so readers who find themselves in this struggle are encouraged to seek additional guidance and support.

8. Masturbation/Self-Pleasuring

What does God say about masturbation? Is it right in light of Christian morality? Does masturbation count as sex? Is masturbation considered unethical?

If you'd like to start an awkward conversation, bring up the topic of masturbation! The longtime sexual taboo is certainly still a common conversational taboo, and as a result, masturbation continues to be surrounded by myths and mystery. When no one talks about something, often we get the sense that it must be something too awful to discuss, at least in polite company or serious conversation. When we do talk about things, we tend to normalize them. Talking about a topic also acknowledges that it is important enough to think about, and it legitimizes your questions and concerns.

Speaking of normalization, masturbation could be considered normal, at least in terms of its prevalence. In study after study, statistics show that more than 90 percent of males masturbate, and about 50 percent of females. There are of course ranges in terms of frequency and within various stages of life, as well as differences within specific populations. Nevertheless, genital self-stimulation is a common activity, even in the face of cultural silence about it.

Caution must be exercised here, however. The fact that something happens often gives us no clue about its moral permissibility. War, poverty, and injustice are far too common. But they are not the way God intended things to be. Whether nearly everyone does something or rarely anyone, reasons for the goodness of any human action must be sought outside statistics. Opponents might see the prevalence of masturbation as little more than a sign of the universality of human fallenness.

Social Norms

In spite of the claim that masturbation is still a taboo topic, the social norms are clearly changing. And while it might still be shrouded in secrecy, there is an emerging awareness that "everyone does it" and that long-established myths are little more than scare tactics designed to control behavior by internalizing fear and guilt. It worked for many people, and for some it continues to have the same effect today.

But the general attitudes are changing, and the following perspective, from the popular medical website WebMD, expresses attitudes that are commonly voiced:

> While it once was regarded as a perversion and a sign of a mental problem, masturbation now is regarded as a normal, healthy sexual activity that is pleasant, fulfilling, acceptable, and safe. In general, the medical community considers masturbation to be a natural and harmless expression of sexuality for both men and women.

The Christian community expresses a more mixed assessment, which we'll examine shortly.

Myths, Medicine, and Health

The myths once associated with masturbation have been dismissed by the medical and scientific communities. Rather than pointing to harmful effects, it's more common to point out that the primary negative effect of masturbation is the (false sense of) guilt that people have been taught to feel about it.

According to the University of Michigan Health System (UMHS), there have been many myths regarding masturbation, but they are all false and without any medical basis. The UMHS list of "corrections" includes

- It does not stunt your growth.
- It does not cause blindness.
- It does not cause deafness.
- It does not cause you to grow hair on your palms.
- It does not cause stuttering.
- You cannot die from it.
- It does not mean your child will be promiscuous as an adult.

- It will not drive a person crazy.

Their conclusion? "It is perfectly healthy as long as it does not interfere with relationships with friends and family, or with doing other activities." In fact, many medical professionals and sex therapists now claim that masturbation has a number of positive consequences for both physical and emotional health. Masturbation may

- create a sense of well-being;
- enhance sex with partners, physically and emotionally;
- help people learn how they like to be touched and stimulated sexually;
- increase the ability to have orgasms;
- improve relationship and sexual satisfaction;
- improve sleep;
- increase self-esteem and improve body image;
- provide sexual pleasure for people without partners, including the elderly;
- provide sexual pleasure for people who choose to abstain from sex play with another person;
- provide treatment for sexual dysfunction;
- reduce stress;
- release sexual tension;
- relieve menstrual cramps and muscle tension;
- strengthen muscle tone in the pelvic and anal areas, reducing women's chances of involuntary urine leakage and uterine prolapse.[10]

The Christian Tradition and Traditional Reasons for Disapproval

Contemporary Christian perspectives on masturbation grow out of a long tradition of disapproval. Even among current Christian moralists, some express serious reservations about giving moral approval to the practice, while others endorse it as a normal and healthy alternative to sex with a married partner.

---

10. Planned Parenthood, "Masturbation," https://www.plannedparenthood.org/learn/sex-and-relationships/masturbation.

Many of the contemporary reasons Christian moralists oppose masturbation have their roots in arguments made centuries ago. Some of those early viewpoints have been dismissed, but some have survived critical scientific and theological analysis. Here is a summary of what I consider the most common arguments still used to explain why masturbation is considered morally wrong.

1. God intended sexual pleasure to be experienced only in the context of marriage, where it is experienced interpersonally. Sexual pleasure, in this view, is meant to be experienced only in a relationship of mutual love. Masturbation is wrong because it is a case of experiencing sexual pleasure in the wrong setting—whether in a state of singleness (outside marriage) or solitude (outside the husband-wife relationship).

The *Catechism of the Catholic Church* (CCC) expresses this view, confirmed by Pope Paul VI in *Persona Humana: Declaration on Certain Questions Concerning Sexual Ethics*: "Masturbation is an intrinsically and seriously disordered act. The main reason is that, whatever the motive for acting this way, the deliberate use of the sexual faculty outside normal conjugal relations essentially contradicts the finality of the faculty. For it lacks the sexual relationship called for by the moral order, namely the relationship which realizes 'the full sense of mutual self-giving and human procreation in the context of true love.'"[11]

2. Along with the first argument, one can emphasize not only the appropriate *context* for sexual pleasure but also God's intended *purpose* for it. The above statement from *Persona Humana* already makes this link. Sexual pleasure is always meant to be associated with the purposes of sex, which God created for procreation and for enhancing the unitive bond between husband and wife. Sexual pleasure separated from its purpose is "disordered"—as in masturbation, through which a solitary individual seeks self-gratification, which is neither procreative nor unitive.

3. Opposition to masturbation is sometimes deeply rooted in beliefs that it is motivated by sinful impurity or by mental or emotional sickness, self-loathing, or social isolation and is also likely to have horribly destructive medical, social, or marital consequences. Perhaps the most common, surviving contemporary example is the claim that there is a tendency for masturbation to become compulsive or addictive and so to interfere with emotional and spiritual health and to have other negative consequences.

These beliefs have persisted even in the face of claims to the contrary by social scientists and medical practitioners. The claims about causes and consequences are empirical ones, and we would expect they can be verified

11. Franjo Cardinal Seper, *Persona Humana*, V.

by evidence if they are true. I suspect that beliefs about negative causes and consequences persist because there is always isolated anecdotal evidence to support the beliefs. Sometimes masturbation is a result of something very unhealthy in a person's life. Sometimes an addiction to masturbation does interfere with healthy sexual activity in marriage or with one's daily personal or professional life. One sad story can have more influence than a multitude of studies. And it's easy to understand why, if someone truly believes a behavior will result in serious harm, he will strongly caution against it.

4. Christians opposed to masturbation also argue that its connection with lust and impure fantasies brings masturbation into conflict with the Christian virtue of chastity. If lust is defined to include unfulfilled sexual desires expressed through sexual fantasy, then masturbation is guilty at least by association.

5. But what does the Bible say? Readers who have noticed the omission of a biblical case against masturbation may be asking precisely this question. I side with those who don't find proof-texts to be very helpful here (or anywhere). There seems to be wide agreement, even among many who say masturbation is sinful, that the Bible does not specifically condemn it. Masturbation just isn't mentioned. Of course not everyone agrees about that! Those who think the Bible does address the issue point to one or two examples.

The first is the story of Onan (masturbation has been called "onanism" for centuries) found in Genesis 38:7–10. When Onan's brother died, he was under obligation to impregnate his brother's wife. But the story says that because Onan did not want a child that would not be his, he spilled his semen on the ground each time they had intercourse. This was displeasing to the Lord, who put Onan to death. What exactly was displeasing to the Lord? Was Onan masturbating? No, he was engaging in an unreliable form of birth control, known as *coitus interruptus*, which is "the practice of withdrawing the penis from the vagina and away from a woman's external genitals before ejaculation to prevent pregnancy. The withdrawal method helps prevent sperm from entering the vagina."[12] The text describes this as Onan "spilling his seed on the ground." Interpreters today generally agree that what the Lord was displeased with is Onan's refusal to carry out his moral obligation to his deceased brother. If that's the case, this text really isn't about masturbation at all.

Another way to understand the Bible as condemning masturbation is to say that it is included in general terms like "sexual immorality" (1 Cor 6:9) or "impurity" (Eph 4:19 and 5:3). The argument here is that whenever

12. Mayoclinic.org, "Withdrawal Method."

a biblical text condemns sexual immorality, it is condemning masturbation. But is it? Or is this a case of first deciding that something is wrong and then reading it *into* texts that don't clearly say it's wrong?

Qualified Permission

Even acknowledging the concerns expressed above, the long tradition of considering masturbation sinful is rejected by many contemporary Christian moralists. They give what I would call "qualified permission." Here's a good example of paraphrased advice from James Dobson, who would usually be considered a conservative Christian: Masturbation is not much of an issue with God, and Jesus did not mention it in the Bible. It does not have harmful physical effects. Dobson isn't recommending masturbation and hopes that people won't find it necessary. But if they do, his opinion is that they should not struggle with guilt over it.[13]

A Roman Catholic ethicist, Margaret Farley, expressing her own view on masturbation, also illustrates what I've called qualified permission. She explains it this way:

> Although there are theologians and church traditions that continue to consider masturbation immoral, many others (most, as far as I can tell, along with most medical practitioners) do not assess it in this manner anymore. Masturbation is more likely to be considered morally neutral, which could mean that it is either good or bad, depending on the circumstances and the individual. It could also mean that, while the practice may raise psychological questions (if it becomes obsessive, for example), it usually does not raise any moral questions at all.[14]

Here is an overview of the qualified-permission approach, which I think demands serious consideration and which reflects the best combination of Christian moral values, scientific evidence, and human experience.

"It's Normal"

The normality of masturbation has moral import, even though it is not the determining factor when considering its moral appropriateness. The statistics that tell this story of normalness differ from study to study, but not widely. It seems reasonable and responsible to summarize them this way:

13. See Dobson's *Preparing for Adolescence* for a more extended discussion.

14. Farley, *Just Love*, 236.

about 90 percent of adult males report masturbating, and about 50 percent of adult women do—although from person to person there is also variation in the frequency of masturbation.[15] This emerging consensus about its normality led the American Medical Association to pronounce masturbation as normal in its 1972 publication *Human Sexuality*.

To call a behavior normal is not convincing to someone who finds the behavior morally reprehensible. In that case its normality can simply be seen as evidence of the pervasiveness of human sin. But it can also be seen as the natural unfolding of the process of human sexual development. The fact that people do something tells us nothing definitive about whether it's right or wrong. It is irresponsible to jump from statistics (what is) to moral claims (what ought to be).

From the perspective I'm calling qualified permission, the wide prevalence of masturbation, which begins in childhood and continues through adolescence into adulthood, is seen primarily as evidence that masturbation is a biologically normal behavior that on its own is morally neutral. If it occurred only rarely, this might give us more reason to see it as an aberration that needed an explanation beyond "most people do it." But it isn't rare, even though the social taboo that limits talking about it might make it seem rare.

Guilt

People often wonder, "If masturbation isn't actually wrong, why do I feel so guilty about it?" (Studies reveal that about half of those who masturbate feel guilty about it.) The most likely reason is that culture, and especially Christian culture, has taught us to feel guilty about it. Sometimes that teaching happens in outward, obvious ways. For example, people write books about why they believe it's wrong, or youth pastors lead discussions aimed to teach that it's wrong. Sometimes the teaching is less obvious. Social taboos often teach us that something is wrong because they make the behavior seem too horrible to even talk about! Lewis Smedes observed, in 1976,

> People used to invent horrible reasons to make youngsters feel guilty about masturbating. Today the reverse is true. People worry now about how to let them masturbate without having guilt feelings about it. The mood today is that masturbation is

15. More detailed information can be found in the online report from the Kinsey Institute, which includes statistics from the 2010 National Survey of Sexual Health and Behavior.

alright; only the guilt is bad. I do not want to dispute the modern attitude.[16]

Is guilt actually a sign that something is wrong? Sometimes, but not always. We feel guilty about things we are taught to feel guilty about. Sometimes we are taught to feel guilty about things we shouldn't really feel guilty about, and other times we aren't taught to feel guilty about things that we really should feel guilty about! The only way to figure out when guilt is appropriate is to carefully discern whether the behavior in question is really wrong or not.

An Important Distinction: The Ideal and the Harmful

Masturbation does not reflect the "ideal" when we think about human sexuality and God's intentions for how it was meant to be a part of positive human experience. Permitting it is not a claim that it corresponds to the ideal. Rather, it reflects the viewpoint that *human activity that falls short of an ideal is not wrong simply because it is less than the ideal.* This is a key claim. God created us as sexual beings with the intent that our sexuality be expressed in relationships of mutual love, where both the celebration of unity and the intent to bring new life into the world would be appropriate. This leads some Christians to say that when sex isn't being used to communicate love in relationship, there is an important and even an essential element missing. It doesn't fulfill the ideal God intends for sex.

There are many normal and morally neutral human behaviors that do sometimes become problematic. Some people overeat and threaten their health. Some not only accumulate possessions but also become hoarders. Some not only drive vehicles but drive recklessly. The fact that good things can become destructive doesn't make the good things bad. We focus our efforts on treating the harmful consequences. A position of qualified permission suggests that we treat masturbation in the same way. If it becomes a compulsive habit or interferes with healthy relationships, we address the abuses rather than issuing a blanket condemnation.

Moral problems more clearly arise when a normal and permissible behavior becomes harmful. There are several legitimate ways to see how this danger might arise with masturbation. In general agreement with comments made by Dobson and Farley (quoted above), moral concerns about masturbation do not arise unless it interferes with one's personal or professional life—for example, by interfering with carrying out one's

16. Smedes, *Sex for Christians*, 138.

personal, marital, or professional responsibilities and commitments. There are some specific harms that Christians would want to avoid.

Lewis Smedes points out that one of the potential problems with masturbation is that it seeks only self-gratification, when sex, he believes, is designed for mutual pleasure in a relationship of marriage. For Smedes, seeking self-satisfaction does not always mean that masturbation is wrong. There is always an element of self-seeking in a sexual relationship. But if a person lets masturbation—or experiencing sexual pleasure on one's own—become a permanent substitute for what God intended, then that distorts God's gifts. One ought never to confuse the less-than-ideal (masturbation) with the expression of love and experience of sexual pleasure that God intended as a *relational* experience.

Settling for solo sex may happen, to some extent, even in marriage. It happens, for example, when one partner seeks sexual pleasure in the context of a self-generated fantasy life. This isn't problematic because fantasy is always sinful but because it is a failure to live out one's vocation as a spouse who is to remain always committed to the health and well-being of the marriage covenant. If masturbation becomes an idealized substitute for a real (and always imperfect) relationship of love, then it becomes a form of marital infidelity.

Conclusion: Qualified Permission

Qualified permission means permission only when one can be reasonably sure that harms like the ones described above aren't part of the behavior. In other words, unless there are clearly identifiable harms that interfere with conducting the rest of our lives in God-honoring ways, it's reasonable to permit masturbation as a normal way some people live out part of their human sexuality.

Giving qualified permission in this way allows those who permit masturbation to also agree with many of the central claims made by those who oppose it. The agreement is focused on avoiding behaviors when they have harmful consequences and seeking to redirect behavior in ways that reach toward God-given ideals.

There are several contexts in which permission makes sense, especially when one sets aside the traditional reasons for opposing masturbation—especially those that seem to be based on myths and misinformation. Sexual self-stimulation does not cause physical or mental ailments or dysfunctions. And except in problematic contexts, it does no harm. In fact, many people believe that the primary harm today comes from the false guilt people feel as a result of internalizing the myths and misinformation.

Consider these contexts:

SINGLENESS BEFORE OR AFTER MARRIAGE

Sexual release is understood biologically as a need. Self-stimulation can serve as a way of helping delay premature or inappropriate relational sex. For younger people, this is especially so when there is such a wide discrepancy between biological development and social conventions about when to get married. For older people, divorce or death leaves people single at a point in their lives where sexual desires remain high.

DIFFERING LEVELS OF SEXUAL DESIRE IN MARRIAGE

While the practice of masturbation is assumed to decline after marriage, statistics remind us that marriage does not automatically eliminate this practice. Within marriage masturbation is sometimes used not to replace marital sex but as an alternative in cases where a partner's sexual desires may not match one's own. Smedes, for example, suggests that in such cases it would be appropriate for a partner to lovingly respect a spouse's occasional masturbation. While masturbation reflects a desire for self-satisfaction, it also reflects respect for the choices of a husband or wife.

Christian authors have also reflected the value of benefits such as those listed earlier. In the absence of harms, it is possible to affirm the ways that masturbation can enhance well-being. This will, of course, sound wildly irresponsible to those who still find validity in branding masturbation a sin.

An approach of qualified permission does not carelessly accept masturbation. But in the absence of the harms discussed above, it does give permission to sexual self-stimulation. In the context of his discussion of masturbation in marriage, Smedes writes that "they are simply satisfying a natural need in a wholly natural and good way." He was writing specifically about a person who had lost a spouse in death. But the sentence, I think, captures the "permission" side of qualified permission.

One final thought: When either single or married people engage in solitary sexual stimulation, it's common for them to find it pleasurable, but not ultimately fulfilling. The pleasure of genital stimulation or orgasm is often unsatisfying because it serves in a mysterious way as a reminder that we are created for more than pleasure. We are created for relationship. What is less than ideal serves as a call to seek what is more ideal.

Bibliography

Bell, Rob. *Sex God: Exploring the Endless Connections between Sexuality and Spirituality.* Grand Rapids: Zondervan, 2007.

Carter, Stephen L. *Integrity.* New York: Basic Books, 1996.

Centers for Disease Control and Prevention. "Key Statistics from the National Survey of Family Growth." http://www.cdc.gov/nchs/nsfg/key_statistics/s. htm#oralsexmalefemale.

Chatterjee, Camille. "Can Men and Women Be Friends?" *Psychology Today,* September 1, 2001. http://www.psychologytoday.com/articles/200109/can-men-and-women -be-friends.

Collins, Raymond F. *Sexual Ethics and the New Testament: Behavior and Belief.* New York: Crossroad, 2000.

Cornell Legal Information Institute. "Marriage." https://www.law.cornell.edu/wex/ marriage.

Countryman, L. William. *Dirt, Greed, and Sex: Sexual Ethics in the New Testament and Their Implications for Today.* Philadelphia: Fortress, 1988.

Delany, Joseph. "Lust." *The Catholic Encyclopedia.* Vol. 9. New York: Robert Appleton, 1910. http://www.newadvent.org/cathen/09438a.htm.

Dobson James., *Preparing for Adolescence: Straight Talk to Teens and Parents.* Ventura, CA: Regal, 1979.

Elliot, Elisabeth. *Passion and Purity: Learning to Bring Your Love Life under Christ's Control.* 2nd ed. Grand Rapids: Revell, 2002.

Farley, Margaret. *Just Love: A Framework for Christian Sexual Ethics.* New York: Continuum, 2006.

Foster, Richard. *Money, Sex, and Power: The Challenge of the Disciplined Life.* New York: HarperCollins, 2010.

Franjo Cardinal Seper. *Persona Humana: Declaration on Certain Questions Concerning Sex Ethics.* December 29, 1975. http://www.vatican.va/roman_curia/ congregations/cfaith/documents/rc_con_cfaith_doc_19751229_persona- humana_en.html.

Freitas, Donna. *Sex and the Soul: Juggling Sexuality, Spirituality, Romance, and Religion on America's College Campuses.* Oxford: Oxford University Press, 2008.

Fullam, Lisa. "Sex in 3-D: A Telos for a Virtue Ethics of Sexuality." *Journal of the Society of Christian Ethics* 27 (2007) 151–70.

Grenz, Stanley. *Sexual Ethics: An Evangelical Perspective.* Louisville: Westminster John Knox, 1997.

Gresh, Dannah. *And the Bride Wore White: Seven Secrets to Sexual Purity.* Chicago: Moody, 2004.

Gushee, David. "A Sexual Ethic for College Students." Paper presented at CCCU Consultation on Human Sexuality, Calvin College, November 2004.

Guttmacher Institute. "American Teens' Sexual and Reproductive Health." May 2014. https://www.guttmacher.org/sites/default/files/pdfs/pubs/FB-ATSRH.pdf.

Harris, Joshua. *Sex Is Not the Problem (Lust Is): Sexual Purity in a Lust-Saturated World.* Colorado Springs: WaterBrook Multnomah, 2005.

Hollinger, Dennis. *The Meaning of Sex: Christian Ethics and the Moral Life.* Grand Rapids: Baker Academic, 2009.

Keyes, Dick. "The Meaning of Shame and Guilt." *L'Abri Papers* #DK04. http://www.labri.org/england/resources/08042008/DK04_Shame-and-Guilt.pdf.

Lebacqz, Karen. "Appropriate Vulnerability: A Sexual Ethic for Singles." *Christian Century*, May 6, 1987, 435–38.

Lewis, C. S. *The Four Loves.* San Diego: Harcourt Brace, 1988.

Ludy, Eric, and Leslie Ludy. *When God Writes Your Love Story.* Sisters, OR: Multnomah, 2004.

McClintock, Karen. *Sexual Shame: An Urgent Call to Healing.* Minneapolis: Fortress, 2001.

McDowell, Josh. *Why True Love Waits: The Definitive Book on How to Help Your Kids Resist Sexual Pressure.* Wheaton, IL: Tyndale House 2002.

McGrath, Alister, *Christian Spirituality: An Introduction.* Oxford: Wiley-Blackwell, 1999.

Meilaender, Gilbert. "Men and Women—Can We Be Friends?" *First Things* 34 (June/July 1993). https://www.firstthings.com/article/1993/06/men-and-women-can-we-be-friends.

Midgley, Mary. *Can't We Make Moral Judgments?* New York: St. Martin's, 1993.

Neal, David T., Wendy Wood, and Jeffrey M. Quinn. "Habits—a Repeat Performance." *Current Directions in Psychological Science* 15 (2006) 198–202.

Nelson, James. "Reuniting Sexuality and Spirituality." *The Christian Century*, February 25, 1987, 187–90.

Nouwen, Henri. *Being the Beloved.* New York: Crossroad, 1992.

Quinn, Jeffrey M., et al. "Can't Control Yourself? Monitor Those Bad Habits." *Personality and Social Psychology Bulletin* 36 (2010) 499–511.

Reeder, Heidi M. "'I like you . . . as a Friend': The Role of Attraction in Cross-Sex Friendship." *Journal of Social and Personal Relationships* 17 (2000) 329–48.

Regnerus, Mark. *Forbidden Fruit: Sex and Religion in the Lives of American Teenagers.* Oxford: Oxford University Press, 2007.

Remez, Lisa. "Oral Sex among Adolescents: Is it Sex or Is It Abstinence?" *Family Planning Perspectives* 32 (2000) 298–304.

Rosenbaum, Janet E. "Patient Teenagers: A Comparison of the Sexual Behavior of Virginity Pledgers and Matched Nonpledgers." *Pediatrics* 123 (2009) 110–20.

Rubin, Lillian B. *Just Friends: The Role of Friendship in Our Lives.* New York: Harper & Row, 1985.

Smedes, Lewis B. *Sex for Christians: The Limits and Liberties of Sexual Living.* Grand Rapids: Eerdmans, 1994.

———. *Shame and Grace: Healing the Shame We Don't Deserve.* San Francisco: HarperSanFrancisco/Zondervan, 1993.

Stein, Rob. "Premarital Abstinence Pledges Ineffective, Study Finds." *Washington Post*, December 29, 2008.

Wadell, Paul. *Becoming Friends: Worship, Justice, and the Practice of Christian Friendship*. Grand Rapids: Brazos, 2002.

Werking, Kathy. *We're Just Good Friends: Women and Men in Nonromantic Relationships*. New York: Guilford, 1997.

Winner, Lauren. *Real Sex: The Naked Truth about Chastity*. Grand Rapids: Brazos, 2005.

CPSIA information can be obtained
at www.ICGtesting.com
Printed in the USA
LVHW032153171121
703614LV00008B/1112